A Practical Guide to
SMALL COMPUTERS
for Business
and Professional Use

Revised Edition

by ROBERT M. RINDER

MONARCH PRESS

MONARCH PRESS and colophon are trademarks of Simon & Schuster,
registered in the U.S. Patent and Trademark Office.
Manufactured in the United States of America
10 9 8 7 6 5 4 3 2 1
Library of Congress Catalog Card Number: 82-63046
ISBN 0-671-47091-4

Contents

ILLUSTRATIONS

FIGURES

TABLES

FORMS

Introduction

This book is about the application of small computers to business-related functions. It is for the small-business person, the professional who has records to keep and reports to write, and even managers in large enterprises who might use a small computer to improve the operations of a limited area of their business. Its aim is to cut through the jargon, the myths and the overblown claims, and to provide straightforward guidance to first-time users of small computers. This book will also be of interest to current users of now-outmoded small computers who want to learn about the new data processing and latest equipment.

You are, no doubt, already aware of recent plummeting prices of computers. Promotional material has hit the airwaves and newspapers. Articles on minicomputers, microcomputers and word processing have appeared in business publications. You may be beguiled by the possibilities, but somewhat hesitant on how to proceed and how to evaluate the claims in the promotional literature. If you are typical, you have no experience with computers, don't know how they work, and are probably both intrigued and a little intimidated by the whole subject. You have no desire to become a computer expert, but you would like to be able to deal with a sales representative intelligently, know what questions to ask, and be able to apply computers effectively in your area of interest.

The book avoids giving pat answers to the many questions confronting the first-time user. The diversity of users and the range of their application needs is just too great to permit single, all-purpose solutions to the problems of planning and selection. Rather, emphasis is placed on showing you how to find solutions that meet *your* specific needs as you see them.

WHO THIS BOOK IS FOR

This book is directed towards three groups that are applying small computers in ever-increasing numbers: small-business persons, professionals and managers who are employed in organizations of various types and sizes. Although each group has its special requirements and constraints, all three are directly or indirectly connected with the world of business. Here are the requirements and what each group needs to know about the planning and selection process.

The Small-Business Person

For businesspeople the first application of a computer is a particularly critical step. The results of early decisions tend to propagate and influence later decisions. Mistakes made in the early phases of computer planning have a way of coming back to haunt you well into the future. The programs and system that you select, and the way you plan to use your system will start you on a path that is not easy to change and you will not find it easy to retrace your steps. Hence, it is crucial that you do as much as reasonably possible in the early stages to get off on the right foot. This means that you must start with a system that is right for *you*, that meets *your* needs, irrespective of how great the same system might or might not be for others.

There are hundreds of different types of small businesses. With respect to computers, they will have some aspects in common and some that are unique. The small-business person who does not have a professional staff of computer experts to fall back on, needs to know how to proceed so that his or her way of doing business will be helped and not hindered by the computer system. Specifically, the entrepreneur needs to know how to plan for a computer system, where help can be found if needed, what kind of help can be gotten, how to select a computer and computer programs, and how to convert from present methods to computerized methods. It is the answer to these, and related questions which is the subject of this book.

Professionals

The situation with respect to professionals is somewhat different. The professional can apply computers to both the business and the professional side of an operation. The business side, although usually modest by comparison with a regular business, can nevertheless be a time-consuming, bothersome chore. The business side of a professional's work requires record keeping, and report writing with respect to clients, contracts, schedules, income and expenses—the typical activities of any business enterprise.

In addition, the computer can be a powerful tool in the performance of professional activities. This is most easily accomplished when the computer is used primarily for its computational ability. CPAs, engineers, architects, tax preparers, investment counselors, are some good examples. Other applications, where the storage and data processing capabilities of the computer are used, although more difficult, are quite possible. Some examples of this type of application are law offices, real estate brokerages, and schools. Other professionals, such as doctors and dentists, are using small computers in the business side of their operations, and usage in connection with their professional activities is being explored.

Professionals will not normally want to use two different computers to process their business and professional applications. They will want to perform all functions on a single system without one area interfering with the other. Although professionals' requirements in many ways are less demanding than those of businesspersons, areas which bear on their relationship with clients are usually of critical importance. Thus, professionals want to know how to plan for both business and professional operations, where needed programs can be obtained, whether they should do their own programming and, if so, what program languages to use.

Managers

Managers in large organizations will view the computer partly as a business-person and partly as a professional. As a businessperson, the manager will be concerned with the application of the computer to business activities. Concerns with respect to planning and selection will be similar to that of the businessperson but with some important differences. As a rule, managers' options are much more restricted than those of businesspersons. These restrictions can apply to what they can do, what equipment they can buy and what programs they can use. All these areas are generally circumscribed by organizational policy, which usually sets standards in order to achieve economies in purchasing, training, spare parts and the sharing of data. However, while working within the framework of the organization's directives, managers are finding increasing applications for small computers. Managers like the greater control and increased flexibility they can get when their applications are processed in their own department instead of on a large centralized computer.

Unlike businesspersons, managers may have access to a professional staff. This can be a mixed blessing. Unless managers know something about the planning and selection of facilities, they may find themselves being led astray. Experienced managers do not take an uncritical view of projects performed by those outside their departments and their control. Therefore, even if a professional staff is available, managers who plan to use a small computer for the first time should pay careful attention to what is said in this book about the planning and selection for business applications.

For the manager, then, there will be certain constraints not faced by the businessperson. But, within these constraints, the planning and selection process will be pretty much the same. Both will be working in a business environment. This will dictate to a large extent what must be done and how to do it.

Finally, managers in small organizations, that is, those that do not yet have their own computer, can find themselves suddenly presented with a computer by an impulsive superior and told to automate operations. In other cases the manager may desire to take the lead in trying to convince a reluctant owner to keep abreast of the times. But whatever the situation, when the computer comes to the small organization, the manager there is going to be in the thick of things. No less than the businessperson, he or she will want to know computer basics, and know how to plan and install a computer system.

In addition to business applications in the conventional sense, small computers open a host of new applications to managers. Some of the more obvious examples are project planning and control, budgeting, resource allocation, scheduling and word processing. Less obvious examples might be those applications specific to the manager's area of operations. And not to be overlooked is the automation of the manager's office operations, personal records, calendar, memos and so on. In all these examples, the small computer might be the "property" of the department, the project team, a work group or just the manager alone. In these cases, the manager's task in the planning and selection process will be similar to that of the professional. The manager may want to apply the small computer to more than one area, and certainly will want to know how to select and evaluate available programs. Finally, he or she may be tempted to try some programming without resorting to any experts.

For those managers and professionals who have had experience with systems implemented on large, centralized computers, there is a danger of blindly transferring lessons learned from this environment to that of small computers. This could be fatal. Both what you have to do and how you do it are different in the world of small computers. This is stressed throughout this book. At all appropriate points, the way things are done in the world of large computers is contrasted with how they must be done in the world of small computers.

Although the book is intended to serve the needs of those working in any of the areas described above, the emphasis is definitely on business applications where the small computer is to be introduced into the main line of a business's operations. This is the most demanding area of application and the one requiring the most careful planning and evaluation. Those whose application is less demanding can eliminate steps that are not relevant to their needs. By using the same methodology, you will at least have given consideration to all points, thereby ensuring that important steps will not be missed.

HOW TO USE THIS BOOK

Use this book to learn about small computers, to plan and select small computers and as a general reference, when information is needed.

First, to learn about small computers, read the book once straight through to get an overview of the whole subject. You can safely skip detailed descriptions on a first reading. There will be far too many new ideas and procedures for you to remember everything. Concentrate on the big picture, and if something is not immediately clear, read on—it will probably be clarified at a later point.

Second, in planning and selecting a small computer, follow the steps outlined in the text. Here, you will find yourself jumping from one section to another, retracing steps and skipping ahead, as needed. An important aid in this process is provided for you by the check lists. The check lists provide a convenient reminder of all the many details that are dispersed throughout the text. Using them will help avoid overlooking important points, and guide you in the proper order in which things must be done.

Third, after you have installed your first system and have gained some computer experience, you can refer to the book for guidance in evaluating that system and in planning your next application.

In the computer field it is common to find things called by several names. The terms used in the text are those that are used most often in the industry. Where there is no clear predominance of use, we have tried to use the term which best describes the subject and is the easiest to remember.

This book tells you what you should know about programs and program languages, but it will not teach you how to program. Programming is a subject in itself, and there are a number of good books dedicated to this task. If you have any interest in learning to program, read what this book has to say about programming languages, select the one best suited to your needs and proceed from there.

It is hoped that as well as providing you with a practical guide to the use of small computers to meet your immediate needs, this book will stimulate you to thinking more broadly about computers and how they can benefit your overall operations.

PART 1
Learning About
Small Computers

Chapter

1

An Introduction to
Small Computers

Small computers are invading the business and professional world at a rapidly increasing rate. Business and professional people working in many different areas are finding that they can cut costs, increase productivity, relieve themselves and their associates of tedious chores and open up new avenues to profits. This is all the result of now having at their disposal the small computer—a powerful tool which a few years ago only a large company could afford but which has recently dropped in price to the point where even the smallest company can realistically consider its use. And the technology has by no means reached its limit. Still more powerful machines are in the offing, indicating that the role of computers will be increasing for some time to come.

What exactly is a small computer, what can you do with it, and, last but not least, should you get one for your own business or professional use? These are the questions we will be dealing with in this introductory chapter.

WHAT IS A SMALL COMPUTER?

Large computers used by big business and big institutions cost many hundreds of thousands of dollars. They take up a lot of space, require a special computer room, and trained operating personnel must be present at all times while they are running. In contrast, a small computer costs in the range of $1,000 to $90,000, with most computers of the type we will be discussing costing well under $20,000. But cost is not the only distinguishing feature of small computers. In addition, they are designed to work right in an office without the need for special construction, air conditioning or electrical facilities. They can be operated by office personnel—managers, clerks and secretaries—after just a few hours training. And programs, the list of instructions that tell the computer what to do, are being mass marketed so that products of reasonable quality and low cost are becoming available. Thus, there is a sharp distinction between large and small computers that involves more than just size and cost.

You may have heard the terms minicomputers and microcomputers used in connection with small business systems. These are the two types of computers that together comprise what we will be calling small computers. In Chapter 4 we will say something about the difference between these two types of small

19

computers. But these differences are not significant for most users. Readers should concentrate on their own requirements without bothering about whether they need a mini- or a microcomputer.

In their role as office machines, small computers are designed to fit conveniently and esthetically into an office environment.

Two popular forms of construction are integrated systems and non-integrated or component systems.

Integrated systems consist of one single unit. Keyboard, display and all other components, except printer, are housed in one cabinet providing a professional, business-like piece of equipment.

Illustration 1–1 A COMPONENT SYSTEM.   IBM's Personal Computer with moveable keyboard. This small computer can be used for word processing, business and mathematical applications. (Photo courtesy of International Business Machines Corporation.)

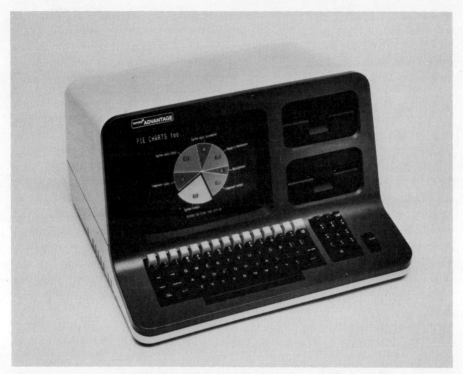

Illustration 1–2 AN INTEGRATED SYSTEM.   North Star's ADVANTAGE computer with built-in keyboard and display. The ADVANTAGE is a business system computer featuring powerful graphics capability. (Photo courtesy of North Star Computers, Inc.)

The component systems usually have a detached keyboard and display. Disk units may also be housed separately. This arrangement provides flexibility in adjusting components for ease of use.

Small computers are easy to use. Ease of use is the result of three features that are typical of today's small computers and critical for their success.

* Entry of data from a typewriterlike keyboard. Office personnel are familiar with it and many are highly proficient in its use.
* Display of results on a TV-like screen. The generation of letters and numbers takes place at electronic speeds, allowing the computer to present information to the user at a fraction of the speed of a mechanical printer. To the user, responses often seem instantaneous.
* Processing is interactive and immediate. There is no waiting for end-of-day, end-of-week or end-of-month processing cycles as is the case with many large systems. Interactive processing means that after an entry the computer can immediately respond with a result, a question, an error message or a request for information. Immediate processing means that if you want a report now, you can request that report and in a matter of seconds a printer will begin banging out what you asked for.

Gone are the unwieldy punched cards and tapes that were the hallmarks of previous computer systems. Today's small computer is designed for direct input of data from the keyboard and the electronic display of results on a TV-tube screen. We will be describing these, and other features of small computers in later chapters, but the above comments should give you a feel for what a small computer is and why it is now a practical device for small businesses and professional use.

WHAT CAN YOU DO WITH A SMALL COMPUTER?

Table 1–1 lists some of the ways that small computers are being used by business and professional people. A scan of its contents quickly reveals something of the variety and scope of what you can do with a small computer.

In order to do the jobs shown in Table 1–1 programs must be entered into the computer. Thus, if we want the computer to perform the operations required for general ledger, we would load a general ledger program into the computer. The same would apply to all the items in Table 1–1—for each job that we want the computer to perform, there must be a corresponding program.

You can get the programs you need in one of four ways.

• Obtain a program and use it as is.
• Obtain a program but have it modified to better suit your needs.
• Have a program written expressly for you.
• Develop or modify the programs internally in your own organization.

Programs obtained from vendors may be purchased, leased or licensed.

The items in Table 1–1 were all taken right out of vendors' program catalogs. In other words, the table lists programs that you can actually obtain and use, if —a big if—they really do the job you need done. For some of the items in the table, there may be only one corresponding program. But for most there will be several. And for others, such as accounting programs, there might be well over a hundred. The number of available programs is continually growing and the quality is improving, providing an ever increasing number of things that a computer can do for you.

Although Table 1–1 lists a good number of applications, still it does not do justice to the scope of available programs. In each case there may be programs written for a specific industry, or even a small segment of an industry. For example, there are accounting programs written for the box industry in general and there are accounting programs written specifically for the corrugated box industry. You can find accounting systems designed for public schools, construction, petroleum and trucking. There are financial programs for handling portfolios, mortgage loans and financial planning. There are numerous programs tailored to the needs of distributors and wholesalers. Complete packages of programs that cover most of the functions performed by professionals have been developed for CPAs and tax consultants.

Table 1–1   Uses of Small Computers

Accounting
General ledger
Accounts receivable
Accounts payable
Fixed asset accounting

Common Business Applications
Billing and statements
Order entry
Open orders
Inventory
Payroll
Budgeting
Information systems
  – Inquiry
  – Update
  – Relational

Specialized Business Applications
Property
Financial management
Project management
Project control
Manufacturing
Bill of material
Forecasting
Job estimation
Job bidding
Job control
Warehouse control
Delivery and distribution
Sales aids and presentations
Commissions and royalies
PERT/CPM
Mailing lists
Word processing
  – Publications
  – Documentation
  – Brochures
  – Manuals
  – Catalogs

Professional
Time analysis
Billing

Statistics
Medical management
Dental management
Patient medical records
Index systems
Investment management
Real estate
Insurance
Library index cards
Dealer catalogs
Tax package for tax consultants
Accounting package for CPAs
Word processing
  – Manuscripts
  – Reports
  – Proposals
  – Letters
  – Catalogs

Office
Mailing list
Appointments
Name and address
Word processing
  — Letters
  — Reports
  — Memos
Electronic mail

Miscellaneous
Graphical output
Text input
Bar code input
Communications
Speech input
Speech output
Engineering
Mathematics
  – Regression analysis
  – Wave form analysis
  – Linear programming
  – Statistics
Education
Stock information
Commodity information

All these examples are given only to indicate what can be done with a small computer. You should not automatically conclude that, in your particular case, you can always use such programs, at least without modifications. Your needs may be met only partly, or not at all, by available programs. How to find programs that do meet your needs is a key problem for users of small computers. We will be discussing this in detail in later chapters.

Note in Table 1–1 the wide use of word processing. It is used in business, professional and office applications. In each case the functions performed are similar although the documents produced tend to be somewhat different. In fact, word processing is sufficiently different and prominent as to merit special attention. Thus, we can designate three primary areas for the use of small computers: business, professional and word processing. Now the key point to note in this regard is that all three areas can be accommodated by the *same* small computer. Businesspeople can do their business applications, but they can also do professional applications and word processing on the same computer. Typical of the type of professional applications business people might want to do is engineering, statistics and even management science. Management science deals with the best ways to perform business functions—from ordering of inventory and the scheduling of deliveries to the planning of new business ventures. Until now, management science has been mostly limited to large corporations. But as computers move into small businesses and programs become available, we can expect the use of management science techniques to become more common.

Similarly, professionals have a need to do business applications on a small scale and they can certainly use word processing to advantage. The result is that the small computer can be viewed as doing more than one function and more than one class of functions. All this, of course, increases the benefits and makes it easier to justify a purchase.

CAN YOU UNDERSTAND COMPUTERS?

Computers are known to be complex devices based on advanced, highly sophisticated technology. Can a nontechnical person really hope to use these devices in his or her day-to-day work? Don't you have to be a mathematician to be able to work with computers?

The answer is that nontechnical people in many fields are using small computers in the home, in business and in connection with their professional activities. The main problem faced by a user is not in understanding how computers work but in knowing how to plan and evaluate prospective applications. Unfortunately, this is the opposite of what one is often led to believe. The computer is promoted as a mysterious but marvelous device that any fool can take to the office, plug into an electrical outlet and start communicating with in English. You will find it easier to understand what the computer should do than to get it to do it.

As you will soon learn, the functions performed by a computer are basically simple. You don't even have to be good at arithmetic to use them because, surprisingly, computers, as used in business, do very little computing. What they do is *data processing* and *information processing.* "Data processor" or "information processor" would be a more apt name than computer. But for historical reasons we are stuck with "computer" and now it would be futile to try to change it.

What is data processing? The updating of records, the insertion and retrieval of records from files, extraction of data from records for presentation in reports—these are typical data processing functions. You do them in your daily business and professional activities. Now you are going to learn how a computer can do the same operations faster and cheaper. The process itself is simple. To make it work there is an incredibly complex process going on within the computer itself. But this doesn't have to concern you any more than the functioning of your brain must be understood in order to use it. Knowing this, you can approach the subject of computers with the confidence that you are fully capable of applying computers intelligently to your area of interest.

Try this experiment:

Put the book down for a moment and try to visualize the business side of your operations that might be performed automatically. Think, in a very general way, of how the paperwork might be handled, how data could be organized for automatic storage and retrieval, what operations might be performed automatically. You don't need technical proficiency for this. Just concentrate on the data used in your business and its flow through one day's cycle of operations.

Now look at Figure 1–1 (page 26). Chances are that your mental picture corresponds to some extent to the diagram shown there. Never mind that the file is shown as a rectangular box while your mental picture may have been of a filing cabinet. It is the organization of data into records and files, and the flow of this data in the entry, update and output operations that is significant here. These elements are common to all business systems, manual as well as computer-based systems. They form the basis of all future discussion of computer operations and will be the focus of our attention throughout this book.

To properly emphasize the importance of the elements of data processing we state them again.

Data Organization
• Files
• Records

Data Operations
• Input
• Update
• Output

Now look at Figure 1–1(b). Did you have the foresight in your mental picture to provide for reports? If you have been working only with manual systems, chances are you missed this one. When you want information you may be used to opening a filing cabinet or scanning indexed cards for the data you need. This can't be done with a computer. There, all data is stored in a form not possible to read directly. Hence the need for report generation by the computer. The report tells you what you want to know about all those wonderful things that the computer is going to do with your data.

Does this mean that you are hopelessly locked out from scanning the data in a computer as you do with printed files? Fortunately, no. There are techniques using televisionlike displays that allow the rapid scanning of data in a manner similar to what you do with printed matter. Most readers will have seen these

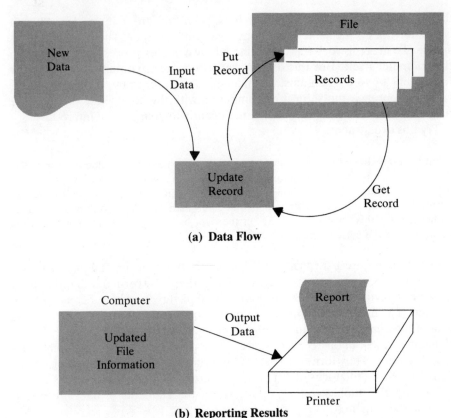

(a) Data Flow

(b) Reporting Results

Figure 1–1   The Elements of Data Processing

televisionlike devices in one form or another. They are used in banks, brokerage offices and ticket reservation offices, to name only a few of the more common places. They are also used in small computer systems, providing a way in which data, otherwise hidden within the innards of the computer, can be called up and scanned. "Browsing" is the apt term often used to describe this capability.

What is information processing and how does it differ from data processing?

Data processing is primarily concerned with performing the traditional business functions on a computer. Accounts payable, accounts receivable, payroll, inventory and order entry are all good, typical data processing functions.

Information processing goes one step further. It takes the information that is gathered as a result of data processing, organizes it, manipulates it and disseminates it in a timely and effective manner. With data processing, information is presented in regularly scheduled reports—daily, weekly and monthly. With information processing, ad hoc questions are entered into the computer and answers are returned in a matter of seconds. Data processing is used to reduce paperwork and cut costs. Information processing is used to find out what is going on and it is used in management analysis and decision making.

Data processing is applied to what has already happened; information processing is applied to planning future steps. Historically, data processing came first. Information processing has been made possible by more recent technological developments. Today it is being used in the larger small computer installations, and is now moving into the mid-range systems. Information processing is broader in scope than data processing, encompassing areas such as word processing and office automation. In time, information processing will become an increasingly important function of the small computer.

In this section we have described in a broad way the capability of computers. But sometimes it is important to know what a thing can't do as well as what it can do. In the next section we will discuss some of the limitations of computers.

WHAT COMPUTERS DON'T DO

In the early days of computers, when the technology was new and there was great excitement about the possibilities of their use, one heard a great deal about "giant brains" and the "thinking computer." As we grew accustomed to working with and living with computers, learning their real possibilities and limitations, this kind of talk died down but never completely disappeared. Now, with the big increases that are being made in computer performance, we are once again hearing about intelligent robots and thinking machines taking over the world.

The fact is that computers are simply very effective tools for processing data and have absolutely no capability for thinking as the term is usually understood. This is easily seen by those with hands-on experience with computers. However, it is important for nontechnical people, planning to use a computer for the first time, to clearly understand what a computer can and can not do. The first step in this direction is to realize that you, the user, will have to do the thinking. The performance and quality of the results derived from the computer will be your responsibility.

The above observations are not meant to deny that there are remarkable parallels between computers and living things. Computers can be made to mimic human behavior and it is often convenient to apply the same terms to computers that we use in describing human attributes. Thus, it is common to refer to the storage of data in computers as "memory." We speak of "intelligent" terminals and "smart" printers. We sometimes say that we will "teach" a computer to do certain tasks and that the computer has "learned" to do an operation. And we talk of the control of computers as "instructions." This manner of speaking has its advantages. After all, one function of language is to be expressive. But we shouldn't be misled by this into thinking that the computer has capabilities that it hasn't.

It might help to think of the computer as a large number of switches all interconnected. Indeed, that is essentially what a computer consists of. A switch turns something on and off. From the keyboard that provides for the entry of data into the computer to the control of the print hammers that record the computer's results, all data is processed and stored by means of switches, mostly in the form of tiny, microscopic transistors. From this it should be clear why computers can't think. Everything they do is simply the result of the opening and closing of a set of switches. As with any machine, it is the user who determines the result.

Since computers can't think for themselves, we must provide the control to make them work. We do this by giving them instructions. Each instruction causes the proper switches to close, thereby causing the proper action to be taken. Each instruction performs only a small, very limited amount of processing. In order to accomplish the complex tasks that are routinely performed by computers, many instructions must be strung together. A group of such instructions designed to perform a specific task is what is called a program. Most readers are familiar with this term. It has been absorbed into our language, so that we talk of programming (and deprogramming) of people as well as computers.

Without a program a computer is an inert device, incapable of doing anything. With a program it becomes transformed into a marvelous machine for processing data at lightning speed. As we have seen, programs have been written for performing many of the normal business functions and also some fairly exotic ones. However, because the application of small computers in business is relatively new, the quantity and quality of the programs available for small computers are not what they should be, although they are improving. Many programs are unusable, some merely passable and a few of really good quality. We will be dealing later with what constitutes a good program and how to identify it.

What the computer likes to do best is to repeat a few simple operations over and over. These it can do at speeds close to the speed of light, endlessly, tirelessly.

How, then, do we get the computer to perform the complex tasks which have to be done? For this it is necessary to combine the few simple tasks the computer can do, that is, the computer's instructions, into larger steps and loops. This process is repeated over and over until a complete program that will achieve the results we want is written. From this it should be evident that writing a good program is a very complex and exacting job. It involves considerable investment of time and money. Most important, it requires a good deal of experimentation. Not even a skilled and experienced programmer can attack a new application and come up with a really good program the first time. Some trial and error is required to find out how best to tackle a given job.

Everybody has a pet horror story (or several) about mistakes caused by a computer. The story usually involves a lone consumer's fight against an impersonal bureaucracy over an erroneous billing charge. After a long, frustrating battle, the weary consumer is told: "Sorry, sir, our computer made a mistake."

From what we have said about computer's thinking capability, and the role of the program in computer operations, the reader should be able to spot where the real source of the mistake lies. However, a few additional words need to be said about errors. They are a key area of concern for anyone contemplating the use of a computer in business operations. No one wants his or her business to be the source of a new horror story.

Computer professionals have a terse expression for the source of errors: GIGO, "garbage in, garbage out." If you enter bad data into a computer, you can only expect bad data to emerge. The quality of output data reflects the quality of the input data. The computer by itself cannot know whether data that is entered is valid or not. But by proper programming, numerous validity checks can be made. It is the responsibility of the users of a computer to provide proper entry data and to see that it is checked by programs. The computer does what it is told, and if you instruct it improperly, you have only yourself to blame.

This is not to say that computers don't malfunction. They do—but almost never in ways that produce the kinds of errors found in the horror stories. The odds against this are very large. When a computer malfunctions it will generally produce unintelligible output, produce no output or just stop running. Errors of the type we find on bills or statements are almost always the result either of a programming error or an entry error.

Because errors can result in expensive and damaging consequences, many safeguards are built into a good program to catch them and alert the user. In what follows we will give due attention to this point.

We have said that small computers are easy to understand and easy to use. Now it is time to mention some things about computers that don't come so easily.

THE HARD PART

Since computers cannot think for themselves, recognize mistakes when they occur or know what to do without being told, a lot of work is required to achieve a successful computer system. This work may already have been performed by the vendor of the equipment. If not, you can hire somebody to do it or you can do it yourself. But one way or another the work must be done and it must be done right.

Just because a small computer *can* do a job doesn't mean it *will* do it. And just because a small computer *can* be easy to use doesn't mean it *will* be. In order to achieve a successful computer system a number of steps must be taken. You must determine your requirements, obtain a good program, select the right computer and then get the computer up and running with your data. (The actual putting into operation of the computer is known in the trade as "cutover.") How well you do these jobs will determine how well the system performs, how smoothly things go and how easy the system is to use.

You can think of the situation as offering you two choices:

(1) Put in a lot of work up-front before cutover to your new system, and little work after cutover.

(2) Put in little work up-front and much, much more work after cutover together with delays and extra costs.

These observations apply in general, but the situation can vary widely in specific cases. Small computers are applied in one-person operations and they are applied in large businesses and institutions. They are given simple, isolated tasks and they are given the job of integrating several complex tasks. Some applications are so standardized that you can buy a small computer and immediately use it as is. Others are so unique that only a customized system can be used. Between these extremes we find all gradations of organization, complexity and uniqueness of application.

Vendors and their sales staff naturally tend to minimize the difficulties and emphasize the benefits. In this book we will proceed differently. Although we certainly don't want to minimize benefits, there will be a great deal of emphasis on the difficulties and problems that can be encountered in converting to small computer systems. Users have found themselves saddled with the wrong equipment—programs that don't work and costs greatly exceeding their original estimates. Avoiding these kinds of disasters is the hard part of installing a computer system and deserves the heavy emphasis we will be giving it. If you are fortunate enough to have a computer application that fits easily into one of the many off-the-shelf systems now available, so much the better. But, in general, the computer is still a long way from being just another piece of office equipment like a typewriter or a copier. Be prepared to proceed with caution and with due attention to what is said later about planning for and selecting a computer.

SHOULD YOU GET A SMALL COMPUTER?

The first-time user is apt to be confronted with a number of doubts and uncertainties. This is especially so if you are not technically inclined and only interested in computers for the possible benefits they can bring to your business or profession.

You will tend naturally to focus on one or two areas where you think you could use a computer. You want to know if it makes sense economically—whether it will contribute to improving operations or prove to be a white elephant that creates more problems than it can solve. These are good questions which must be asked, and a good part of this book is devoted to answering them. However, the basic decision to computerize should be made in a broader context. You have to ask yourself: What is the trend? What part will computers play in small businesses and in professional activities in the coming years? Can I remain competitive if I don't computerize?

The penetration of computers into *big* business was accomplished in roughly three stages. First the questions were: Will it work? Can a computer perform business applications? Then, in the second stage, management asked: Should we get a computer? Will it pay for itself? Now, in the third stage, the only question is: How can we put our computers and computer professionals to the best use? The big computer is taken for granted as a necessary part of doing business and nobody questions whether they should computerize.

The acceptance of *small* computers will develop along similar lines. The penetration of computers into small business and professional use is moving from the first to the second stage. Small computers have proven that they can work in a small business environment. Today small-businesspersons are asking: Should I get a computer? Tomorrow it is expected that computers will be taken for granted in small business or professional work as they are today in large businesses, as common perhaps as the adding machine, the copier and the typewriter. Taking this broad view then, you should be asking yourself how you want to fit into this trend towards computerization. As you will see in later chapters, answers to the question "Will the computer pay for itself in a specific application?" are not always easy to come by even when the computer offers very real benefits. It is a good idea, then, to be alert to the overall trend in other small businesses like yours, and to bear in mind the consequences of being left back.

Experience teaches that three mutually dependent elements are critical to the success of a computer system: the money available, the complexity of the system and the involvement of those responsible.

Money rates high in any decision to purchase, but in computer systems it requires special attention because of the consistent tendency to underestimate costs. There can be numerous hidden costs in converting to computer use; the availability of funds to cover these costs can determine the success or failure of a system.

A business computer capable of performing accounting, payroll and inventory functions with some degree of efficiency currently costs a minimum of eight to fourteen thousand dollars, depending on the model and manufacturer. Although lower-cost systems are available, they are not likely to provide better results than you are now getting, and they could actually make things worse.

For professional use, depending on the application, the minimum cost system can be considerably lower. However, anything less than three thousand dollars rules out important applications that we will be discussing.

User involvement, along with desire, enthusiasm and commitment, are all necessary ingredients required to get past what we have called "the hard part"— installing a computer system. Without a strong desire and willingness to get involved, it is not likely that all the necessary spadework will be done. It is too easy to take the path of least resistance, accept what is offered and take the vendor's word for everything. After all, they are the experts and you are just a layman, so why not follow their advice? This kind of thinking can lead to disaster.

We have already pointed out that readers' applications will vary considerably in complexity and difficulty of implementation. Now we want to consider complexity in conjunction with money and user commitment. It is not money, involvement and complexity by themselves that are significant, but their relationship to one another which determine your chance of success.

This is illustrated in Figure 1–2, which shows three scales for measuring investment, involvement and complexity. The scale of investment increases slowly at first and then rapidly from left to right, corresponding to the increased rate of expenditures for complex, as opposed to simple, computer systems.

The other two scales attempt to gauge involvement and complexity —both nonquantitative items.

Involvement is measured in terms of reluctance, indifference, acceptance and enthusiasm. The first three are all at the low end of the scale. For any but the simplest projects there should be at least some degree of enthusiam.

The scale of complexity requires some knowledge of computer applications and will be better understood after reading later chapters. However, even at this time, it can serve to make some important points.

Four hypothetical readers are depicted in Figure 1–2 and are designated by points A, B, C, and D.

Reader A is possibly a professional, with not much money, but with plenty of enthusiasm. She should have no trouble successfully meeting her modest needs, although her involvement is likely to be all out of proportion to that required by the project. Reader A may also be a member of a small business of one to five people, of which there are many thousands.

Reader B requires a rather complex system. He is underestimating the cost and he isn't overly enthusiastic about getting involved. Maybe he is reluctantly being pushed by competition. Or he could be a manager in a large business or institution in which top management is putting on the pressure. In any case, his

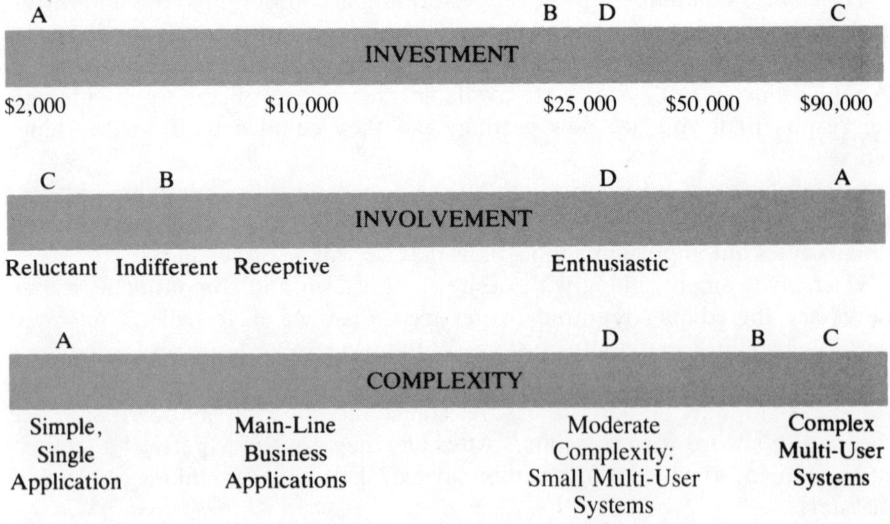

A				B	D		C
			INVESTMENT				
$2,000		$10,000		$25,000		$50,000	$90,000

C	B			D		A
			INVOLVEMENT			
Reluctant	Indifferent	Receptive		Enthusiastic		

A				D		B	C
			COMPLEXITY				
Simple, Single Application		Main-Line Business Applications		Moderate Complexity: Small Multi-User Systems		Complex Multi-User Systems	

Figure 1–2 Evaluating Chances of Success

chance of success is less than good unless he can find a way to generate more enthusiasm about involvement.

Reader B could also be a businessman whose intentions regarding involvement are good, but he just doesn't have the time. Right now he's involved in some major business innovations and this is taking all of his energy and leaving him short of cash. However, he has lots of faith in his manager who has just bought a home computer for his son. Therefore, the manager will be delegated to shepherd the computer system into operation. Reader B is enthusiastic about having a computer and is depending on using it in a new operation he is setting up.

Here we have just about all the ingredients for failure packed into one situation. A computer is being introduced into a changing situation where the man paying the bills won't be directly involved. Yet his manager, whose only knowledge of computers is through his son's hobby, will be under pressure for quick results. When this leads to the inevitable hang-ups, Reader B won't be able to put up the additional money to see the thing through.

Reader C is an interesting case. She has a tough application to computerize but unfortunately is reluctant to get involved and certainly has no interest in computers. However, note that she isn't reluctant to spend money. If she is prepared to pay what it takes to hire outside professionals to do the job, she just might make it. Her noninvolvement will still be a stumbling block, but if she does a good job in contracting for outside help and knows what she wants done there is some hope of success.

Reader D is an obliging individual, in that he presents a picture of the right combination of success factors. His planned investment and willingness to get involved are just right for the complexity of his operations. He should produce a successful system without any wasted money or time. Although he may not exist in real life, he provides an illustration of the rule that a vertical line connecting the three points on the scales is the ideal. However, a line slanting from the top left to the lower right is warning of failure. A line with the opposite slant is warning of wasted resources. A sharply bent line with the bend on the left is warning of danger, while a bend on the right suggests good chances for success if the point for investment is not too far to the left of the complexity point.

Now see if you can place yourself on these three scales and from this come to any conclusion about your chances of success.

Of course, there is no intention to present these scales as any kind of scientific or accurate predictor of success in computer systems. Where you place yourself on the scales is much too subjective a decision. However, the scales can be useful in helping to think about what your computer project might involve, and to provide a warning of trouble when the points on the scales fall into certain patterns.

After reading this book come back to Figure 1–2 and try again. You will find it interesting to see how your position on the scales changes after learning more about each of the subjects that they represent.

How Computers Work –
A Nontechnical Description

You don't have to know the technical ins and outs of a computer in order to use it. However, you should know something about the basic components and how they work together. You should also know how computers go about handling the types of applications you have in mind so you can intelligently plan and select a computer that is right for you. In this chapter we will present a nontechnical description of computers and data processing, and in the next chapter we will describe how computers are actually used in business and professional applications.

THE BASIC ELEMENTS OF COMPUTERS

Computers are composed of six units of equipment which are commonly referred to as computer *hardware*:

- Processor
- Memory
- Storage
- Input
- Output
- Power supply

There is no consensus on the names used for computer equipment. What we will be calling a processor is also referred to as a CPU (central processing unit). What we call memory and storage are often referred to as main memory and secondary memory, respectively. Also, the terms memory and storage are used interchangeably throughout the industry. Even this does not exhaust the terms that are in common use. Table 2–1 (see p. 44) lists some of the more common terms used for the equipment we will be discussing.

If all this sounds confusing to the reader it needn't be. Despite the different names for things, in actual use there is little possibility of misunderstanding. We will stay largely with the terms listed above, but we will use others, when appropriate, so the reader will get used to the terms in common use.

Figure 2–1 shows how these units are related, with arrows indicating the

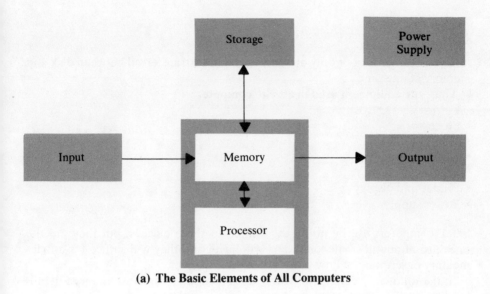

(a) The Basic Elements of All Computers

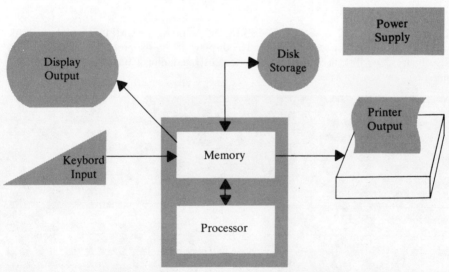

(b) The Basic Elements of Small Computers

Figure 2–1   The Basic Elements of Computers

direction of data flow. Figure 2–1(a) applies to all computers, while Figure 2–1(b) shows the equivalent units that are most often used in small computers. The slanting box symbolizes a keyboard, the rounded rectangle a TV-like display and the piece of paper rising from a box represents a printer. The storage device is a spinning disk whose operation is explained below.

Data is stored in both memory and disk. Data stored in memory is available for processing. The disk is like an overflow area for memory. It costs less than memory, so data is stored on disk and then brought into memory as needed. A large amount of data or only one record might be transferred between disk and memory at one time.

Thus, the equipment used in a *small* computer is:

• Processor
• Memory
• Disk
• Keyboard
• Printer and display
• Power supply

Small computers are by no means limited to these devices, but they are the ones just about all small computers will have, and they will suffice for an elementary description of how a small computer works.

In the following sections we will discuss computer hardware in more detail, but first it will be useful to describe some basics of data processing.

Figure 2–2 illustrates the entry of employee overtime information into a pay-

Illustration 2–1 THE BASIC ELEMENTS OF A SMALL COMPUTER.   Keyboard, printer, display and processor cabinet. The display sits on the processor cabinet, which also houses two disk drives. (Photo courtesy of International Business Machines Corporation.)

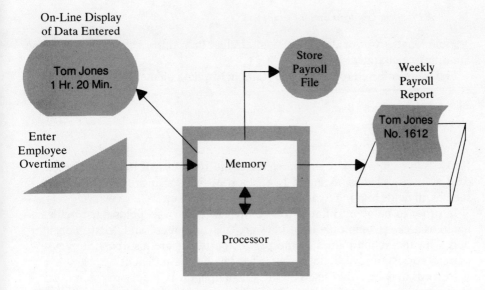

Figure 2–2   An Example of Data Processing

roll system. The overtime data for Tom Jones is entered on the keyboard and immediately displayed, character by character, on the screen for the operator to examine and verify. When satisfied that all the entries are correct, the operator initiates processing with a special entry key. Then, the processor takes over.

First Tom Jones' pay record must be found. It will be stored on disk with all other employee records in a payroll file. With the proper signals from the processor, the disk unit is able to locate Tom Jones' record and read it off the disk into memory, where it is directly accessible to the processor. Then the amount of overtime entered is accumulated in an overtime *field* (discussed below) in Tom Jones' work record. This is a simple addition. Finally, the record is stored back in the payroll file on disk.

At the end of the week a payroll report is prepared with the overtime amount included. If the system has facilities for printing checks, then, of course, the overtime entry will be included in the check amount.

This simple example illustrates the use of the three key units of all data organization: fields, records and files. These are key elements that you will be constantly concerned with in planning and using computers in business applications.

HOW DATA IS STORED

Fields

Fields are the smallest element used in data processing. They are used to store specific pieces of information, such as a customer's name, address, a part number, and so on.

Field lengths vary widely, but most are less than thirty characters and some are only one character long.

Fields are referred to variously as data fields, data elements or just fields.

Records

Records in computers are not much different from records in manual or ledger card systems. That is, a record is a group of fields that are logically related, such as all fields relating to an employee or a customer.

In order to be able to find a record, at least one of its fields must be designated as a *key*. Commonly used keys are "part number" and "customer number," but the actual names of the part or customer are also possible keys. A key can consist of several fields, but often one field is sufficient.

Records may be either fixed or variable in length. If fixed, provision must be made to accommodate the longest possible record likely to be entered into the system. This can be wasteful of memory if the majority of records can be accommodated in a shorter length. If variable, the relative positions of data fields within the record can vary greatly, complicating processing. For this reason, records of fixed length are preferred, unless the application is such that the amount of wasted memory becomes prohibitive.

Files

A file is a group of logically related records, such as payroll records, personnel records and customer records. Records are ordered in files based on their keys, usually in ascending order of the key's characters. This is nothing but the usual filing convention of storing items in alphabetical or numerical order. It provides a ready means of finding a record, basically no different than looking up a telephone number in a directory.

Files are usually too large to be stored in main memory. As we saw in the previous example, the file can be stored out on disk and the desired record brought into memory for processing.

Figure 2–3 illustrates the relationship of files, records and fields, and how they are stored manually and in a computer.

Before you can process data you will have to create files. If you already have a set of records, you will want to transfer these into the computer. This is done by entering the data from the keyboard into memory and storing each record as it is generated onto disk. Once you have your records on disk, only new data will be entered from the keyboard. Whether you're doing a data processing application, or a computational application, the rule is the same: Constant information gets stored on disk, new information is entered on the keyboard. Here we see one of the features that make computers so useful: the ability to store information indefinitely for processing and then call it up as needed.

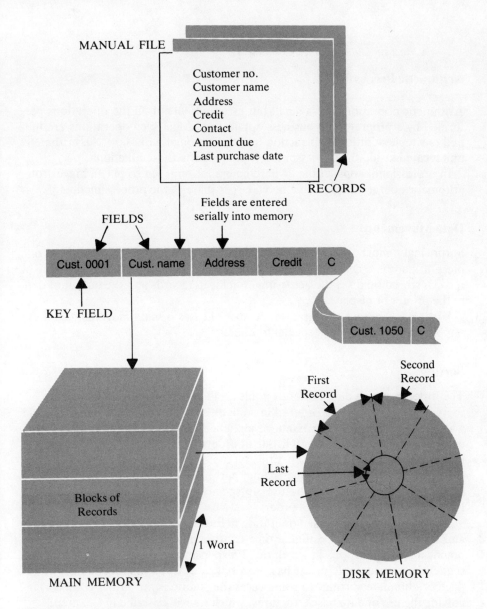

Figure 2–3 Storage of Files, Records, and Fields

HOW DATA IS PROCESSED

The processing of data is controlled by a program. The processor is the unit that is able to interpret a program and perform the operations specified. Data processing operations consist mainly of the following:

- Arithmetic
- Data movement
- Sorting
- Output preparation

Arithmetic Processing

Arithmetic operations are a small but essential part of all the operations performed by a program in a business application. Most such operations are limited to simple addition, subtraction, multiplication and division. An arithmetic unit located inside the processor is used to perform these functions.

In professional applications, where computation is apt to play a bigger role, arithmetic operations take up a much larger share of the processing time.

Data Movement

Surprisingly, most of the computer's time is taken up in moving data from one place to another. Data movement is required for data entry, the accessing of records stored on disk, the accessing of fields in records and the output of data to the printer or display.

Sorting and output preparation are special cases of data movement, but are important enough to merit special treatment.

Sorting

The order in which data is stored in files seldom suffices for all processing activity. Customers may be ordered in a file by customer number, but you might want a listing by customer name in alphabetical order. Further, within each customer file you might want a listing of orders by part number and within part number, by date. In order to get this type of report, you tell the computer to sort by the three keys: customer name, part number and date. This requires a sort program which allows the user to specify which data elements are to be used as sort keys, and in what order.

Sorting is a frequently used operation in business applications. For large files and several sort keys, it can be a time-consuming operation. At best, it is not practical for applications in which rapid response to inquiries is required. Consequently, considerable effort has been put into developing techniques to reduce or eliminate sorting. In some cases the solutions are rather complex, involving the use of data base structures, which we will describe in Chapter 3.

Output Preparation

The output of data is the ultimate goal of data processing, since this is how the results are communicated to the user. In order to make these results comprehensible and easy to use, the computer must format the data and present them with proper page numbers, dates, page headings, column headings, and so forth.

Data output is primarily of three types: output presented on a display screen, output of printed reports and the output of documents, such as checks, invoices, text, and so on. Requirements for each type of output varies, but in all cases the data is organized and formatted by a program. This provides great flexibility in the presentation of output data and allows changes to be made as the need arises.

In the typical business application, most data output is in the form of printed reports. Accordingly, a large portion of programming in these applications is devoted to report generation, and special programming languages have been developed to make this task easier. A report must contain—besides the reported data—page headings, column headings, page numbers, dates, total breaks and other miscellaneous items. All these are specified by the program and positioned in memory, so that when the data is moved to the printer a properly formatted report is generated.

THE PROCESSOR AND MEMORY

Figure 2–4 shows a simplified version of a processor and its relationship to memory. The work of the processor is performed by just two components: a control unit and an arithmetic unit. The control unit is the device that carries out all the program instructions. The arithmetic unit is the heart of a computer. The other units—memory, storage and the control unit—exist only for the purpose of feeding the arithmetic unit, where the data is actually processed. From this you might conclude that the arithmetic unit must be quite a

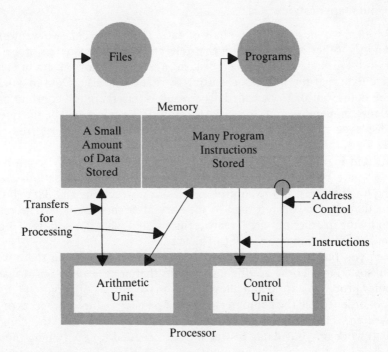

Figure 2–4   The Processor and Memory

complex piece of equipment. It is not. You will be interested to learn that the arithmetic unit of a computer often consists of little more than an adder. Surprisingly, all the complicated things that computers do in business, engineering or science can be done with nothing more than a device that can add two numbers together! When companies and governments spend millions for large, extremely powerful computers, at the heart of all their expensive equipment is simply an electronic adding machine. How is this done?

The trick is to build up complex operations from simple ones. By using negative numbers, the adder can be made to subtract. Multiplication is repeated addition. Division is repeated subtraction. Comparison results from subtraction. From these five operations others are derived. In this way, starting from the single operation of addition, all the computer's functions are generated by performing millions of simple steps. The computer compensates for its limited abilities by its fantastic speed, performing millions of operations a second. Knowing this should give you a different perspective on computers than most nonexperts have.

We can think of the functions of a computer as consisting of a hierarchy of operations, starting with the simple and building to the complex, as follows:

- Add
- Arithmetic operations
- Computer instructions
- Computer programs
- Computer applications

In storage we must have two kinds of data. One is the data we want to process and the other is the program that tells the computer how to process this data. Both types are split between disk storage and memory. Data in memory is active data that the processor is using or is about to use. Data in storage is inactive data, waiting to be called. The result is that there is a constant flow of data between memory and storage. Also stored in memory will be the information displayed on the display screen and the information transferred to the printer for output.

Notice in Figure 2–4 that instructions get transferred into the control unit. That is where they perform their work. In memory the instructions are just waiting for their turn in the control unit. Both instructions and data go to the arithmetic unit and are returned to memory after modification. The reasons for modifying instructions are largely technical, but what it amounts to is an increase in the size of memory that can be used.

When you buy a computer, there is no data in memory, but there will be some instructions. These are the instructions that are necessary just to get the computer properly started and allow you to make entries of additional instructions. In order to use the computer you will first have to buy a program or have one written. This program will provide the instructions that the computer needs to work on your data. Instructions are needed for everything the computer does—for processing, for input and output transfers, and for transfers between memory and storage.

Each instruction does one simple operation, such as ADD, COMPARE, MOVE, TEST FOR ZERO and so on. MOVE is one of the most frequently used instructions. As we have seen, a large portion of any business-oriented program is involved with moving data. Every transfer of information within the computer requires a program instruction to move the data. At this rate, it takes thousands of instructions to get useful work out of a computer. In order to simplify programming, programming languages have been developed which bypass the need to work with machine instructions. These languages will be explained in Chapter 5. For now, it is only necessary to realize that whether you plan to do your own programming or have somebody do it for you, there will be no need to work on the elementary level of machine instructions—there are much simpler techniques available.

If you buy or lease your programs, they will probably come to you on disks, or, for low-cost computers, possibly on tape cassettes. When you insert the disk, the computer will know how to transfer the instructions from disk to memory. If you have programs written for you, they will have to be entered from the keyboard. However, once entered, they can be transferred to disks for storage, so that keyboard entry is no longer required.

When your programs and data are loaded, processing can start. The control unit reads the first instruction. The instruction says two things to the control unit. It tells it what to do and where the data is that needs processing. One of the control unit's main jobs is knowing how to find data stored in memory. It gets the data, runs it through the arithmetic unit in a manner dictated by the instruction and then returns the data to memory. The return position in memory may or may not be the same as the original position. Then the control unit fetches the next instruction, and the process is repeated. Little by little, in small steps your job gets done. When complete, the result is either shown on the display screen for immediate action or printed for a permanent record. This is how a computer works.

STORAGE AND MEMORY

Since storage is simply an extension of memory, it is appropriate to discuss them together. As noted before, the terms storage and memory are used interchangeably.

We speak of *levels* or a hierarchy of memories, from the fastest to the slowest. Table 2–1 (page 44) shows six levels of memory, their characteristics and the terms used to designate them. The ruling elements in establishing memory hierarchy are speed, size and money. The higher the speed of memory the more it costs. Ergo, very fast memory is supplied in small quantities, whereas slow memory is used for storing large masses of data.

Computers used for business or word processing applications need huge amounts of storage. A very small computer could require over 500,000 characters of storage, while a large small computer could easily use 14 million or more characters. A main memory of this size would be prohibitive for the

Table 2–1   Levels of Memory

Terms Used in this Book	Level	Device	Characteristic	Other Terms Commonly Used
Memory	1	Register	Smallest capacity. Fastest access. An integral part of the processor. Not expandable.	Register storage
	2	Cache	A staging area for feeding registers. Seldom used in small computers.	Cache memory. Cache storage.
	3	Semiconductor memory	Most of what we call memory is at this level. Expandable.	Main memory. Main storage. Primary storage. Working storage. Working memory. Semiconductor memory.
Storage	4	Fixed disk	Very large capacity. Fast access. Good reliability. Expandable.	Memory. Mass memory. Winchester disk. Secondary storage. Disk memory.
	5	Removable disk	Large capacity. Acceptable reliability. Expandable.	Disk memory. Mass memory. Floppy disk.
	6	Tape	Largest capacity. Slowest access. Used primarily for back-up for disks.	Memory. Mass memory. Cassette. Cartridge.

respective systems. However, the cost of disk storage for the same amount of memory is now quite reasonable. Hence, files and programs are stored on disks. As the computer needs either instructions or data, it moves the stored information from higher levels to lower levels.

Registers are the fastest type of memory. This is where data is stored when actually being processed by the control unit or the arithmetic unit. A computer may have sixteen or more registers. Some have less. The number need not concern you because you have no choice in the matter. Unlike other types of memory, the number of registers is not expandable. They come as part of the processor. They will not influence your selection or use of the computer. You could work with computers for a hundred years and not hear of them again.

Cache memories are staging areas, used to store items that are to be processed next. They hold more than registers but much less than working memory. They are mostly used in the high end of small computers, but at the rate small computers are increasing performance, they may become common at the low end also. The presence of cache memory should signal to you high performance. However, like registers, a cache is not something a small user would ordinarily be concerned about.

You will however, be very much concerned with *main memory and disk storage*. Very few things are certain in this world, but, unless your situation is unusual, you can bet that no matter how much memory and storage you have, you will wish you had more.

Main Memory

Main or working memory is made from thousands of microscopic transistors connected in such a way that they can store information. The amount of memory that comes with a computer is not fixed. You order the amount you need in fixed size modules. However, computers vary widely in the maximum amount of memory they can accommodate, from 64,000 characters to well over a million characters for small computers.

One of your major tasks in planning for a computer will be to determine the amount of main memory you will need. Memory cost is a significant portion of your computer cost. For this reason you will want to keep it to a minimum. On the other hand, memory size is an important contributor to performance. If it is too small the computer becomes difficult to use and your application may become unfeasible. Thus, in planning for a computer, you will be concerned with finding a reasonable trade-off between performance and cost of memory.

Disk Storage

The disk is the unit most widely used for storage in computers. Magnetic tapes are also used, but their role is quite secondary to disks. Those who plan to get a small computer will find themselves giving a lot of attention to disks, both in the planning stage and in the operation of the computer. We will therefore describe disks in more detail than the other components of the computer.

Disk units store data on a spinning disk whose surface is coated with a magnetic material. As shown in Figure 2–5 (page 46), the information is stored in the form of tiny magnets. The process is similar to that of recording on magnetic tape used for sound recording, but instead of recording sound, data (letters and numbers) are written on the disk. Data can be read and written over repeatedly, so that if we want to update a record stored on disk we merely write the new data over the old data. The device used to perform the read/write functions is called a *read/write head*.

The read/write head is attached to a movable arm and data is recorded on concentric tracks of the disk. When you want to write a new record, it is placed at some selected location on the disk, just as you would select a place to put a new card in an index file. The position on the disk will be determined by moving the read/write head to a disk track and then waiting for the spinning disk to turn to the right track location.

Later, if we want to retrieve the record, we will go to the same track and track location and tell the head to read instead of write. Here we see why disks

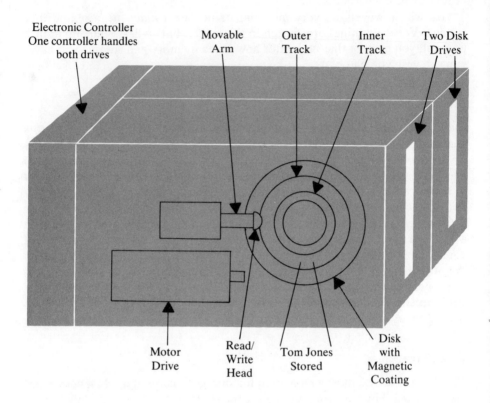

Figure 2–5   A Disk Subsystem Consisting of Two Disk Units and a Controller

are used and have replaced tapes in computers. The moving head can cover much more territory in less time than the fixed head used with tapes. To find a record on a tape you must wind the tape from reel to reel. On the average, you will have to pass through half the records before you find the one you want. With the disk you move the head straight to the desired track and then wait for the short time that it takes the rapidly spinning disk to turn to the right location. With a disk unit, one out of a million characters can be accessed in well under a second, and disks available in small computers can store from 500,000 to over 10 million characters. No wonder disk units are the favorite storage devices of computer users.

There are several methods for adding records to a file. They may be inserted in sequence or inserted into overflow areas where their position is automatically recorded in tables. In all cases, additional space must be provided in anticipation of the added records. Also, some reorganization of the file may be required, either when the record is added or at periodic intervals to place the records, temporarily stored in overflow, in their proper location.

In a properly designed business system all the details of creating disk files, adding records, changing records, and deleting records are done automatically by a facility called "data management system." When you specify a particular record and the operation to be performed, the data management system will take care of positioning the read/write head and then will either read or write the selected record. Thus, the user does not have to be concerned with where records are actually stored on disks and the mechanics of retrieving them from storage.

Figure 2–5 shows the three basic components of a disk unit. Besides the disk itself, there is the *disk drive* and the *disk controller*. The disk drive provides for housing the whole unit, the mechanisms for spinning the disk and moving the read/write head. The controller provides for controlling the head position and transmitting data between memory and the disk. As a user you should know that controllers can be used with more than one drive, thereby reducing the cost of multiple-disk systems.

There are several types of disk units. In some, the disks are sealed in a protective enclosure and permanently attached to the device. In others the disk can be removed, stored temporarily in a disk library and replaced by another disk withdrawn from the library and inserted in the unit. This provides almost unlimited storage although the storage available to the computer at any one time remains limited. The most popular type of removable disk is flexible and is called a floppy disk, commonly known as a "floppy". Floppy disks cost only $3.50 to $9. Thus, although each fixed disk may store more than each removable disk, you can store a large amount of total information at low cost on a floppy. With the floppy costing so little, it is common to develop a library of floppies which will grow as the application of your computer grows. These features of the floppy have led to its almost universal use in small computer systems. You may or may not use a fixed disk, but until a new technology comes along, chances are you will be using floppies extensively.

Illustration 2–2 DISK STORAGE.   The two verticle slots on the right provide for two 8″ floppy disks on the Radio Shack TRS-80, Model 16, multi-user computer. (Photo courtesy of Radio Shack, a division of Tandy Corporation.)

A new type of memory not included in Table 2–1 because its use is yet to be established, is *bubble memory*. This is a magnetic device which gets its name from the fact that the magnetic domains look like water bubbles when viewed with suitable magnification. They are about one ten-thousandth of an inch in size and have been tightly packed, 16 million to the square inch. Bubble memories are faster than disks in terms of access time and are competitive in storage capacity. They have the added advantage of having no moving parts to wear out or fail. By the time you read this, bubble memories may be in use in small computers.

Memories of all types must do two things. They must store information and they must provide a means for accessing that information when it is wanted. These operations are, of course, performed by the control unit in the manner specified in the instructions. When you buy memory you will be primarily concerned with how much it can store, that is, the capacity of the memory. You will also be concerned with the speed with which information can be accessed. Balancing these two considerations against how much you want to spend will determine how much working memory and how many disk drives you will buy. Working memory accesses data in millionths of a second or less; disk units in several thousandths of a second or at least 10,000 times slower than working memory. From this it is easy to see the need to provide adequate working memory, although disk storage is considerably cheaper.

INPUT-OUTPUT DEVICES

Keyboards, displays and printers are the input-output (I/O) devices most commonly used with small computers. Readers will be somewhat familiar with their operation from their use of typewriters, office machines, television sets, and display screens seen in pictures and at various places in the business world or in home computers. In fact, it is just this familiarity which makes the small computer an acceptable tool for office personnel. Since we will deal with them when we discuss equipment in Chapter 4, little need be said here except to explain to those not familiar with it the use of the *cursor* on the display screen.

Typists, working with a typewriter, always know where the next character will appear on the paper, and they have the means for moving the print location to any part of the paper by using the space bar, tabs, rolling the paper up and down, and so on. Operators working with a keyboard and display need equivalent capabilities to control where characters will appear on the screen. This critically important function is performed by a special marker called a cursor. One type of mark commonly used for the cursor is the underline, "_."

When a key is hit, the keyed-in character will appear where the cursor was and the cursor will move to the next available position. At the end of a line, the cursor will wrap around to the start of the next line. Keys are provided on the keyboard for moving the cursor to any desired position on the screen. Individual systems differ in what cursor positioning features they supply, but the minimum will allow the operator to move the cursor left, right, up and down, to position it at any allowable screen position.

Notice that the printer has been left out of the picture completely. In computer systems the keyboard does not activate printing as it does in typewriters or calculators. Rather, the printer is strictly under control of the processor. The program will tell it when there is data to print. This data will be sent to the printer together with control signals for positioning the paper, tabbing and so on. Obviously, you must insert the kind of paper that the program expects to be in the printer. If you run out, you will have to add more. And ribbons will have to be replaced. This sounds like a negligible amount of work, but if you have a heavy print load, you will find that your printer requires a good deal of attention.

There is little that need be said here about the actual operation of the printer. In the chapter on equipment we will have a good deal to say about specific types of printers that can be used, so we can defer further details of how printers work to that time.

POWER SUPPLY

Note in Figure 2–1(a) a box labeled "power supply." What is a power supply doing in a nontechnical description? It is there to impress on you the importance of the computer's life line to the electric utility. As we all know from experience, this life line can be broken at various points. Less well known is that there is a limit to what computers can tolerate in terms of having other electrical equipment, like large motors or electric switches, working off the same line. Lightning can also be a problem. Designers can design power supplies that protect against most electrical problems. But the better the protection, the higher the cost.

When competition gets tough, the power supply is a tempting place to cut corners. Performance won't suffer and the cabinet still looks great. But every time the machine in the next room goes into operation, mistakes start creeping into your records. Protection against power failure or surges is an important area, but one often overlooked by owners of small computers. This is something that must be kept in mind when planning for a computer. We will not treat it further here, but will return to questions of reliability and the protection of power supply in the last chapter.

TECHNIQUES FOR PROCESSING

There is always more than one way to do a job, in data processing no less than in other activities. In some cases the advantages of one method over another may not be significant, but in other cases they can be decisive. Techniques of data processing may seem like an overly detailed subject for nonexperts, but the serious user should understand certain basic approaches in order to assess competing products and alternative solutions to data processing problems. Accordingly, we will describe in this section techniques for accessing data, the handling of files and the two major approaches to processing: *batch* and *on-line*.

How does the computer know where information is stored? One solution is to divide the total available storage space into fixed size units. A unique address is assigned to each unit. In the same way that you can find a building if you know the address, the computer can locate information if you tell it the memory address. We can make the address divisions large or small, but in any case, our view of memory and storage will be of a large number of consecutive blocks, each having its unique address.

From what has been said previously, it is evident that the computer must constantly get data from memory for processing and put it back in memory after processing. The method used for accessing from and restoring data to a specific address in memory will have a critical bearing on how fast the computer performs the job. Two major methods of accessing data are serial (sequential) and random. These methods can be quite involved, but the ideas behind them are not.

Sequential Access

Consider records stored on disk. The records are stored sequentially in concentric tracks. One way to access the data is to start at the beginning of the outermost track and read each record sequentially, one after the other. When all records on one track have been read, the read/write head is moved to the next adjacent track and the process repeated. This method of accessing data is called sequential access. It is very efficient if we have a reason to read all records in the exact order that they are stored. An example of an appropriate use of sequential access is the weekly processing of a payroll where all records are updated and then printed in alphabetical order.

Random Access

Suppose, however, we wanted to inquire about Kenneth Zimmerman's last pay check. It is not efficient to scan all the records just to get Mr. Zimmerman's. A faster method is to scan a short index as we do in looking for something in a book. When we find Zimmerman in the index, it will give us a disk address consisting of track storage location. We can then go directly to the track containing Zimmerman's record, wait for the disk to spin into position and then read the record into memory. This method of accessing data is called the *indexed access method*. Records can be stored randomly on the disk and we can always find them—as long as the index is maintained up to date. Updating of the index will be done automatically by the system and neither the operator nor even the programmer of your application has to worry about it. Instead, the operator simply enters some such command as:

GET ZIMMERMAN

The system will then automatically look up the right track, search the track and then display Zimmerman's pay record on the screen. Methods other than the indexed access method are available for the random access of records. However, the details are rather technical and need not concern us here.

If you want to enter a record for a new employee, and assuming the records are stored in employee number order instead of by name, the computer will try to store the new record in employee number order, in order to increase

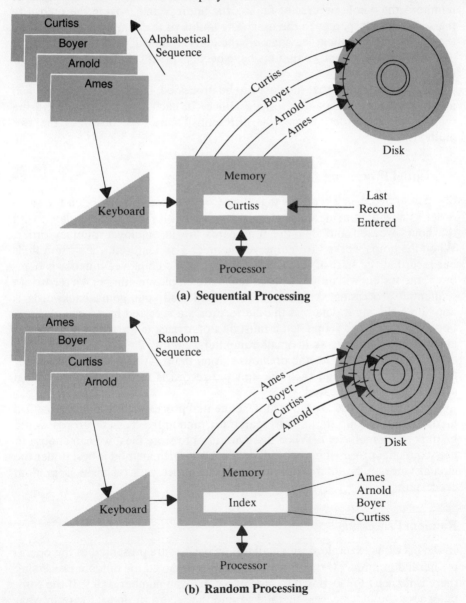

Figure 2–6   Sequential and Random Processing

efficiency for sequential operations. But first it must check to see if there is an empty slot on the disk. If not, it will be forced to go to overflow area. All this requires that the system maintain a map of storage, telling it exactly which slots are occupied and which are empty. If an empty slot is found, the slot address is entered together with the employee number in the index for the payroll file, and the slot address becomes the address for the new record. Now the record can be stored and retrieved simply by specifying the employee number—the whole process of finding the address and moving the record to the screen is transparent to the user! The ability of the computer to handle all the details of processing, leaving only the entry of new data to the operator, is one of the reasons small computers have become practical machines for the office.

There are two ways that the data can be processed, corresponding to the two methods of accessing data described above. In each case the results are the same—only the order of entry is different. Figure 2–6 illustrates the two methods.

Sequential Processing

Sequential processing requires that the records stored in a file be in the same order as new data being entered. Suppose a payroll file is to be updated with the hours worked and that the time cards are in employee number order. When the hours worked for employee number 1 are entered, the system finds her record at the start of the file. If the next active employee number is number 4, the system will move ahead in the file to employee number 4's record. In sequential processing skipping records is allowed, but going backwards is not—both the input data and the file records are accessed in a forward direction. When a record is updated it must be stored back in the file in its same relative position. When, as in small computer systems, the storage device is a disk, the system waits for the previous slot on the rotating disk to come under the read/write head and then the updated record is recorded in the original slot, or a new file is created.

When tapes are used to store files, sequential processing is the only practical method—backing up the tape to search for randomly accessed records would be impossibly inefficient. When disks are used to store files, we can choose to use sequential processing or not, depending on which method is best under the circumstances. The alternative to sequential processing on disks is random processing.

Random Processing

In the previous example, assume all the time cards are presented to the operator in random order. If the payroll program is designed for random processing there is no need for sorting the cards into employee number order. If the computer uses the index access method to find the record, it doesn't care in what order the input data is presented to it.

It is probably apparent to the reader that random processing has many advantages over sequential processing, opening up applications not otherwise possible. If a customer calls on the phone to ask how many units of an item you can ship immediately, random processing allows you to quickly bring the inventory record up on the screen and give the customer an immediate reply. Then, if the customer places an order, the record can be updated and confirmed before you hang up. This is just one example of fast inquiry and response made possible by random processing. It provides you with a whole new time scale with respect to your operations—that is, knowing what's happening *now* and being able to enter changes as they happen.

Master Files and Transaction Files

A file which stores records such as payroll, inventory or customers is called a master file. A master file stores current and historical information on a single subject, such as vendors or parts.

A file which stores new data for entry into the master file is called a transaction file. Thus, in the previous example, the time cards form a transaction file. In the more conventional approach shown in Figure 2–7, the cards are first

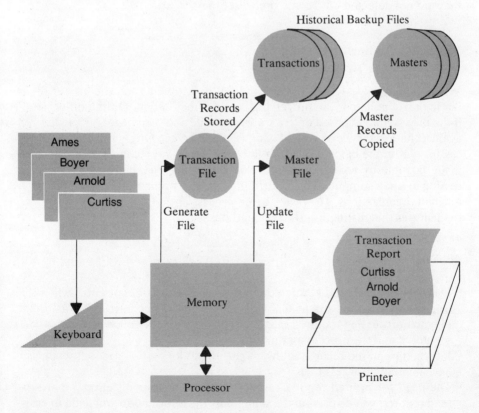

Figure 2–7   Master Files and Transaction Files

transcribed to disk, in which case the file records would constitute a transaction file, which would then be run against the master. The process is essentially the same as described above when the data was keyed in and used immediately to update the master. However, once the transaction file is created, it can run against the master without further operator intervention—the master, under complete control of the computer, is updated, record by record, automatically.

A very large amount of data processing consists of running a transaction file against a master. After processing there will again be two files: the updated master and the unchanged transaction file. The transaction records are usually retained for a period of time in a historical file. Then, if errors are found in reports, they can be traced back through the transaction files. It is also important to make a copy of the master file before each processing run or at periodic intervals. Then, if problems occur it is always possible to rerun the old transaction file against the old master until the run is completed satisfactorily.

Finally, it may be found desirable to print a report periodically, usually at end of day, from the transaction file. The report shows under clearly formulated headings the changes that have occurred in the system as a result of transaction entry. One format sometimes used is a "before" and "after " printout of the modified data. This helps trace source of errors, especially when they are not detected until some time after they occur.

Batch and On-line Processing

When data is processed as it is entered on the keyboard and the master file is immediately updated, the processing is said to be on-line. On the other hand, if the data is first recorded onto a transaction file and then processed in one run against the master file the processing is called batch. Originally, all data processing was in the batch mode. On-line processing was a considerable advance made possible by technological developments. The capability of on-line processing in small computers has contributed greatly to their practical application in small organizations. However, batch processing still has its place. Here are the features that distinguish the two methods:

On-line Processing

- Data is validated, and corrected if necessary, at the time of entry when the original document is still available to the operator. In contrast, errors found in batch processing require that the original document be located, retrieved, reentered and the processing run repeated.
- Information in the records is always current. With on-line capability you can have immediate access to it.
- The need for printed reports can be reduced. In place of lengthy, hard-to-read reports, you display on the screen just the information you need in easy-to-read format.

Batch Processing

- Programs are simpler and less equipment is required.
- Operator time at the keyboard can be less, a significant consideration when large masses of data must be entered.
- The processing time of the computer can be used more efficiently.
- If the system goes down in the middle of a run, it is a simple matter to rerun from the beginning (assuming you have retained a copy of the master). In an on-line operation it may not be known if a record was updated or not. Additional logging facilities are required to provide for this.

In order to obtain trade-offs between the advantages of on-line and batch processing, the two methods are often combined. Thus, input data may be validated on-line, but stored on disk or tape for later processing in a batch run. Or, updating of records may be batched but inquiry to data on the master file may be on-line.

Applications not requiring on-line capabilities, and, therefore performed in batch mode are:

- Accounting functions, such as accounts receivable, accounts payable and general ledger.
- Billing
- Ordering of inventory and supplies
- Activity reports, such as orders, sales prospects, and inventory trends.

This is not to say that the entry of data for the above functions might not be entered and validated on-line, but, if so, this data will be batched for later processing.

Applications particularly suitable for on-line processing are:

- Inventory
- Processing of orders
- Production monitoring
- Customer accounts
- Order entry

In these applications it is the need for fast response to inquiries and the supporting need to maintain records that are current, that dictates the use of on-line processing.

BITS, BYTES, AND WORDS

Although "bits," "bytes," and "words" are technical terms, you can't be around computers long without hearing a good deal about them. Just as all drivers learn about miles per gallon and miles per hour, even the most casual user of computers learns about bits, bytes, and words.

Bits

In an earlier chapter we mentioned that computers could be thought of as a large number of interconnected switches. Taking this view, one switch would comprise one bit. If the switch is open, we say that the bit is equal to zero. If the switch is closed, we say that it is equal to one. Thus, one bit is able to store either a zero or a one and nothing else. It is the smallest possible piece of information. All larger amounts of information can be expressed in terms of the number of bits, just as we can express miles in terms of inches. However, inches can be further reduced to halves, quarters, eighths, and so on, forever. But the bit is incapable of being divided into subunits. A switch is not half-open or half-closed, it is one or the other.

In computers, numbers and letters, instead of being stored in the printed form we are familiar with, are stored as combinations of ones and zeros. Just as the number two has the symbol "2" in our notation and the symbol "II" in the Roman numeral notation, it has a symbol in a computer composed of ones and zeros, namely 0010. If you could look inside a computer memory and see what was stored you would find the equivalent of long strings of ones and zeros in various combinations. Fortunately, the computer is able to translate these ones and zeros into the letters and numbers we are used to working with. Other than for an understanding of the term bit, you will never have to be concerned about strings of ones and zeros and the internal workings of memory.

To store all the digits, zero through nine, requires more than three but less than four bits. Since, as noted, bits can not be subdivided, we must use four bits per digit. To store all twenty six letters plus space requires five bits. If we want to include both upper- and lower case letters, numbers and all the many other symbols that are used in text, then we need seven bits. Note that to go from four bits for the ten digits to seven bits for all the upper and lowercase symbols on a typewriter keyboard requires the addition of only three bits! But we do something similar all the time. If we want to count nine things we use one digit. If we want to count ninety things, ten times as many, we add only one more digit! The rule we use is that each time we want to increase the number of things by ten, we add only one digit. With bits, the rule is that every time we want to *double* the number of things, we add one bit. To put the same thing another way, if we add one bit we double what we can do. This is why things like memory size increase in multiples of twos.

Bytes

Eight consecutive bits are called a "byte." When you hear the term byte, think of one keyboard or print character, such a "B" or a "5." Bytes are strung together in memory to form numbers, words, sentences and paragraphs. The byte is a very convenient unit to work with. In small computers data is handled almost exclusively in terms of bytes and memory sizes are specified in terms of the number of bytes they can store. Since "byte" can be loosely translated to mean alphabetic or numeric character, the term should offer no problems.

However, if you are more curious about precisely how and why bytes are used, here is the answer:

• A byte can store all upper- and lowercase symbols, seven bits, and still have one bit left over to use for checking or control.
• A byte can store one digit (four bits) with four bits left over, or it can store two digits with no space left over. In the former case the digits are said to be *unpacked* and in the latter they are said to be *packed*. Packed digits save memory, but require more processing. In any case, the programmer takes care of these details.
• The byte provides some standardization in the grouping of data. Bytes transmitted by a computer can be recognized by a communication network. Or they can be transmitted and received by another computer without special processing.

Words

A "word" is the number of bits that the processor handles at one time. It is a key indication of the power of a computer. A word can be as small as one bit, but word lengths used today in small business computers are as follows:

• 8-bit words. Most low-end computers fall in this category. Here the word length is equal to one byte.
• 16-bit words. These computers handle twice as much data in the same time as the 8-bitters. As prices fall, newer processor designs are shifting to 16 bits, or two bytes per word. This is a very common word length in the minicomputer.
• 32-bit words. The ultimate in small computer power, at least so far. These computers should be powerful enough to handle anything a small business can throw at them.

Two things happen when you increase word length. The speed of the processor increases, because more data is processed at one time. And the size of the memory that you can attach to the processor increases, because larger word lengths allow for more memory addresses. The larger memory, again results in faster processing. Although you can do everything with an 8-bitter that you can do with a 32-bitter, the time required may be so long that from a practical standpoint you might say that more applications are made possible by increasing the word length.

COMPUTERS AND COMPUTER SYSTEMS

Strictly speaking what we are calling a small computer is actually a computer system. The actual computer is really only the processor and memory. The terms "computer", "computer system", and "system" are often used interchangeably to describe the same thing. However, the terms are not really the same, and it is time, now, to take a closer look and see what the difference is and what it implies for the small computer user.

The two essential units that we must have to do any kind of computing are the processor and some memory. The keyboard, the display screen, the printer and disks could all be replaced by other devices that would perform the same functions, although in different ways. That is why the computer itself consists of the processor and memory. When we start adding other equipment—keyboards, disks, displays and printers—we are starting to build a computer system. All the equipment that is used in a system is the hardware component of a system. The other required component is the software—the programs used to instruct the computer. When these are added to the equipment, we have a complete, working *system*.

The point is that while there is little that you can do to change the processor, there is a great deal you can do in building or changing a system. Thus, you might want to use a different type of printer, or add more disks or use a different display. This is possible providing there is hardware and software compatibility. Also, with respect to programs, you might find software on the market that you would rather use than that supplied by the vendor of the computer.

Thus, computer systems can change. If you need more storage, you don't have to get a new computer. Rather, you add more disks to your system. If you want more speed you might be able to get it by adding memory. As your business grows and as your use of the computer increases, you will expand your system to accommodate your new requirements. Obviously, there is a limit to how big a system a computer can handle. When this limit is reached, it will be time to start shopping for a new, more powerful computer.

There are two system configurations that are of sufficient interest to warrant special discussion. These are systems with multiple work stations, and systems having communication links. While the computer system depicted in Figure 2–1(b) is expected to serve the needs of most readers, some will require the more sophisticated systems discussed below.

Multiple Work Stations

Figure 2–8(a) depicts a small computer system having multiple work stations. The figure shows three stations, but more or fewer are possible. A work station is the input-output equipment which enables an operator to submit work to a computer and receive results. We have shown about the minimum equipment that a work station would be likely to have—a keyboard and a display device. Conceivably, a work station could have all kinds of other facilities. Often a printer is included. However, we want to keep it simple and the basic ideas can be presented with no more than what we have shown in the figure.

The combination of a display device and a keyboard is also commonly called a *terminal*. You may hear the term applied in small computer systems, even when there is no communication line, so that the keyboard and display is called the computer terminal and a system will be single-terminal or multi-terminal.

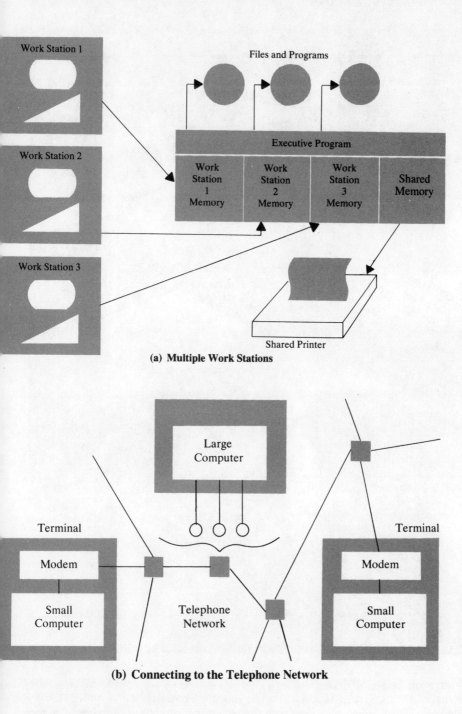

(a) Multiple Work Stations

(b) Connecting to the Telephone Network

Figure 2–8   Alternative Computer Systems

Illustration 2–3 A MULTI-USER SYSTEM.   Two users share a printer in this config-
uration of IBM's System/34, but as many as eight work stations are possible. This is a
mid-range, small computer system with communication capability. (Reprinted courtesy
of International Business Machines Corporation.)

Another way of designating the type of system we are discussing here is as a *multi-user system*. A computer or program that can handle more than one user at a time is said to have multi-user capability.

The primary feature of the system shown in Figure 2–8, is that three operators, one at each work station, can all be entering and receiving data at the same time, yet there is only one processor, one memory and one set of disks with one master file. How is this possible?

Remember that disks are mechanical devices. The processor runs several thousand times faster than the disk. In a system such as we have been discussing until now, with only one work station, the processor would spend most of its valuable time waiting for the disk to move or for the operator to hit a key. The spare time that the computer has can be utilized by processing more than one transaction at a time. To do this, each work station gets a piece of memory for its exclusive use, at least for the time it is processing a transaction. Overseeing all that's going on and acting something like a traffic cop is EXEC, an executive control program. The EXEC decides when to let a work station have access to the computer and how long that access will last.

The processor itself can do only one thing at a time. But since its speed is so fast, it appears to each operator that he or she has exclusive use of the computer. In a well-designed system the operator should not have to wait more than a few seconds to receive a response. However, if the number of work stations is more than the system can handle, the response time will rapidly increase to over five seconds. Then an operator becomes very aware that others are using the system.

There are a number of ways that the EXEC can assign computer time to the work stations. One method gives each station a time slot. When a station's time slot arrives, it receives access. When the time slot ends, that work station is thrown out and the next station gets its turn. This method is called time-sharing. It would not be a good choice for the system shown in Figure 2–8 because all work stations are sharing the same master file. It would be better to give exclusive control of the disk for one record update. This would prevent conflicts and ambiguous results if two operators try to update the same record at the same time.

While the head is being moved to the desired disk position, or as data is entered on the keyboard, processing can be performed for the other work stations. In this way processing of several work stations can be overlapped.

Multiple work stations are used for three reasons in small computer systems:

(1) There is more data to enter than can be handled by one operator. In this case it is cheaper to add a work station than to add another computer. If, as in Figure 2–5, there is only one master, the multiple work station solution is the only practical one.

(2) The nature of the business requires simultaneous access to the computer. A good example is a distributor. If a customer calls with an order, the distributor wants to be able to check inventory immediately and not have to

wait while a previous customer is being serviced. Multiple work stations provide the solution.

(3) Points of entry are separated. Consider a small computer located in an office where most of the computer operations take place. But packing clerks in the warehouse and shipping and receiving clerks on the dock need to record entries. Multiple work stations, or terminals, solve this problem.

It is a big step to go from the single work station that is provided in the typical small computer to multiple work stations. The latter are considerably more complex, requiring special programs and additional memory. Also, planning for a multiple system should not be undertaken by a first-time user without professional assistance. However, once the first big step is taken, going from two stations to three or four is not such a radical departure. The main thing, as noted above, is not to exceed the capability of the processor.

Communication Networks

The use of communications with small computers has developed at a phenomenal rate. Microcomputers came on the scene just when a revolution was taking place in communications and data processing. Extensive communications were linking terminals, computers and data bases into information systems. It is only logical that small computers of all sizes—right down to personal computers and word processors—should be connected to these networks.

Public vs. Private Lines

There are two types of communication facilities available for use with computers: the public switched networks and private lines (also called dedicated or leased lines).

The telephone system that we use with our home and business phones is referred to by communication people as the public switched network. It is available to the public for a fee and the public shares the facilities. To use it we, of course, have to dial the number of the person at the receiving end. Similarly, when a computer is connected to the public switched network a dialup operation is required. When a connection is established with the called station—which may be a computer—information can be exchanged. Connection is confirmed by having the called computer return an audible signal to the calling station. Then, by pressing a button, the computers are free to "talk." The process of dialing, acknowledging and responding can, and often is, automated via the computer and modem.

The public switched network provides inexpensive communication between any computers that have access to a telephone. However, speed of transmission is relatively slow, and there is always the possibility of receiving a busy signal when line usage is heavy. To get around these limitations private lines can be leased from the telephone companies. Private lines are reserved strictly for those who lease them, so the user has much more control over their usage. Speed is higher and reliability is better than on public lines. Hence private lines are used almost exclusively by large users of communication facilities.

Local Area Networks

Local Area Networks, or LANs, provide for communication over short distances—within an office, a building or between closely adjacent buildings. Their primary function is to connect office equipment so that data can be sent from one unit to another, substituting the electronic transfer of documents for physical transfer. Of course, small computers are an important link in LAN architecture whenever they communicate with large main-frame computers, other small computers, printers and electronic files.

How Communication Is Used by Small Computers

Although there are numerous applications for the exchange of data between computers, today most small computer users want access to either a public information utility, their own private data bases or other users of small computers.

Information utilities such as The Source, Dow Jones News/Retrieval Service and CompuServe (*see* Chapter 6) can be accessed through the public switched network by dialing the number of the information utility. The small computer then becomes a window to all the extensive data and programs that these utilities maintain on their large computers.

Extensive private database and communication networks are maintained by businesses, governments and universities. Personal computers can tap into these networks, becoming a terminal/processor that can receive data and programs from large computers (down loading), store results for later use in large computers (up loading), and exchange information between small computers (electronic mail). The potential for increasing productivity by communicating in these ways is only now beginning to be explored. However, it is being pursued vigorously and is expected to become routine procedure in a few years.

What You Should Know About Communication

Since communication has become such a prevelant adjunct to small computers, users will want to become familiar with some of the more common terms and concepts. Here are brief descriptions of the most important.

Modulation. A method of transmitting information. As in FM (frequency modulation) or AM (amplitude modulation) the varying of a signal (the carrier) is in accordance with the information to be transmitted. The information can be speech, music or, in the case of computers, data. At the receiving end the reverse process, called demodulation, is performed.

Modem. A device for performing modulation and demodulation. Required for connecting computers to a telephone line.

Integrated Modems. A modem built into the cabinet of a computer instead of being a separate piece of equipment.

Point to Point. A private line with only two stations.

Multi-Point. A private line with more than two stations. Requires some method for designating who is allowed to transmit and receive, since only one message can be accommodated at a time.

Protocol. The rules governing the exchange of data between stations. Computers must use the *same* protocol to be able to talk to one another. A commonly used protocol is IBM's Binary Synchronous Communication (or BSC). Many protocols are determined by manufacturers. Lack of standards means implementing communication between different systems can be difficult or impossible if their protocols are different.

Polling. A method for controlling access to a multi-point line, whereby each station is sequentially invited to send a message and will either decline or accept.

Simplex. Data can be sent in only one direction. The same stations are always the transmitter and receiver.

Half Duplex. Data can be sent in both directions, but not simultaneously. Requires only two wires. IBM's BSC protocol is half duplex.

Full Duplex. Data can be sent in both directions simultaneously. Requires four wires.

Digital Transmission. Transmission of computer signals without modulation. Can't use the public switched network. Telephone company provides special digital equipment. No modem required. Reliability is better.

Synchronous Transmission. A form of transmission that requires the receiver to keep in time with the transmitter for the period of a complete message. Advantageous for high volume traffic to get good line utilization. Used on high speed lines.

Asynchronous Transmission (Async). A form of transmission that requires the receiver to keep time with the transmitter only for the period of a single character. Advantageous for low volume communication to reduce modem cost. Used on low speed lines and where character timing is variable.

3

Examples of Computer Processing

In the previous chapter we gave a general description of how computers work. In this chapter we will give specific examples and discuss key points of which users should be aware.

HOW COMPUTERS PROCESS BUSINESS APPLICATIONS

In business applications the emphasis is on storing, updating and reporting of data. The amount of computation is small compared to other operations, and what computations there are usually will be on an elementary level—add, subtract, multiply and divide. It follows that in dealing with business applications we will be primarily interested in files, records and data manipulation.

In order to illustrate the processing of a business application we will expand on our previous example: the entry of overtime pay for an employee.

Figure 3–1 (page 66) shows the computer elements we have been discussing applied to this application. The payroll file is stored on disk. Each employee has, among other things, a number, a name, a regular pay rate and an overtime rate. The operator first starts up the computer according to a well-prescribed procedure consisting of throwing one or two switches and, possibly, hitting some keys.

The operator, who may be you, a clerk, a bookkeeper or other employee, sits at the keyboard and views the display screen.

Before an employee's overtime can be entered, the computer must have access to the program that processes payroll and it must also have access to the file which stores employee payroll data. Both of these we will assume to be stored on two separate floppy disks.

There should be two disk libraries—one for files and one for programs—conveniently located near the operator. Files must be updated and, therefore, you must be able to write on them. But you don't want to be able to write on program disks because of the danger of damaging your programs. Hence, you will try to keep the two on separate disks. If the payroll program and file disks are not already in the disk drives ready to go, the operator retrieves them from the libraries and inserts them into the disk drives.

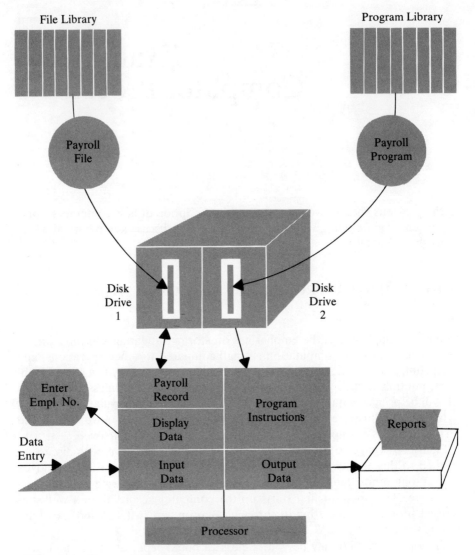

Figure 3–1 Processing a Business Application

The first thing the program might do is ask you to sign on with your identification code (ID) and then enter the date. The screen might look like this:

—PAYROLL PROGRAM—

PLEASE ENTER YOUR ID_

DATE (MM/DD/YY)

The ID is an assigned code that allows the computer to determine who is authorized to do what. In the present example, you would not want employees to be able to make overtime entries whenever they needed extra cash. Use of the ID allows you to limit access to the payroll program to those whose business it is.

Use of an ID varies widely. Some programs get fairly sophisticated, requiring three or more different entries. Others don't require an ID at all. The ID itself may be simply the person's name, or it may be a code such as a string of numbers. Some systems have the ability to suppress the display of the ID as it is entered on the keyboard so inquisitive bystanders can't see the code.

Besides providing security the ID can be used as an audit trail for tracing activity and questionable entries back to individual operators. If you have strong requirements for security, you will want to give close attention to features such as ID codes in the selection process.

The underline mark "_," following PLEASE ENTER YOUR ID is the cursor described in the previous chapter. The program has placed it right where the first operator entry is to take place.

After entry of the ID, the operator is prompted to enter the date. This might be the current date or another date that the operator wants the program to use in processing the entry. In the present example, the overtime might have occurred in off-hours so that entry was not possible on the day it occurred. The operator needs to be able to date entries for the date of occurrence, not the date of entry. On the other hand, reports and audit trails should bear the current date, so that both entries might be necessary. At this point in the program it is better practice to enter only the current date for audit trail purposes.

The date-prompting message indicates in parentheses how the date is to be entered, that is, two digits for month, two for day and two for year.

When the operator has keyed in her ID and the date, she will hit the ENTER key. If the computer finds the ID to be invalid, it will return a message on the same screen:

INVALID ID. REENTER

If the operator actually is not authorized to use the payroll program, hopefully she will be dissuaded from trying again with the thought that the computer can't be fooled. More likely, the operator is authorized but made a keying error and she will try again.

When the ID and date are validated and accepted, the program will return a new screen to display a list of the operations that the program can perform, and asks the operator to select one of them. Thus, the screen might look something like this:

—PAYROLL PROGRAM—

PLEASE SELECT OPERATION _

1. INQUIRY

2. ENTER NEW EMPLOYEE

3. DELETE AN EMPLOYEE

4. CHANGE AN EMPLOYEE'S RECORD

5. ENTER PAYROLL DATA

6. POST TO PAYROLL FILE

7. PRINT PAYROLL

8. PRINT EARNINGS REPORT

9. PRINT OVERTIME REPORT

10. PRINT CHECKS

The position of the cursor is automatically set to where the operator is to make an entry of one of the ten basic payroll operations. Now if the operator hits the "5" key, a five will appear above the cursor. The number 5 corresponds in the list to ENTER PAYROLL DATA, which is what must be done to enter overtime hours.

Lists such as those shown above for the payroll program are commonly called "menus." They tell you what's available and you take your pick. Menus can appear at the start of a program, as in the present example, or any other place in a program where there is a choice of operations.

When the operator hits ENTER, the computer picks up the data displayed on the screen, analyzes it to determine the appropriate response and immediately displays the next screen, which might appear as follows:

—ENTER PAYROLL DATA—

ENTER EMPLOYEE NUMBER (3) _

The first line is merely feedback from the computer to reassure the operator and remind her that the data entry routine was entered, as requested in the menu. The word "routine" is a valuable, all-purpose term to designate a program, or part of a program. Since we have referred to the set of instructions on the program disk as the payroll program, it is convenient to have another term with which to designate parts of the payroll program. Other ways to say the same thing could be data entry "route" or data entry "path".

The second line asks for the employee number, and the cursor is positioned at the first digit position waiting for a keystroke by the operator. The "3" in parentheses tells the operator that an employee number has three digits. If she enters less, she will get an error message.

Now assume the overtime hours are to be entered for employee number zero, one, one. The operator hits the zero key and the screen displays the second line as:

ENTER EMPLOYEE NUMBER (3) 0

Note how the cursor has moved automatically to the next character position. When the full number is entered the second line will be:

ENTER EMPLOYEE NUMBER(3)011

All three digits have been entered so the cursor rests under the last entry—it has no place else to go because there are no more entry positions on this screen.

The operator hits ENTER, but this time the response is not immediate. The computer is looking for the employee's record no. 011 on disk. But the wait time is only a second or so, and then the next screen appears:

—ENTER PAYROLL—

TOM JONES	
EMPLOYEE NUMBER	011
STANDARD RATE	3.40
STANDARD HOURS	8
OVERTIME RATE	5.10
ENTER UNDERTIME (HH-MM)_	
ENTER OVERTIME (HH-MM)	
ENTER DATE (MM/DD/YY)	07/01/80
MORE SCREENS WANTED (Y/N)	N

Note that on this screen *constant data* is separated from *variable data*, that is data entered from the keyboard. It is only necessary to enter the nonstandard data. If the hours worked are exactly eight in one day, there is no need for the operator to make any entry since the computer can calculate the wages from the standard amounts. Arranging things so that only the exceptions need be entered into the computer can greatly reduce the necessary operator time.

Note also that although a payroll record may contain information on job title, address, dependents, deductions and other data, only items pertinent to pay rate and entry of hours worked are displayed. Why clutter up the screen with unwanted data? The simpler the screen, the less chance of error, and reduction of errors is what computers are all about. Refer to the menu to see which routines you might select to get this other stored information displayed.

The cursor is now waiting for an entry of undertime hours worked. This is not the entry the operator has in mind. Now she must take control of the cursor. There are keys allowing the operator to place the cursor at any allowed position on the screen (not all positions are necessarily allowed).

Therefore, the operator hits a "down cursor" key which moves the cursor down one line on each hit, placing the cursor at the start of the overtime hours field. The screen, displaying (HH-MM) is asking for a two-digit entry for both hours and minutes. Assume the operator enters 01 30. The last four lines will now display:

ENTER OVERTIME(HH-MM)   01 30

ENTER DATE(DD/MM/YY)   07/01/80

MORE SCREENS WANTED(Y/N)

The cursor is sitting under the first digit of the date. Here the system is providing a way to enter an effective date for the transaction entered, that is overtime on a specific day. Remember that on the first screen (shown on p.66) the date called for was the current date of entry. This is now displayed on the screen. If the transaction date is the same as the current date the operator does not have to make an entry. The current date is treated as a default value which takes effect if no entry is made by the operator.

Default values are used extensively in programs to save operators from making unnecessary entries. Defaulting to the most probable value eliminates entries except in exceptional cases.

If the transaction date is not the current date the operator can make a new entry overriding the default value. Only the part of the default value that is different need be changed. Thus, the year and month will seldom be changed.

The last line of the screen asks if more screens are wanted. What the computer is doing is offering the operator a chance to view more of the data in the record without going back to the first menu. "(Y/N)" tells her to enter Y if, yes, she wants more employee record screens and N if, no, she doesn't. If Y were chosen the program would probably display a new menu to allow the operator to pin down just what data she wanted to work with.

However, the screen shows an N over the cursor. This is the default value. If no entry is made the N routine will be selected. Only if the Y routine is wanted is an entry required.

Assume in our case the operator wants the default value. Then she just hits ENTER. At this point the program would probably return her to the previous screen:

—ENTER PAYROLL DATA—

ENTER EMPLOYEE NO(3)_

The program is betting that the operator has more entries to make. This is a good bet because it is more likely than not that a number of entries will be accumulated before going through the procedure of sitting down at the computer for a session of payroll processing.

How does the operator get out of this loop? Several approaches are used. Hitting ENTER when no data has been entered can signal the program to back up one screen. By repeated hits, the operator can eventually exit the program.

A more positive and faster method is to display at the top or bottom of each screen the question:

RETURN TO FIRST MENU?(Y/N)   N̲

By overriding the default value with a Y, the operator can immediately start from the beginning.

On the first screen the question is:

END OF SESSION?(Y/N)   N̲

At this point, if the operator overrides the default with a Y, she might see the following:

PLEASE ENTER TOTAL HRS. & MIN.(HHH-MMM)_

The program is asking the operator for a three-digit total number of hours and total number of minutes entered. (To save effort total minutes greater than 60 are not converted to hours.) The program is, in effect, saying, "I know you are a careful operator, but errors do happen so just in case, let's check. I'm not going to allow posting these entries to the file until I know they are correct."

If the operator has more than just a few entries she will have added them up on her desk calculator before starting the session and will now have the adding machine tape at her side. The program, for its part, will have been accumulating totals each time an entry of hours and minutes was made in the session. It is, therefore in a position to immediately compare the two values. This is a reasonably good check on whether the operator entered the values correctly. Unless there are offsetting errors, an improbable event, this procedure will detect an entry error. Unfortunately, it won't tell you in which entry the error occurred.

If the total entered by the operator doesn't agree with that computed by the program, the program assumes that it is correct and that the operator made an error (an assumption sometimes hotly contested by the operator) and will return a message something like this:

ERROR. CHECK TOTAL OR REENTER ALL VALUES

PLEASE ENTER TOTAL HRS. & MIN.(HHH-MMM)_

In other words, the program recognizes that the source of the error could be in making the entries to the calculator or to the computer and tells the operator to try again. The cursor is set to receive a new entry of totals.

This simple example for the entry of overtime to a payroll record illustrates many of the features and techniques of processing with small computers. Many details will vary from program to program—the content of the screens, the way menus are implemented, procedures for moving from screen to screen, the terms used, and so on—but the basic approach and the methods used remain pretty much the same. These methods are so central to the successful operation of small computers that they are worth additional emphasis and elaboration.

Some Favorable Points

The display screen and the way the display is manipulated by the program make the computer easy to use. The need to learn rules is kept to an absolute minimum. Rather, the operator is led step by step—by means of menus, questions and messages. For experienced operators this step-by-step procedure can become tedious and reduce the entry input rate. Therefore, more advanced programs provide the best of both worlds—they allow experienced operators, at their discretion, to skip ahead, while inexperienced operators can call up additional instructions on how to proceed.

The type of processing performed in the payroll example is referred to as *interactive* or *conversational* processing. Interactive processing allows the user to interact with the program, responding to questions, selecting routines and making decisions as the circumstances require.

Another, more traditional type of processing, called *batch* provides no interaction. Data for entry is accumulated and sent to a computer site where it is entered all in one batch, processed, and reports are sent back. The user and the computer are always remote from each other.

Readers who have experience with service bureaus' batch processing systems will appreciate the advantages offered by conversational processing. Although we have discussed them before, it is appropriate to list these advantages again while the previous example is fresh in your mind.

- Tests made by the computer on the validity of operator entries can be corrected immediately while the source document is there in front of him or her.
- Data in the file can be kept up to date. It is only necessary to make entries promptly to have timely file data.
- Business information is continually available in a matter of seconds. An inquiry entered on the keyboard can immediately be followed by the display of information on the screen of your output unit.
- Computer entries can be made directly from source documents, eliminating transcription of data which is a source of error as well as being time-consuming.

In the first point above it was stated that the computer can check the validity of operator entries. How can the computer know if an entry is correct? It does this by checking the allowable *range* of the field. The programmer, knowing what data to expect, can program checks for:

- Required alphabetic or numeric characters in a data field.
- A minimum or maximum allowable number of characters.

- Missing data.
- Absolute bounds, such as dates not having month fields between 1 and 12.
- Logical bounds, such as a person's age or a dollar amount on a check.
- Comparison to a stored value when a unique entry is called for, as for an operator's password.

Although the above validity checks are useful they are far from sufficient for numerical data. That is why in the example the system asked the operator to enter totals from the calculator tape.

Mistakes in the entry of alphabetic data, although certainly undesirable, are by no means as critical as for numeric data. Wrong letters or transposition of letters do not always make a word unreadable, and have still less overall effect on the comprehensibility of a full sentence.

Finally, in discussing ease of use, something has to be said about the display screen itself. Even the short payroll example should be sufficient to convey how its speed and flexibility lead to more efficient business processing, to say nothing of saving wear and tear on the operator. You can buy a computer with only a printer for output and save money. But unless you really have to count pennies this is no place to economize. There are compelling reasons why the display has become an almost universal adjunct of small computers. Take advantage of it!

Some Unfavorable Points

The reader probably also noted some not so favorable things in the payroll example.

The operator had to enter an employee's number to get his record. What if all she has is the employee's name? Then she has to look up the number on a computer printout of the payroll. Or an index that relates employee name to number may be stored in the computer.

Why this inflexibility? It is simply that it is much easier to store and access records by numbers rather than names. Except in the more advanced programs, it is not felt that the extra cost and complications can be justified. The problems that result when there are more than two identical names in the file can require programming and procedures all out of proportion to their frequency of occurrence. In writing a program, the programmer must provide for all contingencies, no matter how infrequent. Thus, using numbers that are unique and individually assigned sidesteps some thorny problems. On the plus side, fewer keystrokes are required to enter a unique number for an item than its name.

In order to run a program, the operator had to manually remove the program and file disks from the disk library and insert them into the disk units. This manual handling of disks, besides being a nuisance, can be a source of damage to your precious records. Those who are going to *use* the disks must be impressed with the need for proper and careful handling techniques.

In order to reduce costs, most users try to keep the number of disk drives to a minimum. The need to copy files and programs makes two disk units a practical minimum.

By copying disks, you protect yourself against loss of data. Data can be lost in a number of ways. Damaged disks, computer malfunctions, program errors, disk unit crashes and operator error are all potential causes of lost data. Therefore, wise users see to it that they always have a spare copy of their programs and their files. When you buy a computer the ability to copy from one disk file to another should be a standard feature of the system.

These are typical of some of the types of problems that arise in data processing. Most of them are minor and can be handled. A more serious problem is the handling of files.

In business operations files are rarely independent of one another. More often than not, it is necessary to transfer data from one to another. This is certainly the case with respect to order entry, inventory, customer and other files concerned with main-line business operations.

It doesn't make much sense to enter the same data into the computer more than once in order to get it entered into more than one file. If the data is modified in one file it doesn't make sense to print the data out so it can be reentered by an operator into a second file. Proceeding in this way could call into question the computer's value as an investment.

In order to avoid excessive data entry, methods must be provided for transferring data from file to file without human intervention. The problem must be solved both on the hardware level and the software level.

On the hardware level two approaches are used. In one case, transfer between files is on-line. That is, both files are available to the computer on disk so that entries or update can be made at any convenient point in the program. Upon completion of the program both files are current. Note that the program may be an application program such as order entry, or it may be a utility program whose only function is to transfer data from one file to another. In either case the result is the same.

If both files are on-line they must reside on disk storage that is inserted in a drive unit. If both files are small they may be on a single disk. Then, a two-disk drive system would suffice, one drive for the program disk and one drive for the two files.

More likely, each file will be on its own disk, requiring three disk drives to perform a data transfer and when more than two files are related, additional drives may be required. Or you can adopt the procedure of transferring data one file at a time, saving on disk drive cost but complicating and increasing the system processing procedures.

Another approach is to store the data to be transferred between files in memory. Then, as long as this data remains where it is, it is available for transfer to any file in the system at the discretion of the operator.

From these observations it should be clear that the transfer of data between files is no easy task that can be taken for granted. The following considerations apply:

- Transfer of data between files requires careful planning and preparation.
- Files should be designed so as to minimize duplication of data across files and the number of files.
- Many software products will not provide for data transfer. If they do, they offer a big advantage and any buying decision will be weighted heavily in their favor.
- The number of disk drives required will be determined by multiple use of files as well as total storage requirements.
- The smaller the computer system the harder it will be to justify the additional cost and complications of multiple files.

Ultimately, the solution to the handling of files and data transfer must come from the development of programs that perform the required functions. Such programs are now becoming available in the form of data base systems, as described later in this chapter.

PROFESSIONAL APPLICATIONS

Even if you are a professional planning to use the computer primarily for computations, you should have read the previous section on how business applications are processed. In that section many basic features of processing with small computers were discussed and will not be repeated here. Conversely, some business applications are predominantly computational in nature so that points treated in this section may be of interest to businesspersons and managers as well as professionals.

Professional applications often, although certainly not in all cases, place more emphasis on calculations than the handling of records. The scope covered by the category of professional applications is so broad that it would be hard to make any statements about it without requiring a host of qualifications.

High-level Computation Without Files

Often a professional will have a number of formulas which model some process or device. Examples can be taken from numerous areas, financial planning, market research, engineering design, scientific research, and stock and commodity trends to name a few. The model will be general in nature so that it will have been programmed and will reside on disk. When the user wishes to apply the model to a specific problem, he or she has to supply data or parameters to the model. Then the program can grind out the solution.

Figure 3–2 (page 76) diagrams the processing of a professional application where the emphasis is on computation and a good presentation of the results. First the program is transferred to memory from disk. Now the professional enters the data. These could come from test instruments directly, but in the kind of small computers we are discussing, entry will most often be through the keyboard. The input data may be large or small, but in any case the program operates on this data directly without having to pick up a record—in this example there are no files in the business sense.

When data entry is complete, the engineer signals the program to start computing by entering a key word such as GO, START or similar command. Key words are special words reserved for the computer by which the user can tell the computer to do various operations. When the program recognizes the GO

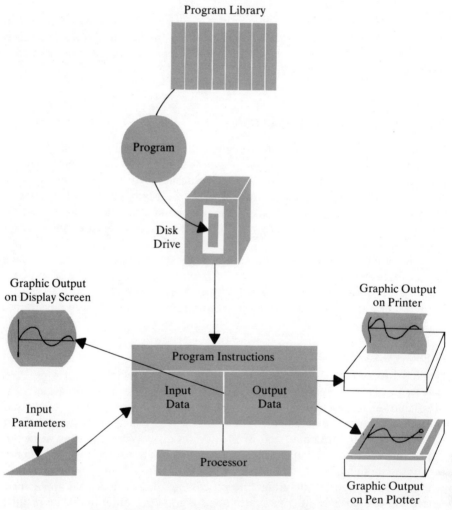

Three Possible Ways of Producing Graphic Output

Figure 3–2   Processing a Professional Application

command, it will start its calculations. Depending on the method selected by the programmer, the results can be presented either numerically or graphically. In some programs both types of output may be possible with the actual choice left to the user at run time.

In Figure 3–2 graphic output is shown on three different devices. Graphs can be presented on a display screen which has the advantage of speed but is of course not permanent. For a permanent copy, some printers have graphic capability.

The types of displays and printers that come with small computers have limited capability for graphic output. This is because their *resolution*, the amount of detail they are capable of handling, is small. For high-resolution, permanent graphic output, devices known as *plotters* are available. A plotter is symbolized as the third output device in Figure 3–2. Plotters have a pen that can be moved around a writing surface by the computer. It is capable of a great amount of detail and some models allow selection of several colors of ink under control of the program.

All three output devices are capable of combining graphics and alphabetics so that labels and numbers can be assigned as required.

Any but the most elementary graphics require extensive programs and large memories. Hence, sophisticated graphic systems are not seen on the low-end small computers. However, at the rate computer performance is increasing, graphic presentations can be expected to become a prominent tool of small computers in the not too distant future. In the meantime, graphics, while limited, can still be effective for presenting output data.

When the professional in our example sees the results he is unlikely to be satisfied the first time. He will want to ask "What if . . .?" questions. He will raise the bounds of some parameters and lower others. If the program is designed right, he will only have to enter the changes at the keyboard; the computer will remember the other entries. This process is repeated until he is satisfied that the solution is optimal. Here is where the power of the computer manifests itself. It allows the user without laborious calculations and input to try numerous approaches to a problem, guided by the latest results as to what to do next. For some types of problems it is even possible to let the computer find the optimum solution by itself.

A computer system dedicated to problem solving can live with one disk unit, if necessary. There will be little or no need to work with files and records. A simple tape cartridge can serve for backing up programs and data. However, this would be a minimum system. For really strong computational power, the processor should have a 32-bit word length and all the main memory you can afford. Also, the computer's performance in benchmark tests should be investigated.

Benchmark tests are "typical" problems run on several different computers. From such tests you can tell which computers excel in statistical-type problems, matrix handling, numerical analysis, text processing, business processing, etc. From benchmark tests you can get an indication of whether a given processor is suitable for the class of problems you will be working with.

Unfortunately, benchmark tests are difficult to run. Therefore, they are not performed often and are usually limited to just a few (three to six) of the many available computers. You will sometimes find results of benchmark tests in computer magazine articles and possibly in publications of firms specializing in the computer industry. Check the ads in the computer publications for leads. One organization that does bench-mark testing is the Association of Computer Users which publishes the results in their "Benchmark Reports." You may contact them by writing to:

ACU
P. O. BOX 9003
Boulder, Colorado 80301

An important point to recognize in connection with applications of the above type is that a *small* computer has to be regarded in a different light here than when used for data processing. A small business almost by definition has relatively small files. This makes the small computer a natural and appropriate tool.

However, a professional, a small-business person or a manager doesn't necessarily have "small" problems to solve. The complexity of a problem may have nothing to do with the size of the organization trying to solve it. A professional might contract to do an analysis for a large organization and find a small computer wholly inadequate. A scheduling problem, even for a small business can quickly swamp the capacity of a small computer.

The power and accuracy of a computer for complex calculations drops rapidly as the size decreases. At the low end, the computer is just one notch up from a programmable calculator. Therefore, just because small computers can work for small businesses, it doesn't follow that they can also work for small professional organizations.

One way to meet this problem is to use a small computer for the less demanding computations, and use a time-sharing service for the really big jobs, with the computer serving as the terminal into the telephone network.

Low-level Computation With Files

At the other end of the computational scale is the professional who needs to do only calculator-type operations, but does a great many of them. CPAs and tax consultants are good examples. Here, the advantage of the computer over the programmable calculator is its larger memory, speed, ability to display many items at a time and ability to work in an interactive mode. Other benefits can be derived by storing customer data in files and printing financial statements or other reports.

With the facilities provided by a small computer, there is more flexibility for exploring alternative tax strategies involving things like depreciation, rent-lease-purchase, investment strategies, and so on.

Because the market for professional accounting and tax programs is large and doesn't ordinarily require customizing by the user, software for these applications should be less of a problem than in other areas of professional use.

Where the application is specialized, professionals will often be forced to write their own programs. However, many of the standard mathematical and statistical operations are available and can reduce programming effort considerably. Lack of available programs is often used to advantage, allowing the professional to provide a unique service not available elsewhere.

WORD PROCESSING

In no other application is the power of the computer so immediately apparent as in word processing. Word processing allows the operator to compose, manipulate and alter text so much faster than previous methods that anyone who has had to cope with the composition and revision of written material can't help becoming enthusiastic. If your work involves the writing of anything from letters to many-paged documents, you should look carefully into how you might benefit from a word processing system.

Word processing provides for (1) the storage of previously prepared text and (2) commands that allow the operator to change or use the text in numerous ways.

Figure 3–3 (page 80) illustrates word processing on a small computer. Text is originally entered from a keyboard and stored on disk. Portions of this text can then be called up for viewing on the display screen. The operator has a number of edit commands at his disposal with which he can make changes in the text. Word processing programs have certain basic editing features more or less common to all word processing. Then they will have additional features which vary from program to program and the program's sophistication.

When the operator is satisfied with the text as he sees it on the screen, he can start output to the printer or he can store the text back on disk for later printing or for further changes.

Figure 3–3 shows a text being displayed in which a letter and a space are missing. To correct this the operator would use an insert command. There are various ways of doing this, one of which is to use the cursor to designate to the computer where an insertion is to be made. The operator sets the cursor under "R" which says to the computer: "Insert to the left of this 'R'." Next the command INSERT is given the computer which now waits for the operator to key in the inserted text. In this example the inserted text is simply the single letter "O".

When the operator types an "O" on the keyboard the text on the screen opens up to allow the "O" to be inserted. This means that all the text on that line must be shifted right one character position. If the text bumps into the right margin, there will be overflow into the next line which now also must be shifted. This might be repeated for several lines but the operator need not

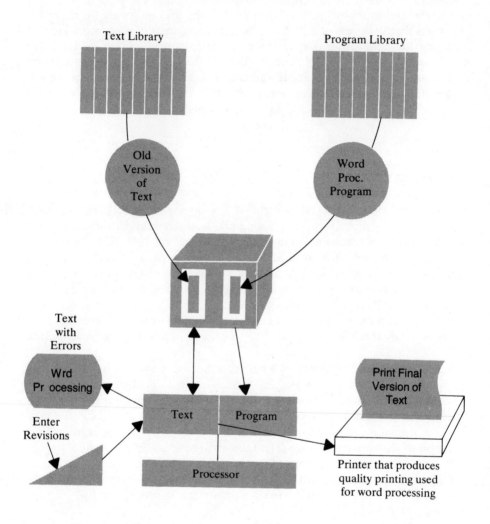

Figure 3–3   Word Processing

know this or be concerned with anything but giving the computer an INSERT command. He will then see on the display screen his keyboard entry with the text shifted to the right the necessary amount and the necessary number of lines.

This simple example of an elementary edit operation is enough to indicate how powerful the computer can be when used in word processing. The speed of the computer and the versatility of the display screen are used to advantage in a way that just has no equivalent with pencil and paper, or even with an electric typewriter.

How does the operator give a command like INSERT to the computer? There are about as many ways as there are word processing vendors. Sometimes specials keys are supplied whose only purpose is to signal a word processing command. In other cases, dual-function, or even triple-function keys are used with a shift key to designate which of the symbols on the key is active. Or the command may be keyed on to the screen into a reserved section which accepts messages from the operator and sends messages to him from the system.

The display in Figure 3–3 still has one uncorrected error, a space between the "R" and the "O." This is eliminated by setting the cursor under the blank and giving a DELETE command. Now the characters to the right of the cursor all shift left, closing the gap.

We have described two of the fundamental commands found in just about any edit program or word processor. Many other possibilities exist. If you think of some of the more complex documents you might have worked with or seen—government specifications, operating instructions, repair manuals, scientific and technical documents, for example—you can appreciate the sophistication required of a word processor that is capable of manipulating this variety of data. Not all word processing assignments require this sophistication, so that you can find a whole range of levels of word processing equipment on the market.

The commands that even a low-end word processor should be able to handle are:

- Insert
- Delete
- Move
- Copy

These commands are used with a single character or a group of characters. Thus, you can move whole paragraphs or pages from one part of a document to another. Or copy or delete them.

In addition to the basic edit commands, you can find commands which enable you to call onto the screen, by name, any document stored on disk. Another very useful and necessary feature is scrolling. Scrolling allows you to move the text on the screen up or down as if it were one long scroll of paper so that as text leaves the screen at the top it appears at the bottom, or vice versa. Some systems can scroll a line at a time; others, half a page or even a whole one. Continuous scrolling while keying in text is another possibility.

With just the features mentioned above very useful work can be done. Yet these would comprise just a bare bones word processing system. At higher levels of sophistication, you can expect to find the following:

- Justification, or straight margins on both the left and right side of the page, which produces the professional-looking copy found in most publications.
- Automatic page numbering.
- One or two underlines.
- Subscripts and superscripts.
- Tab setting.
- Centering, which allows the automatic centering on the page of such things as titles.
- Pagination, or the linking of sections into full pages.
- Left and right scrolling as well as up and down scrolling to provide viewing of documents that are wider than the screen's width.
- Search, or the ability to find and display the first occurrence of a character or group of characters. A very powerful and necessary command when working "blind" with most of the text out of sight in memory or on disk.
- Global commands, or the ability of the commands to apply to all occurrences in a document. For example, CHANGE ALL 'WORD' TO 'TEXT', will cause the change to be made for all occurrences of "word" in the whole document.
- Repeat last command. For example, this command used following a search command would allow you to step progressively from one occurrence to the next at your own rate of speed.
- Upper- and lower-case letters.

In addition to the above, word processing systems have various capabilities for formatting a page of text when printed, for selecting names for a mailing list from a master list, for calling up standard business letters, standard paragraphs or phrases, and so on. Based on the above, it should be clear why word processing has become one of the fastest-growing applications of computers.

Word processing is a different type of application for the computer. In processing for business, the subject of the processing is data and the unit of processing is the record. In processing for professionals, as described above, the subject of processing is numbers or the parameters entered on the keyboard, while the unit of processing can be said to be the problem at hand. In word processing the subject is text and the unit of processing is the page. Thus, these three areas of application can be said to have their own domain, resulting in the need for different features in the equipment used for each.

Inasmuch as the unit of processing in word processing systems is the page, it is often cumbersome to work with screens whose capacity is less than that of an 8½ x 11 inch page. Scrolling helps in this regard, but it isn't a fully satisfactory solution. This is why the more powerful and expensive systems have high-resolution display tubes that can display about 65 lines at 100 characters per line. An 8½ x 11 inch page can store about 58 lines at about 80 characters per line. Unfortunately, small computers not specifically meant for word processing use display tubes that seldom have a capacity greater than 24 lines at 80 characters per line. This is less than half a standard page. Even with this limitation, word processing systems are proliferating for business and professional use at an accelerating rate, due to the vast improvement over the typewriter that even a small screen affords the user.

It is apparent from Figure 3–3 that the same components are used for both data processing and word processing. Here is one of the big payoff areas in small computers. With the same computer you can do both types of processing merely by switching disks, just as for any program change. Originally completely separate operations, the trend is now to integrate word processing with data processing. The end product of many business and professional activities

Illustration 3–1 WORD PROCESSING.   The Xerox 860 full-page display unit provides for efficient word processing. This system combines data processing and word processing in one unit. (Reprinted courtesy of Xerox Corporation.)

involves the submission of some document—a letter or a report—to a customer, client or colleague. Thus data processing leads naturally into word processing.

However, when you do word processing, although the equipment may be the same, you will want different capabilities than for data processing or problem solving. We have already discussed the advantage of having a screen that can display a full page of text. Other screen features you may want that are not always available on standard displays are underline, upper- and lower-case letters and special alphabets.

How much emphasis you put on these in selecting a system will depend on the proportion of word processing you expect to do. If word processing comprises a very major part of your operations you might consider a word processing system designed specifically for this purpose. Be prepared to pay $12,000 and up for such a system.

Despite the power of word processing systems, they are not for everybody. If you are not used to working with a typewriter, or if the volume of your work is small, you should carefully consider before buying. Remember that for quickly scanning from page to page or section to section you can't beat working with printed pages. With a word processing system you will have to enter data on a keyboard, and you will only be able to view one screen of data at a time.

INFORMATION PROCESSING AND DATA BASES

Raw numbers and letters stored in computer memory or on disk are data. When this data is applied to some useful purpose it becomes *information*. One of the big advances of today's small computer over earlier generations is its ability to perform what is called information processing. Information processing should be a major consideration in any decision on the use of a computer.

Figure 3–4 shows the basic components of an information processing system. It is immediately apparent that these are the same components as are used in a small computer, with the addition of the one item—a *data base*. The data base is portrayed inside a cloud-like envelope to bring out the fuzziness that exists with respect to the data base concept and information processing in general. This fuzziness results from the fact that there is no sharp boundary between information processing and data processing. Usually the former is the result of the latter. With the data that is entered and stored in the computer for performing the routine business functions of ordering, billing and accounting, we find that all kinds of data that can provide information for improving operations become available. Further, information processing in its broadest sense is not limited to business applications, but can be applied to non-data processing functions as well.

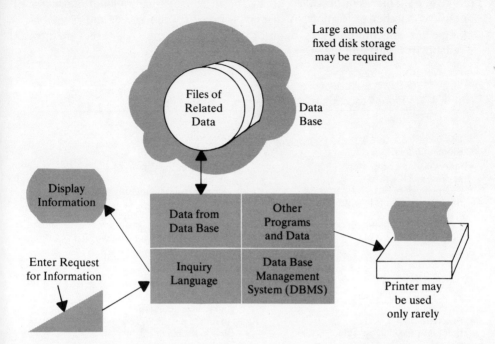

Figure 3–4 Basic Elements of an Information Processing System

Table 3–1 (page 86) should make the distinction between data processing and information processing clearer. In the first column are listed several common computer application areas, some fairly specific, others quite general, together with the traditional data processing operations that go with them. In the second column are examples of information processing applied to these same areas.

Note how many of the information processing items relate to time and the ability to get up-to-date information quickly. Another feature that shows up often is the use of existing data as input to analysis for getting better results or avoiding undesirable results. For example, data on past sales can be used to analyze customer buying patterns, allowing for better planning of resource allocation for the future. Also, the display and manipulation of data is seen to result in the use of that data for information purposes.

From these observations it should be clear why the small computer now lends itself to information processing. Changes can be entered in the keyboard to update a file record on the spot. Information can be instantly called up on the screen and appropriate action taken. The disk can store millions of characters of data which can be called up by the processor, manipulated and exhibited in a number of formats. A display, a powerful processor, and plenty of storage are the prerequisites of information processing. All three are now available in small computers.

Table 3–1   Data Processing and Information Processing

Data Processing	*Information Processing*
Customer Orders	
• Store customer orders for packing and delivery • Create invoices • Enter into accounts receivable system • Provide order reports	• Maintain current status of order • Answer customer questions on status of order quickly • Spot delays or other conditions requiring special action • Maintain statistics on items sold for guidance on future ordering strategies
Company Purchases	
• Store purchase orders for purchasing • Receive bills • Enter into accounts payable system • Provide purchase reports	• Flag orders overdue for immediate attention • Maintain records of vendor deliveries and quality • Follow up on returns
Inventory Control	
• Update count of inventory • Trigger a reorder • Enter new items • Enter into purchasing • Provide inventory reports	• Provide inventory status of any item immediately • Maintain statistics on inventory patterns • Maintain current lead time data for factoring into reorder calculations
Medical	
• Patient accounts: billing and payment	• Diseases and injury history • Allergies • Prescriptions
Professional	
• Client accounts: billing and payment	• Word processing • Modeling • Project planning • Data banks of specialized financial, demographic or other salable information
Job Shop	
• Conventional small business accounting	• Schedule jobs • Allocate machine time • Monitor job steps • Quote new jobs quickly on basis of above information

In its broadest sense a data base is a collection of data that is accessible to the user. Disk memory provides the storage for the data. Programs exist that allow the processor to pick up individual items from the millions that may be on disk, when so requested by the operator at the keyboard. The requested items are presented on the display screen, and the computer waits for the next action by the operator. Data bases are by no means limited to on-line use, as in this example, but for small computer users, on-line operation is where the big payoff is.

There are two types of programs you will often hear mentioned in connection with data bases. One is the data base management system or DBMS. The DBMS performs the job of finding the data asked for by the user and changing that data when told to do so. The other programs associated with data bases are often called a "query language" or "inquiry facility." These allow the user to work with the data base with simple, English-like commands, such as:

GET ALL CUSTOMER RECORDS WITH ZIP CODES EQUAL TO 10017 AND SEX EQUAL TO MALE

In its simplest form, a data base system might simply search a file, looking for all the records that meet the user's request. In the previous example, this would be all men with zip code 10017. Searching all records is a slow process and for on-line operation is impractical. There are two ways to speed the process up.

One method of speedup, familiar to all readers, is the use of an index. We create an index of zip codes which tells us where to look for records having zip code 10017. We can then examine the record to determine if the sex criteria is met. However, the process can be speeded up further by creating a set of second indexes for sex. The zip code index points to one of the sex indexes which point to the records. It's not hard to see that the complexity is increasing rapidly.

The second method of increasing speed of access is to include pointers in the records themselves. The first record with zip code 10017 has a pointer which tells us where the next record with zip code 10017 can be found, and so on, forming a chain throughout storage. Again, it is easy to see that to have a useful system, we will need several pointers pointing in several directions. Again, the complexity of the system grows rapidly.

All data base techniques use one or a combination of the above methods for accessing data. Data base designers play a losing game. The more they try to make a data base easy to use, the harder it is to use. That is, the faster, more versatile the data base, the more complex it becomes, which in turn makes changes more difficult, recovery from failure more of a problem and overall costs greater.

All this would limit the use of fast data base inquiry to large computers if technology hadn't come to the rescue. Now, with costs rapidly falling, fairly sophisticated data bases are being used in high-end small computers and are moving into those in the $15,000 range. As prices drop further, readers can expect increasing capability in this area.

There are several so-called data base management systems available for low-end micros costing from about $200 to $800 for the data base package. These tend to be file handlers and report generators, with some capability to use English like sentences to retrieve data. However, since large memory is the key to powerful data base managers and memory prices are plummetting, low-end micros will be seeing increasingly powerful data base systems.

Earlier in this chapter we discussed the problems associated with transferring data between files. Data base systems greatly reduce this problem and sometimes eliminate it completely. In addition, data base systems greatly reduce programming difficulty and make the computer easier to use. In fact, it can be said that without data bases, really effective business data processing is not possible.

Here are the key points that make data bases so useful in business applications:

• All data, the data base, is held in one storage area and shared by various programs. This eliminates the problem of passing data from program to program, as from order entry to accounts receivable.
• The data is independent of the programs, making programs easier to write and easier to change.
• Files and data can be linked through indexes and pointers, providing fast access to data and reducing time-consuming sorting operations.
• Files can accommodate variable entries. For example, one customer may have one order and another ten orders. In conventional files this would require that all records accommodate the maximum allowable number of orders (variable length records are a possible solution here, but they are very difficult to process using conventional files).

The reader is warned that not all programs marketed as data base software will have the above features, especially in the microcomputer area. However, when computer professionals speak of data bases, they refer to programs with the characteristics given above.

When shopping for real data base capability, check which of the above features are provided. Also, be sure to check and evaluate what facilities are provided for making changes to the data base and how you can recover your data base if, for any reason, it becomes unusable. Good recovery facilities are a must.

We have described how computers work and given some examples of computer processing. Now it is time to describe what equipment is available to perform these functions.

Equipment Used in Small Computers

We described the basic units that make up a small computer at the beginning of Chapter 2. In this chapter we will discuss these units in more detail, giving features, sizes, speed, costs and an indication of market trends where appropriate. This information is presented to give you a feel for what is available and how much it costs. It can be used to make rough estimates and compare costs of various alternatives. However, with the rapid rate at which both the technology and prices are changing, these figures will change. Therefore, before making any final decisions, it is important to obtain the most current information.

MICROCOMPUTERS AND MINICOMPUTERS

It is common practice to divide computers into three classes:

• Computers or main frames
• Minicomputers ("minis")
• Microcomputers ("micros")

Computers (without a prefix) are the large machines that have been around from the beginning of the industry. They require specially trained, full-time operators. They may also require special installations, such as raised flooring, and temperature and humidity controls. They are not suitable for the small user, and, consequently, are not the subject of this book. We refer to them only to point out and highlight the differences between them and small computers.

Minicomputers and microcomputers are both considered small computers. They do not require professional full-time operators or special facilities for installation. Secretaries, clerks and bookkeepers can operate small computers with minimal instruction time. Some air conditioning may be required, but this is usually a convenience for those working in the area rather than a requirement of the computer. All this makes the small computer suitable for placing in an office and using office personnel to operate it.

Within the category of small computers there are a number of models of various sizes. The largest minicomputer is not much different from the smallest of the large computers. Similarly, the largest micro is not much different from the smallest mini. In other words, within the class of small computers there is available a broad range, from those almost matching the large computers down to small micros not very different from those sold to hobbyists or for use in the home.

If present trends continue, micros will replace minis in most of their traditional functions. Micros are expanding their turf in all directions, so that there are now several sub-classes of microcomputers. Those of particular interest to readers of this book are:

- Business computers designed primarily for the plant and office.
- Personal computers designed for business, the professionals and education.
- Portable or "briefcase" computers designed for trains, planes and general commuting.

In this book we will be concentrating on those features which are important for the planning, selection and application of small computers irrespective of the class of computer used.

PROCESSORS AND MEMORY

The processor and memory are usually sold as one unit, packaged in a single cabinet. Nothing about the processor will change during its lifetime. It will be neither modified nor expanded. Memory, on the other hand is fully capable of expansion. You can start with a small memory and then, as your use of the computer grows, you can expand it upward to the maximum allowable by the type of processor you have. This maximum is determined by the manufacturer's design. One consideration is the number of spare slots in the cabinet that have been provided for additional memory. Typical values for the amount of memory small computer systems can accommodate are 32K, 42K, 64K, 128K, 256K, 512K and 1M bytes. Remember a byte can be considered to store one character of data. In business, "M" stands for a thousand. However, in the computer industry, "K" stands for a thousand and "M" stands for a million. Thus the above figures indicate that memory capacities are mostly in the range of 32,000–1,000,000 characters. In working with computers you will have many occasions to speak of memory in terms of 32K, 42K, etc. The term "bytes" is often left out, but it is standard practice to always measure memory capacity in terms of bytes.

ROM and RAM Memory

In catalogs and brochures memory is often referred to by the technical terms

ROM and RAM. Readers, therefore, should understand what these terms mean.

ROM stands for "read only memory." You can read information stored in a ROM, but you can't write new information into it. RAM stands for "random access memory." You can both read from and write into a RAM, an obvious advantage, with the result that RAM constitutes the greatest part of memory in a small business or professional computer.

However ROM has some definite advantages: permanence of information, low cost and high speed.

When power is turned off, all the information in a RAM is lost. Not so with a ROM. The ROM, once set, retains its information and there is no danger of accidentally overwriting it with extraneous data. Thus, ROMs are used whenever the permanence of data is essential. Examples are "bootstrap" programs that are used to get the computer up and running. With a RAM, it is always necessary to reload information from disk or tape when power is first turned on. System software that is never changed by the user—such as program language translators and data management systems—is also often stored in ROM. In this case, the lower cost and faster speed of ROM memory is used to advantage.

ROMs can be used to quickly and conveniently change what a computer does. Pull out one ROM and replace it with another and you can change certain capabilities, such as character fonts on a display or the type of language being used for programming.

ROMs are buried deep inside the computer, and users have very little occasion to deal with them. It is RAM memory that is used by the application programs to process data and manipulate information. If your requirements grow, it is RAM memory which you will buy to expand and increase the capability of your system. Typical costs for additional RAM are:

Bytes	Cost
16 K	$140–$160
32 K	$200–$300
64 K	$350–$600
128 K	$1,200–$3,500
256 K	$2,400–$4,300

The range of costs for RAM are determined by a number of features, such as speed, error detecting capability, reliability and the type of vendor.

Prices of RAM are falling faster than any other component of computers. The above figures should be considered as top prices.

Types of Processors

The main thing that distinguishes one processor from another is word length. Remember that a word is the number of bits processed at a time. The larger the word length, the faster the processor and the easier to address memory. The most commonly used word lengths in small computers are 8 bits, 16 bits and 32 bits. Occasionally you will find 12-bit or other nonstandard word lengths used. Telling a computer professional that a computer is an 8-bit machine tells him a lot about the processor and what it can do. To a nonprofessional, the word length doesn't mean much, but it still is a convenient way to scale the broad range covered by small computers. Knowing that a computer is an 8-bitter is like knowing that a car is a subcompact. A 16-bitter would be a compact, and a 32-bitter a standard model.

Processors vary in their ability to handle add-on equipment such as disks, printers and terminals. Some provide for substantial expansion of the basic system, allowing growth in a number of directions. Others don't. This is one of the key areas for consideration in selecting a computer.

The devices that are attached to the processor and memory are often referred to as *peripheral units* or *peripheral equipment*. In the following sections we will describe peripheral units used in small computers, presented roughly in the order of their importance in the planning process.

DISKS

The disk is a key element in the successful use of small computers for business applications. Only with disks can the necessary low-cost storage and fast access to information be achieved.

In selecting a storage device, such as a disk, three features are of primary interest:

* Storage capacity—the total amount of data that can be stored
* Access time—the time to find data in storage
* Transfer rate—the speed with which data can be transferred between storage and memory

Your concern for these features will vary with the intended application. In general, the smaller and less complex applications will require attention only to storage capacity. As you move up to larger, more complex systems, access time tends to become significant. Finally, for multi-user systems or very demanding single-user systems, the transfer rate also becomes significant. Since requirements of applications can vary widely even within the designations of "simple" and "complex", there will be exceptions to these rules.

As you plan your computer system, you will find yourself giving a good deal of attention to disk storage requirements. Here are the devices that are available for you to choose from.

Floppy Disks

Floppy disks get their name from the fact that the disks themselves are flexible. They are made of Mylar plastic coated with a thin layer of magnetic material. They are sandwiched inside a square, thin, cardboardlike protective cover that remains permanently on the disk, even when in use. The disk spins inside the cover and a slot in the cover allows the read/write head to come in contact with the magnetically coated disk.

One's first impression of a floppy is that it seems more appropriate for a toy than a business computer system, where important records must be safely processed and stored. Actually, floppies work surprisingly well. Although they are not as reliable as some of the other components in a computer system, they have been found to be practical and are now used in just about all small computer systems.

As pointed out previously, a major feature of the floppy is that the disk and its cover are removable from the disk unit itself. You can build a library of programs and files stored on separate disks, as needed. When you want to run a program, you insert the disk on which the program is stored in a slot of the disk unit, the *disk drive*, and close a latched cover over the slot. Depending on the data needs of the program to be run, you might do the same thing with another disk used for the master file. When the program has been run, the disks are just as easily removed.

Floppy disks cost only $3.10 to $9.00 each, depending on the quality, type, source, and quantity. At these prices you can afford a sizable library of programs and files for insertion into the computer. One word of caution. The quality of the disks varies considerably, and disks will wear out after repeated use. Therefore, for use in business or whenever valuable data is stored, only the best quality disks should be used, and these should be periodically replaced. Check with your supplier for replacement time. In addition, you can afford to make copies of your files for use as backup. All it costs you is a few dollars for the disk itself and you have a copy that can be used if the original is lost or damaged. No wonder the floppy has become the prime storage device in small computers. Nothing else can touch it in terms of low cost, reasonable access time and total storage capacity.

Figure 4–1(a) (page 96) shows the disk enclosed in its protective envelope. In 4–1(b) the disk itself is shown with the envelope removed. The reader can see here how address locations are composed of a track number and a sector number.

Floppies come in two sizes, a standard size which has 8-inch square jacketed disks, and the mini-floppies which have 5¼-inch square jacketed disks. The standard size can store between 220,000 and 350,000 bytes of usable data. By "usable data" is meant space for data that is available to you, the user. The total storage capacity of a standard floppy is about 400,000 bytes. But a large number of these bytes must be used for formatting and control, so that the controller in the disk unit will know where to store and find data. Thus, only little over half of the total capacity is available for *your* use. You must always make sure when investigating all types of storage devices, to determine how much of total storage is actually available for use. You wouldn't be the first to make the mistake of planning a system based on total capacity, only to find you don't have the storage space you thought you had. Articles and brochures don't always make clear whether they are referring to total or usable capacity.

Because the usable capacity is what is left over after all the formatting is provided for, it has become common to refer to total storage as *unformatted* storage and usable storage as *formatted* storage. Representative values for both types are shown in Table 4–1 for various recording methods. You will note a considerable range exists for the values in the table. Since storage capacity determines the size of the programs and files you can use, you should understand what is behind these figures and what trade-offs are involved in disk selection.

Look again at Figure 4–1(b) and note that there are 77 tracks and 26 sectors.

If you want information stored on track 1, sector 6, the arm which moves the read/write head must move from where it is resting to track 1. When the head reaches track 1, it will have to wait for sector 6 to roll around. Sector 6 might

Illustration 4–1 FLOPPY DISKS.   In foreground floppy disks provide programs and data for graphical displays on DEC's Rainbow™ 100 personal computer. (Photo courtesy of Digital Equipment Corporation.)

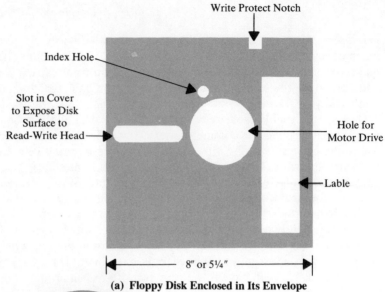

Write Protect Notch

Index Hole

Slot in Cover
to Expose Disk
Surface to
Read-Write Head

Hole for
Motor Drive

Lable

8" or 5¼"

(a) Floppy Disk Enclosed in Its Envelope

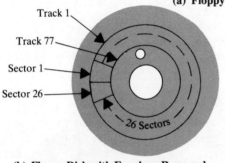

Track 1

Track 77

Sector 1

Sector 26

26 Sectors

**(b) Floppy Disk with Envelope Removed,
Showing Tracks and Sectors**

Table 4–1 Floppy Disk Characteristics

| | Storage in Bytes (Characters) | | | |
| | 8-inch Floppy | | 5¼-inch Mini-floppy | |
Recording Method	Unformatted	Formatted	Unformatted	Formatted
1. Standard density, single side	400K	240–350K	110K	66–90K
2. Double density, single side or double side	800K	480–700K	220K	132–180K
3. Quad (double density and double side)	1.6M	960K–1.4M	440K	264–400K
4. Quad-half track	3.2M	1.9M	880K	528–800K

K = thousand
M = million

Access Time

Average Access Time: 0.2 to 0.4 seconds

be the next record to come up or it might require a complete revolution before it appears. This waiting time for the sector to show up is called *latency* and is added to head positioning time to give the access time to get the desired information. In on-line systems access time is a critical figure in determining system performance.

When the desired sector is found, its contents are read into or written from memory. Each sector carries *format data*: data to identify the sector, to separate sectors and to provide for error correction and detection. The amount of format data required by *each* sector is the same whether 8 sectors or 26 sectors are used.

The more sectors used, the more total available storage must be "wasted" in format-type data, resulting in less usable data. The trade-off is between short sectors which allow you to pinpoint your access to specific data but which reduce usable storage, and long sectors which force you to read and write in big gulps but which use available storage space more efficiently. The range of values in Table 4–1 for formatted storage reflects, to a large extent, the effect of different sector sizes.

When sectors are identified by formatted breaks between sectors, as described above, the disk is said to be *soft sectored*. That is, the number of sectors and their size is under control of the system software and is not dependent on the equipment.

Another approach is called *hard sectoring* and depends on identifying each sector by the presence of a hole in the disk located at the start of each sector. Hard sectored disks usually have 26 or 32 sectors per track. Their big plus is that they can store up to 50 percent more data than soft sectored disks by doing away with the format space between sectors. The trade-off is more expensive equipment, less flexibility and hence less interchangeability between different units.

Some disk drives can accommodate both soft and hard sectored disks.

Table 4–1 shows several recording methods and the storage that can be achieved with each type. Standard single-sided floppies were the first, highly successful floppies. However, users' need for ever more low-cost storage led researchers to improve the technology until an eightfold increase was achieved! And the end is still not in sight.

The first advance was the double-sided floppy, which had to be turned over by the operator, so that only one side was available to the computer at a time. The next step was to double the density of the recording, effectively packing twice as much data on the same size disk. This was followed by the use of two read/write heads—one on each side of the disk, so manual turning of the disk was no longer necessary.

Combining double-density and double-sided disks with two heads has led to what is called *quad capacity*—a quadrupling of the original capacity of 400,000 characters for 8-inch disk and 110,000 characters for mini-disks.

Finally, another doubling of capacity can be achieved by making the tracks half as thick as previously. This can bring the 8-inch floppy into the 2-million-character range and provide the mini-floppy with a capacity of over half a million characters. With this achievement, practical low-cost processing of business applications can take a big step forward.

In Figure 4–1 the most common format for 8-inch disks is shown. It is based on an IBM product and is known as the IBM format, or IBM standard. It has 77 tracks, 26 sectors per track and 128 bytes per sector for 256,000 usable bytes per side.

A 5½-inch disk commonly has 35 tracks per side, 16 sectors per track and, again, 128 bytes per sector or 71,680 usable bytes per side.

When double-density recording is used, the number of bytes per sector will double. When half-track recording is used, the number of tracks per side will double.

Price ranges are summarized in Table 4–2.

Other formats are in common use. Check with the vendor of any equipment you are considering. As you will learn in the chapter on selection, the programs you choose will determine the disk units you will need.

As an example of the use of the above figures, suppose you had a 110-character record in a file of 1,000 items. Your records would easily fit into a single-density sector of 128 bytes. However, you need a total storage of 110,000 bytes. This is too large for the 5¼-inch mini-floppy. You could go to a single-sided 8-inch disk or a double-density mini-floppy.

Table 4–2 Some Floppy Disk Equipment Prices

Size in Inches	Storage	Equipment	Approximate Price Range*
5¼	140,000	Drive	$500
	140,000	Drive & Controller	$645
	160,000	Drive, uncased	$220–$570
	160,000	Drive & Controller	$790–$800
	200,000	Drive & Controller	$580–$600
	320,000	Drive	$325–$600
	400,000	Drive, Controller & Buffer	$800–$1,000
	640,000	Drive	$400–$700
	800,000	Drive, Controller & Buffer	$1,600–$1,800
8	500,000	Drive, Controller & Buffer	$1,200
	1,000,000	Drive, Controller & Buffer	$1,500
	2,400,000	Complete two drive subsystem	$3,300

*Low end prices are from discounters who may not provide support.

This example provides for only one file. If more files or other data were to be stored on the same disk, similar calculations would be made and total storage determined.

Which is the best approach, an 8-inch floppy, using low-density recording methods or a mini-floppy at high density?

The mini-floppy has the lowest initial cost. Offsetting this is the greater reliability of lower-density recording. Other things being equal, high-density recording will always be more error-prone than lower-density recording. Also, the cost per stored character is less in a large floppy than in a mini-floppy. Choose the large floppy, unless you really can't afford it.

Floppy Disk Subsystems

The use of a floppy disk requires several components:

- The disk drive which spins the disk and moves the head to the desired track
- The disk controller which supplies the signals and processing to operate one or more drives
- Cabinet or cover
- Power supply
- Programs consisting of a disk data management system and utilities which provide the commands for the use of floppies

All these components taken together comprise a disk subsystem. They will all be present in a working small computer; however, the form they take may differ. For example, the disk subsystem may be packaged as a unit with a small computer, in which case the user is hardly aware of its existence, except when disks must be inserted and removed from the drives. Alternatively, a disk system might be packaged separately with, say two or four drives (dual or quad drives), which can be added to a small computer for expansion of storage capacity. In this case the subsystem would be packaged in its own cabinet. It may have its own power supply or it may use that of the computer to which it is attached. Sometimes a small computer will have provision for the addition of disk drives which share all other subsystem components with existing drives.

The point is that there are considerable options on how disk storage is provided and how it can be expanded. Table 4–2 gives some examples of floppy disk equipment and their price range. Price is determined by a number of factors other than storage capacity. Reliability and performance can vary considerably. Some specific features that can increase costs are:

- Faster access times.
- Special interlocks that prevent removal of the disk when the drive is not set for release.
- Compensation for the change in data density that occurs between outer tracks and inner tracks. All tracks have the same number of characters, although they vary in diameter.
- More rugged construction.
- Provision for adding several more drives.
- The source. Some systems houses or computer manufacturers, when they sell

a system, mark up components such as disks and printers considerably more than other vendors.

Cartridge Disks

The cartridge disk, like the floppy, provides for removing one disk and replacing it with another. However, the cartridge disk is a much higher performance device, with a much higher price tag to match.

Cartridges can be lifted off the drive unit and stored in racks until needed. Each disk cartridge costs about ten times the price of a floppy, or around $70 to $90 each, depending on the model, quantity and source.

There are numerous types and capacities of cartridge disk drives. One popular arrangement is to combine one fixed, high-performance disk with one removable cartridge disk. One such unit has 10 million formatted characters on the fixed disk and 10 million formatted characters on the cartridge disk. Average access time is 25 ms (milliseconds). Compared to floppies, these are very impressive figures. However, the cost of such a unit is around $14,000. This, together with the high cost of the cartridges themselves, limits the use of cartridge disk drives to the high end of small computer systems. If you are plan-

Illustration 4–2 CARTRIDGE DISKS.   The disk drive is conveniently located by the operator in Univac's BC/7-900, a small business system that provides multi-user and multi-processing capability.
(Reprinted courtesy of Sperry Unvac, a Division of Sperry Corporation.)

ning a large data base system or a multi-user system with several work stations, cartridge disks may be justified. Otherwise, you will want to look for less expensive alternatives.

Winchester Disks

The Winchester disk, together with the floppy, is the second type of disk appropriate for low-cost, small computer systems. However, Winchesters differ in several fundamental ways from the floppy. Most significant, the disk is not flexible, but hard and rigid, and it is not removable from the drive. This places Winchesters in the category of fixed disk units, of which there are several types other than the Winchester. With the fixed disk, we immediately lose the capability we had with the floppy for low-cost storage of many files, programs and backup copies in case of damage. In addition, Winchesters are more expensive.

Offsetting these shortcomings, the Winchester has these decisive advantages over the floppy:

- About ten times the capacity
- Better than one fifth the access time
- Between two and three times the transfer rate
- Roughly 25 percent more time between failures
- One tenth the error rate

Illustration 4–3 WINCHESTER DISK.   This unit has two disks with 12 megabytes of unformatted capacity. With less or more disks, units with 4- or 20-megabytes are available. (Reprinted courtesy of the Kennedy Company, a Subsidiary of Magnetics & Electronics, Inc.)

Table 4–3 Winchester Disk Prices and Access Times

Size in Inches	Storage	Features	Price Range
Special Cabinet	5MB	Virtual File System	$2,700
5¼	6MB	For insertion directly into a floppy slot	$1,200
	12MB	Drive	$1,300–$1,800
	10MB	Complete subsystem	$2,500
8	5MB	Full subsystem	$2,500–$3,000
	10MB	Full subsystem	$3,100–$3,700
	12MB	Full subsystem	$3,100–$3,900
	20MB	Full subsystem	$3,800–$4,800

Average Access Time = 0.05 to 0.018 seconds
MB = Megabytes = Millions of bytes

Table 4–3 shows some examples of what you can expect from Winchesters. Note the wide range of storage capacities. There is also a pretty good spread in access times. This amount of variety is both good and bad. While it provides a lot of hardware to choose from, it also indicates that approaching a standard isn't in the cards until all these offerings get sorted out and some kind of dominance is established.

The term "Winchester" is not the name of the manufacturer of the device; it was IBM's code name for a new type of disk introduced in 1973. At the time, it represented a big advance in disk reliability, because it practically did away with a major problem for disk users, the tendency of the disk heads to "crash," that is, gouge the surface of the disk and thoroughly destroy a good day's processing. The term "Winchester" now stands for a certain type of disk technology in which featherweight heads are very lightly pressed against a lubricated disk, providing crash-free operation and the kind of reliability necessary to operate in a business office rather than a special computer room.

As small computers were applied to small businesses, it became apparent that more storage and faster access was required than could be provided by floppies. The result has been the adoption of the Winchester technology to the needs of small computer users. Now, some twelve manufacturers are producing Winchesters, with each manufacturer solving the problem in a somewhat different way. However, they have generally focused on rigid disks of 14, 8 and 5¼ inches in diameter. Consequently, these disks are referred to as hard disk drives, or simply 14-inch and 8-inch disks, mini-Winchesters, micro-disks—there doesn't seem to be a consensus yet on what to call them. We will continue to call them Winchesters.

The newest addition to small computer disks is the 3¼ and 4-inch Winchester. It is too early to give prices on these units.

As of this writing, vendors are scrambling to find a suitable backup for Winchesters. Backup means that you have *copies* of the data stored on the Winchester disk. In case of disk failure, the copy can be loaded in its place. Even though Winchesters are reliable, you can't risk not having the duplicate files. Everybody agrees that backup is necessary, but there are wide differences of opinion on how to achieve it. Tapes? Floppies? Removable Winchesters or other hard disks? It is too early to say what the industry will finally adopt. If, by the time you plan your system the industry has arrived at a consensus on this issue, fine. However, if vendors are telling different stories, move cautiously with Winchesters. Determine what the vendor is offering for backup and evaluate it in the context of your applications.

Floppies, cartridges, and Winchesters are not the only types of disks available. You can attach much larger and faster hard disks to a small computer and run data base management systems on them. But disks of this type are much more expensive and not necessarily suited to an office environment. It is felt that readers of this book should stay with products designed expressly for the small computer market and for use by nonprofessionals. In addition, most of you are not going to want to pay the stiff prices of the larger disks. However, if after investigating Winchesters, you find you need something bigger and faster, and are still determined to go ahead, then you should get the help of a computer professional to plan at least this part of your system. For these reasons we will not be describing the other types of hard disks in this book.

Before leaving the subject of disks and the need for increased capacity, it should be mentioned that the limits for floppies have not necessarily been reached. Floppy manufacturers will try to challenge the hard disks with greater storage capacities of their own. If they are successful, users will get an extra bonus in the advantages of backup that floppies offer. Thus, users have more than one possible answer to their storage problems, making the future of business processing with small computers increasingly attractive.

PRINTERS

The first-time user might easily jump to the conclusion that a printer is merely something necessary for computer output, and requires little consideration of what it does and how it does it. The following questions should quickly convince you that printers are a key element in a computer system, and that they should be selected with considerable care.

- Do you want your printer to produce quality documents or can any readable copy suffice?
- Will the printer be able to keep up with your system or will it be a bottleneck?
- Will you have to print on preprinted forms or can you use any kind of paper for all your printing needs?
- Will you get the kind of printer that can stand up to your printing load, or will you find it breaking down after a few months' operation?

Printers are the weak link in small computer systems. They tend to be noisy, slow, and subject to failure, and they don't always produce the nice-looking, clean copy we would like. And to add insult to injury, they are expensive. All this despite some heroic efforts on the part of designers to improve all these aspects. Since it is a rare computer system that doesn't require some form of printed output, we have to live with them and hope that we can choose a type of printer that will reduce our problems to a minimum. There *are* printers that are quiet, fairly reliable and fast, but unfortunately, for practical reasons most users will be forced to rely on types that don't have these qualities. The reasons will become clear as we describe the different types of printers and the features which make them useful or not useful for a given application.

You have two broad categories of printers to choose from: non-impact printers and impact printers.

Non-impact Printers

Non-impact printers use some pretty sophisticated technology to print at high speeds without banging metal type against paper. Consequently they are quiet and more reliable than impact printers. And there is no inked ribbon to replace or fuss with. Non-impact printers use a device called a writing head, which glides across the paper horizontally, line by line. The head works either by heat, or by electricity. In either case, a specially coated paper is required, either heat sensitive or electrically sensitive. Print is not produced from fully formed characters, but from an assemblage of dots. Most readers will recognize these dot patterns from documents they have received from the government or business firms, since this form of printing has become quite common both for impact and non-impact printing.

As the writing head skims past the paper, elements in the head are selectively activated to apply heat or electricity to the paper in tiny dots, no wider than the thickness of a printed line. The application of heat or electricity causes a change in the color of the paper to these tiny areas, which are arranged in the form of characters. Print elements on the head are arranged in a matrix of rows and columns as shown in Figure 4–2. By selective activation of the dots, a large set of characters can be produced.

The more dots, the smoother the characters and the larger the character set. About the smallest dot matrix for producing acceptable characters is a 5×7, shown in the figure. This is a widely used matrix size, about the lowest-cost matrix that is practical. The 7×9 matrix is also popular, being used where better print quality is desired. The trend is to larger matrices, so that matrix print quality is approaching the quality found in formed character printers.

Readers might be interested to know that some display screens in small computers also use a dot matrix to form characters. Although the technology is vastly different, character formation is similar in that dots of light are arranged on the screen surface into characters, just as they are in printing.

Despite their important advantages, non-impact printers have a number of drawbacks. Here are the problems you will encounter in their use:

• They require special paper that doesn't lend itself to printing on forms such as checks, bills, statements, etc.

Figure 4–2   The Formation of Characters by Dot Matrix Printers

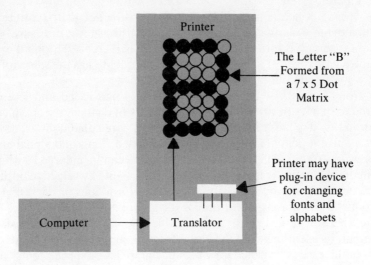

- The special paper costs more, about five times as much as plain paper. If you do a lot of printing, you will notice the difference.
- They can only make one copy at a time. Multiple copies require a separate print cycle for each copy!
- The quality of print is inferior to that of impact printers. In fact, you may not consider them satisfactory for documents used outside the organization.
- Some of the special papers tend to become degraded over a period of time. Newer products seem to have solved this problem.

Non-impact printers find wide use where the above points are not a problem, such as terminals in communication systems, and for computer printouts in professional applications intended for internal use only. Since impact printers, on the other hand, can use plain paper and can produce multiple copies, they are the types of printers usually selected for business systems.

Impact Printers

If you ever looked inside your typewriter, you were probably impressed by the number of parts, the complexity and the manufacturing know-how required to produce these by the thousands. Your typewriter is an impact printer and computer impact printers work in essentially the same way, that is, by pressure against an inked ribbon. However, computer printers are designed to go much faster. In order to achieve high speed and maintain reliability at these speeds, designers have devoted considerable effort toward simplifying the printing mechanisms and reducing the number of parts to rock bottom. Thus, they look and operate quite differently from the familiar typewriter.

There are two types of impact printers, both of which have their place in small computer systems.

One type of popular impact printers is the wire dot matrix printer. This works in a manner similar to non-impact printers, as shown in Figure 4–2, except that the matrix is formed from thin wires. Characters are printed by pressing selected wires against an inked ribbon. Print quality has the same rough appearance and limitations as for non-impact printers.

The strong points of wire matrix printers are high speed and low cost as compared to quality printers, and great flexibility of character sets. Since character formation depends only on the selection of wire combinations, computer programs make it possible to select from a variety of fonts and alphabets, such as Hebrew or Arabic. Also, the size of characters can be enlarged with proper programming. Finally, graphic output is made possible by selective positioning of the write head and the activation of wires to form lines or darkened areas. The production of graphs with printers (or any other device) requires special and extensive software. If this can be justified, graphics can add considerably to a computer's usefulness and the ease of interpreting its results. Matrix printers vary in the ease with which they produce graphics or special fonts. Ideally, these should require only a plug-in unit that contains the necessary instructions. Investigate carefully if interested in these features.

Non-impact printers, with their matrix writing heads, have similar flexibility for producing graphics and switching between fonts, but the cited problems limit their usefulness in these areas.

The other type of popular impact printer is the daisy wheel. The illustration shows how the daisy wheel printer gets its name. "Petals" on "stems" have one character embossed on the surface facing the paper. The wheel is rotated into position, and then a hammer hits the back of the petal, forcing the character against an inked ribbon. Compare the simplicity of this operation to typewriters or other print mechanisms you might have seen. Most electric typewriters used in the home and office are actually mechanical devices with power assist from an electric motor. They have about 600 moving parts, while the daisy wheel printer has only about 10 or fewer moving parts.

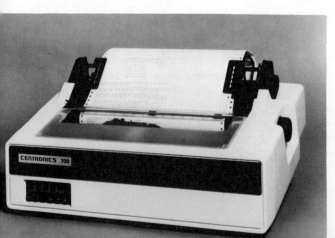

Illustration 4–4 A DOT MATRIX PRINTER. Typical rates for these printers are 60, 120, and 180 characters per second. (Reprinted courtesy of the Centronics Data Computer Corporation.)

Illustration 4–5 A DAISY WHEEL AND RIBBON CARTRIDGE. The daisy wheel has formed characters at the tips of its "stems," providing quality printing. (Reprinted courtesy of Qume.)

Although slower and more expensive than a matrix printer, the daisy wheel printer is widely used for the following reasons:

- It is the lowest-cost printer that can produce quality print at reasonable speed.
- The small number of moving parts and simplicity of design permits reasonable speed combined with acceptable reliability.
- Print wheels are easy to take off and put on and they are available in numerous fonts and alphabets.
- Each print wheel can accommodate some ninety-six characters, sufficient for both upper- and lower-case letters with plenty left over for punctuation marks and special characters.

A variation of the daisy wheel is the NEC Spinwriter. In the Spinwriter, the "petals" and "stems," instead of being in the form of a daisy, are in the form of a cup. Despite this and certain other differences, both printers are in the same class and suitable for quality printing.

Recent developments in dot matrix printers are enabling these printers to approach daisy wheel printers in print quality. To do this the dot matrix printer prints fewer characters per second. But when high print quality is not required it can run at full tilt. This is like having two printers in one, and is a very promising development for small computer users.

For some time, letter quality printers could not be purchased for under $3,000. Now they are available for under $900, and as low as $650 from discounters, greatly increasing the affordability of small computers as word processors.

Changing Printers

Can you change printers easily to accommodate different requirements? Or can you substitute one printer in a computer system for another? In some cases, yes. Printers will be attached to your computer by means of a cable and

Table 4–4   Printers—Representative Characteristics and Price

Type of Printer	Characters per Second	Columns	Price Range
Letter quality	15	126	$650–$895
Letter quality	18	80	$1,200
Letter quality, heavy duty	33	130	$2,500
Letter quality, heavy duty	40	130	$1,500–$2,000
Letter quality, heavy duty	55	130	$2,600–$3,300
Letter quality, heavy duty	80	130	$3,500
Electronic Typewriter Adapted for Computer	—	—	$350–$800
Dot Matrix, Thermal	40	80	$350–$400
Dot Matrix, Impact	80	132	$600–$800
Dot Matrix, Impact with 15-inch carriage	80	132	$900–$1,000
Dot Matrix, Graphic printer	100	—	$700–$800
Dot Matrix, with 4-color Graphics	150	132	$1,700–$2,000
Dot Matrix Impact Graphic Printer with 1.5K Buffer	200	—	$1,600–$1,800

a connector. If compatibility is present, you can unplug one printer and plug in another. But for compatibility three things are required.

(1) The connector on the new equipment must be of the same type as the one it replaces. Unlike plugs and sockets used in homes and offices, there is no universal standard for computer equipment. There are not too many variations, however, so your chances of finding compatibility here are good.

(2) The electrical signals used by the new printer must be the same as the old. The story here is about the same as for the connector—no universal standard, but not a large amount of variation either. In the case of both connectors and signals, suppliers often offer more than one type: a standard and an optional type. If both the connector and electrical signals of two printers are the same, the printers are said to have the same *interface* to the computer. One industry standard for printers is the Centronics interface based on the connector in the printers of the Centronics Data Computer Corporation. The wide adoption of this interface increases chances of being able to plug different printers into the same computer.

(3) The most difficult compatibility problem involves the programs. Printer action is controlled by programs. The format of reports or other printed document is a function of printer characteristics. If you substitute a printer having fewer columns than the program expects, you're in trouble. Other, less obvious incompatibilities can also cause problems. Therefore, even if the printers seem to be identical except for speed or type of print head, subtle differences may be present, making the two printers incompatible. You must test before you buy. On the other hand, if you know that a program is written to work with a certain printer, there should be no problem. Software vendors can be consulted on the type of printers their programs are designed to work with.

Upward Compatibility

Changing printers is facilitated if the manufacturer of your printer produces a line of printers that are upward compatible. Then you can start with low-cost, slower units and move up to faster, larger-capacity units with more features. Upward compatibility should be an important consideration if you are looking for a system that can accommodate growth. You don't have to go to the printer manufacturer to find out about upward compatibility. If it's available, the vendor of your computer system can answer your questions. Therefore, be sure to take into account your printing requirements before selecting a program. If you do this, changing printers is indeed possible.

Printing on Preprinted Forms

In the business world a good deal of printing is done on forms such as checks, invoices, statements, packing slips and so on. Printing companies provide preprinted material in a form that can be fed to the printer and properly registered so that the characters are entered in the spaces on the forms. The forms may be printed right on the paper or attached as separate pieces. Check with your computer vendor or a supplier of computer accessories and business forms. Prices are around $12, $33 and $22 for statements, two-part invoices and payroll checks respectively in orders of 6,000 pieces.

If you are going to print on forms, your printer will have to have pin or tractor feed. The tractor has a set of pins that engage holes in the paper on which the forms are attached. Unlike friction feed, which is commonly used in typewriters, tractor feed allows accurate control of the form's position. Tractor feed is common on 132-column impact printers. Smaller printers may be a problem.

Number of Copies

Non-impact printers make a single copy. Impact printers can make several copies, but the number varies from printer to printer. Multi-part forms or blank sheets interleaved with carbons are used.

Paper Handling

Printers accept paper in sheets, rolls or fan-folded stacks. Some printers can handle all three types, some only one. Which kind of printer you need should be determined in conjunction with your form-printing requirements and how these will be supplied by the printing company that prepares your forms.

Low-cost Printers

The appearance of low-cost computers has generated a huge market for low-cost printers, that is, printers costing less than $1,000. Buyers purchasing low-end small computers in the range of $2,000 to $5,000 don't want to spend over $1,000 for a printer. They neither want nor need all the features of the more expensive units. The result is that now there are a number of models priced well below the magic $1,000 figure.

Low-cost printers include both impact and non-impact printers. They can print at impressive speeds, zipping along at over 100 characters per second, and as high as 225 for non-impact printing. Many are limited to 80 columns, but there are models that can print 132 columns. A limited graphic capability is becoming a standard feature.

Low-cost printers may be an excellent choice for professionals or managers who are looking for a personal computer. For use in business applications, it is not likely that a low-cost printer will be suitable. For one thing, the paper widths handled by small printers are likely to be too narrow. Or the number of copies may not be sufficient. But most important is reliability. Will maintenance and repair costs offset the money saved by purchasing a low-cost printer? Probably.

In a later chapter it will be explained how to estimate printer loading. Unless loading is unusually light, heavy-duty printers will be the cheapest selection in the long run.

Special Requirements

The printers described in this section should meet the needs of the large majority of readers. However, we have by no means covered the whole field of printing. There are printers that are very much faster than the ones described. There are color printers for graphical output. There are special printers for printing things like tickets and tags. So if, in reading this section, you haven't found the kind of printer you need, that doesn't mean it doesn't exist. Consult one of the sources described in Chapter 6 to find what you need and to determine what steps should be taken to use it effectively.

DISPLAYS

In terms of their qualities, displays are the opposite of printers. They are silent, very fast, reliable and require no attention. Some people complain that they are tiring when viewed for any length of time. Others don't mind them at all.

There is not much variation in a display unit from one small computer to another. Most use a display of 80 columns, or character positions, by 24 rows, for a total of 1,920 character positions on the display screen. This has been found adequate under most circumstances. It can be used to image an 8½-inch wide page which is certainly one of the more common widths. And 1,920 characters has been found sufficient to present the menus and prompting that is an important element in small computers.

Illustration 4-6 A LOW-COST DAISY WHEEL PRINTER. Smith-Corona's TP-1 provides quality printing at under $900, substantially lowering the cost of word processing. (Photo courtesy of SCM Corporation.)

However, situations always exist where more display is needed. Now, some vendors are offering displays of 132 columns to better match the formats produced by the most popular small computer printers. However, display capacity will not be a major concern for most users of small computers.

There are two types of applications in which large displays are more than a luxury: word processing and graphics.

In word processing it is desirable to be able to display a whole page at a time so the user can see at a glance what a page looks like. This makes it much easier to adjust formats and to allocate text. Some word processing systems do have this capability, but so far it is found mostly in the more expensive, dedicated word processing systems. A page display will have about 66 lines of 100 characters per line.

With the displays now used in small computers, only very limited graphics are possible. It is possible to do curves, simple bar charts and so on, but nothing approaching what engineers, architects, designers or artists would like to have.

Good graphics capability requires more expensive displays. These are available and are coming into widespread use as graphics generating software becomes increasingly powerful.

Other features that you may find important when considering a display are:

• Freedom from glare and neck strain. Does this sound trite? If so, remember that it is one thing to view a display for a few minutes in a showroom and quite something else to work with one for an extended period. A display that can be positioned to reduce glare and neck strain can measureably reduce fatigue and the accompanying errors and lost time. If your application will require long sessions at the keyboard and display, give this item the attention it deserves.

- Ability to control what can, and what can not, be written in various portions of the screen. Thus, a field might accept only numbers or only letters. The most important use for control of fields is in providing for constant and variable data. For example, a menu contains constant data that shouldn't be overwritten—new data is acceptable only in fields set aside for data entry.
- Sound alarms to warn the operator of certain conditions, such as the end of a line or entry errors.
- The ability to designate fields that will blink off and on to capture the operator's attention, and fields that can be displayed at higher intensity or in reversed contrast, that is, dark figures on a light background.
- Color. Colored displays result in ease of use and esthetic appeal, particularly in graphic applications. Despite their higher costs, they are finding an increasingly large user base. Most small computer users will find their price range of $4,000 and up too high.

If your data entry requirements are light, you might consider all these features as luxuries, not worth much attention. However, if you expect a lot of data entry, the specific features of your display could have a big impact on productivity, enough to be the deciding factor in equipment selection. The ability to move quickly about the screen and not miss key items in a display could make the difference between a successful and an unsuccessful system.

KEYBOARDS

A low-cost system may have a keyboard little different from that of a typewriter. However, most keyboards for use in business applications come with several keys for cursor positioning, a numeric pad and special-function keys. The numeric pad, consisting of a calculatorlike grouping of the numerals zero through 9, greatly speeds entry of a long column of numbers. Function keys enable the operator to initiate a function in the processor simply by hitting a single key rather than having to call up an appropriate screen and then enter a command. Here again, you should try to match the keyboard to your needs. Considerable operator time can be saved by having a keyboard that reduces keystrokes and operator strain. On the other hand, for some applications special keyboard features may be nothing more than a luxury.

SOFTWARE AIDS FOR DISPLAYS AND KEYBOARDS

Some features of displays and keyboards, although implemented mostly by

Illustration 4–7 A SMALL COMPUTER KEYBOARD. Keyboard functionality is provided in DEC's Professional™ 350 personal computer. A 16-bit processor addresses 256K bytes of memory. (Photo courtesy of Digital Equipment Corporation.)

software, do require some provisions in the equipment to make them successful, and are best discussed in this section.

Split Screens

A particularly useful feature for displays is that of split screens. In split-screen mode, the display screen is divided into two parts, sometimes called windows. Each window can display different types of data and the data in each window is subject to the same manipulation as it is in the single, large screen.

   An example of a split screen might appear as follows in a word processing application:

PAGE 20

A RESEARCH REPORT PREPARED BY THE CAMBRIDGE INSTITUTE, A MASSACHUSETTS THINK TANK, STATES FLATLY THAT SOLAR POWER CAN NEVER PROVIDE MORE THAN A TOKEN CONTRIBUTION TO OUR ENERGY NEEDS IN THIS CENTURY. THIS VIEW HAS BEEN HOTLY CONTESTED BY THE ENERGY ALTERNATIVE GROUP, AN ORGANIZATION OF

POWER

COAL	3, 4, 10, 15, 25, 26, 27, 40
OIL	3, 7, 76, 17, 8, 41, 42
SHALE	3, 8, 16, 9, 10, 11
SOLAR	3, 9, 17, <u>20</u>, 21, 22

In the top window is the text, and in the bottom window is a portion of the index. The text has been selected by placing the cursor under page 20. Either window can be scrolled up or down independently.

In business applications, split screens allow simultaneous viewing of separate files, or different parts of the same file.

Some display programs allow more than two windows on a split screen. Hewlett-Packard has systems that provide as many as thirty-two windows.

Scrolling

Scrolling allows the user to shift the data on a display screen as if it were on a scroll that is rolled up or down. If data is shifted down, the screen lines disap-

Illustration 4–8 SPLIT-SCREEN DISPLAY.   A fine example of using the screen to present numeric and graphic information simultaneously. (Reprinted courtesy of Wang Laboratories, Inc. One Industrial Ave., Lowell, MA 01851.)

pear at the bottom and new lines appear at the top. If data is shifted up, the reverse process occurs. Figure 4–3 illustrates scrolling.

Scrolling can be a line at a time, a half or a full page at a time, or continuous. These functions are usually controlled by special keys on the keyboard, making scrolling a simple, rapid way of compensating for the relatively small amount of data that can be presented on even a large display screen.

In addition to the vertical scrolling described above, horizontal scrolling is also used. When the number of characters or columns per line exceeds the capacity of the screen, horizontal scrolling is a practical necessity. With data formatted for a 132-character printer an 80-character display screen needs horizontal scrolling for the user to work with this format on the screen.

Programmable Function Keys

A useful feature to look for in keyboard display combinations is the programmable or "soft" function key. This is a key whose function is not built into the equipment by the manufacturer. Instead, it is defined by the program and it can be different for each program.

One program may cause a menu to be displayed when a programmable key is pressed. Another program may interpret the same key to be a call for help. It will then display an explanation of its previous action, so the operator has a better understanding of how to proceed.

A system may provide several programmable function keys. They could be special keys located on the keyboard, or they could be located on the display unit adjacent to the screen. In any case, to be easy to use, their function should be displayed on the screen in short, clear descriptions. Thus, a line at the bot-

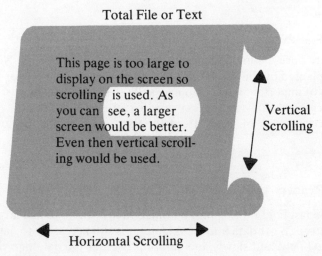

Total File or Text

This page is too large to display on the screen so scrolling is used. As you can see, a larger screen would be better. Even then vertical scrolling would be used.

Vertical Scrolling

Horizontal Scrolling

Figure 4–3   Scrolling

tom of the display might appear as follows in order to describe the functions performed by keys P1 through P6:

P1: HELP P2: RETURN TO MENU P3: BACK ONE SCREEN P4: FORWARD ONE SCREEN P5: SPLIT SCREEN P6: IGNORE ENTRIES

Nonstandard Languages

For computers manufactured and sold in the United States, standard keyboards will have English characters and special characters that are customarily used in the United States. However, some vendors can provide keyboards for other languages, or with special symbols that are commonly used in other countries, such as currency symbols. All nonstandard keyboard characters must have matching nonstandard character generators in order to display these characters on the screen. Similarly, printers must have corresponding character sets. In daisy wheel printers this may be accomplished by selecting the appropriate daisy wheel. Matrix printers require special facilities which may or may not be available on a particular model. These might cost $100 to $200 per character set.

SPECIAL DEVICES

We have covered the basic and most commonly used components of small computers. However, there are other devices that can be added to a system. Here is a brief rundown of the most important.

Magnetic Tapes

Tapes were once the main storage medium for data processing. Now they have been supplanted by the much faster disks and are used mostly for storing backup copies of important data. You may still see some very low-cost systems that use tape cassettes for actual processing, or large systems that have a lot of sequential processing and can afford the extra cost of high-performance tape units.

Optical Readers

One of the last hold-outs against automation in both small and large computers is data entry. To get data into a computer it is still necessary to have somebody sit at a keyboard and slowly and laboriously enter the data one character at a time. There should be a better way, and optical readers are an attempt to provide one. Unfortunately, the attempt has not been entirely successful. Optical readers work something like TV cameras in that they convert what they see into electrical signals. An optical reader is focused on an input document and it converts the numbers and letters into computer code. This is no mean task. Accordingly, optical readers are expensive and the number of rejected documents can be high. Nevertheless we mention them here because, if you have the right kind of application, optical readers can save you lots of time and money.

Here are the requirements for successful application of optical readers:

• A high volume of input data to justify the cost of the optical reader.
• No handwritten characters. (Some readers can accept handwritten numbers but none accept letters.)
• Cleanly printed characters with good contrast under all conditions of handling.
• Documents that are easy to feed to the reader and not subject to bending, tears, etc.

Not all optical readers read numbers and letters. Consider the items you buy in a market. The dark and light bands on the packages are bar codes that can be read by an optical reader. Since codes are easier to read than characters, bar code readers are much cheaper than character readers. The larger the bar code the easier to read and the lower the cost. Special printers are available for printing bar codes for inventory, bins, boxes, and so on.

Plotters

Plotters are automatic drawing machines. A pen controlled by the computer traverses a piece of paper and the result can be a graph, a map, an engineering drawing, a cartoon, an address design, a music score or any other of the many things that we put on paper, including letters and numbers of all sizes and shapes. Add to this the ability to use four or more colors and you have a device that should eventually greatly increase the utility of small computers for professionals. As of now, the use of plotters is limited by present capabilities of small computers. To exploit their real potential requires lots of software, lots of storage and lots of memory. As these all come down in price, the use of plotters in professional use can be expected to grow rapidly.

Starting from about $1,000 for the simplest, bare-bones plotter, numerous models are available at costs up to several hundred thousand dollars. A low-cost plotting system suitable for professional use can be had for $1,400 to $5,000.

Digitizers

Digitizers convert things like graphs, maps and drawings to signals that can be fed into a computer for storage and processing. In a sense, they perform the reverse operation of a plotter. An operator holds a pointer or pair of cross hairs over the document to be fed into the computer. The cross hairs are moved along the lines of the document and the coordinates of each point are simultaneously sent to the computer. Provision is also made for the entry of labels and commands on a keyboard.

There is a big potential for the use of digitizers by professionals. Graphic data and complex functions can be quickly entered into a computer using a digitizer. But, as with plotters, their use requires the purchase of a good deal of specialized software.

Modems

Modems are devices for connecting computers, printers, displays or other devices to communication lines. Their principal function is to convert the signals used to carry messages on the telephone lines to the different type of signals used by computer equipment. Modems sit quietly in a corner doing their job without requiring attention as long as they are in working order. The thing to keep in mind is that (1) you can connect to a communication line if you want to, (2) if you do so, you will have to figure in the cost of a modem, (3) modem cost depends on how fast you want to send your messages, and (4) you will need special programs for sending and receiving data.

The simplest modem to use is the type that incorporates an acoustic coupler. The acoustic coupler has a cradle into which you put your telephone. Beeps generated by the coupler from computer data are "heard" by the telephone and sent on their way down the telephone line to any telephone number that has been previously dialed.

At the other end, the signals are received, and new ones are transmitted. These come out at your telephone as a new set of beeps. On "hearing" these sounds, the acoustic coupler converts them to electrical signals and sends them to your computer.

Acoustic couplers are limited in both speed and reliability, but are widely used for low-volume applications, especially for communicating with time-sharing services. For high-volume applications, it is better to dispense with the acoustic coupler and use a direct electrical connection.

The cost of modems is determined primarily by speed, usually specified in bits per second (BPS). Speeds vary from 75 to 9600 BPS. Users of small systems will not often exceed 2400 BPS and will more likely find 300 to 600 BPS adequate.

Costs for modems that operate in the range of 75 to 600 BPS are $200 to $500.

Almost any vendor of equipment or a time-sharing service can provide the equipment and assist you in hooking your computer into the telephone network. Other specialized features discussed in this section will be more of a problem.

Ask vendors about optical readers, plotters, digitizers and so on. Ads in computer magazines and *Thomas Register* are good sources for leads. Manufacturers don't usually sell directly to users, but they can tell you who does.

STANDARDS FOR EQUIPMENT

You can buy an electrical appliance anywhere in the country, knowing that you can bring it home, plug it into a wall socket and turn it on. Standard plugs, sockets and voltages are so common that we take them for granted in our everyday life.

While there are some standards in the computer industry, they cover a very small part of the total equipment. Unlike home appliances, the peripheral units we have described above can not just be plugged into any processor. Plugs and sockets may be different, electrical signals may be different and the programs in the processor may not be right for generating and receiving the commands—"hand shaking"—between processor and peripheral unit.

Although everybody recognizes the advantages provided by standards, their development and acceptance in the computer industry is limited because of the speed with which changes in equipment occur and the vested interest that manufacturers have in their own way of doing things.

Lacking official government or industry standards, we find vendors adopting de facto standards that are the result of economic pressures to produce pieces of equipment that can talk to each other.

De facto standards are set primarily by dominant companies or sometimes by small, innovative companies who are first to market a successful product. Consequently, many of the de facto standards are set by IBM. Small companies know their market will be bigger if their products can connect and work with IBM equipment. At the low end of the market, Radio Shack, Apple, and Commodore's PET computers set de facto standards by virtue of the many smaller companies who want to be able to connect to this widely-used equipment.

Another important de facto standard used at the low end of the market is the S-100 bus. A *bus* is a group of wires used to connect peripheral units and memory to a processor. The S-100 bus has specific signals assigned to each wire, so if an S-100 device is plugged into an S-100 processor, they can work together. S-100 products are mostly low-end systems, suitable for professionals or very small businesses. Buying an S-100 bus computer has, in the past, insured the buyer that a host of other products could be attached with minimal interface problems. However, the future of the S-100 bus is in doubt as larger firms, with no commitment to the S-100 bus, move into the small computer business.

Since de facto standards are the result of consensus, it is not surprising that some variation can be found between different implementations of these standards. You can not assume that all products advertised as conforming to a de facto standard are identical at the interface. Variations are possible, and may require adjustments or rejection of a product.

Two *official* standards adopted in the computer industry that you should know about are described below.

ASCII

ASCII stands for American Standard Code for Information Interchange. It specifies how all the letters, numbers and other characters are coded into signals for the computer. Keyboards, processors and printers designed for the ASCII code can talk to one another.

RS-232C

RS-232C is a standard used where a piece of equipment is to be connected to another. While ASCII specifies coding of characters, RS-232C specifies signals, voltages, etc. If manufacturer A and manufacturer B both use RS-232C, you can plug one into the other and they will work together electrically. Many manufacturers use RS-232C, but those who don't often supply it as an option.

RS-232C is intended for serial movement of data, that is, only one wire is used for data and only one bit of data is moved at a time. This is slow but cheap. For faster data movement, parallel transmission is used, in which one byte (8 bits) or one word is moved at a time over a bundle of wires.

Although RE-232C uses only one line to transmit data in a given direction, it actually specifies 25 lines—or 25 pins on a connector. Included in these 25 lines are lines for electrical paths and for hand-shaking between equipment such as, "Request to Send."

While the RS-232C standard is fairly explicit, its implementation by various manufacturers varies significantly. All 25 pins are rarely used and usage of pins varies. The result is that when a connection is said to be RS-232C you can't count on compatibility—investigate before buying.

RS-232C is found in many printer and modem connections to computers. When not RS-232C, the chances are a printer will use the Centronics parallel-type interface.

PUTTING IT ALL TOGETHER

When the various devices described above are connected so they can work together, you have a small computer system. It should be clear by now that the capability and cost of this system will depend on such things as the word length of the processor, the amount of memory, the types of disks used, the quantity of each type and, finally, the type of printer you select.

The typical small computer buyer will pay between $1,500 and $15,000 for his or her equipment. However, as we will see in later chapters, costs for a number of other items must also be considered.

What You Should
Know About Programs

In order to make the computer work for you, you must supply it with the right programs. Depending on how it's programmed, a computer can be made to do a great number of things. Your task is to get it to do the things you want. The only way to do this is with programs that have the right fit for your applications.

For example, if your interest is in an inventory system, it is not enough to just pick up a program package labeled "A General Purpose Inventory System." There are many types of inventory and many different requirements from one business to another. If you try to apply the wrong program package to your business, you will find yourself forced to change the way you operate, not able to provide for various situations unique to your industry and lacking in some of the information necessary to monitor operations and make decisions.

Thus, programs are of critical importance to anyone using a computer. Most readers of this book may never come close to programming or learning about it in detail. Nor is it necessary. But there are definite things every serious user should know about the subject. Accordingly, in this chapter we will present an overview of the world of programming. Then, in later chapters we will describe the role of programs in computer selection and how to determine what program is right for you.

HOW PROGRAMS ARE WRITTEN

Programmers string together computer instructions in the proper sequence to get the computer to do a job. This task is referred to as both programming and coding. The programmer writes each instruction on a standard coding sheet, and when the program is complete, the instructions are keyed in at the computer keyboard and the entries verified by inspection of the display. Short programs can be entered directly without using coding sheets. However, many programs can have several thousand instructions, in which case the use of coding forms becomes necessary.

Computers can be programmed using the instructions built into the computer hardware by the manufacturer. However, these built-in instructions are complicated and hard to work with, making their direct use a laborious, error-prone activity. Programmers, naturally enough, began looking for a better way. The result was programming languages.

Early workers on computers soon realized that they were continuously repeating certain sets of instructions, such as those for inputting or outputting data. Why not code these instructions once, and give the whole group a name? Then, whenever the instruction group was needed, they could use just the name instead of the whole set of instructions. This was the beginning of program languages. Program languages simplify the writing of programs. They use one word to specify a large number of computer instructions.

There are several levels of program languages, each successive level reflecting an increased power and ease of use for the programmer. Most programs written for computers today are written in what are called *higher-level languages*.

Another key advance was the naming of data. Remember that the computer memory can have millions of addresses, each address representing where a different piece of data is stored. Imagine the programmer's job if he or she had to keep track of all these addresses in order to store and retrieve data! The solution is simple and ingenious: Let the computer do this work. How? By assigning meaningful names to data, such as NAME, OCCUPATION or NET-PAY. The computer keeps an index of where each such name's data is stored. Then, for example, if the programmer issues a GET NET-PAY, the computer knows the exact address where the data is stored.

The computer also keeps track of memory space used and memory space available. Then, when the computer sees a name it hasn't seen before, it finds a place to store the named data in memory and then makes a new entry in the index.

Combining names for instruction groups and names for data we get what are called "statements" in higher-level languages. Each statement written by a programmer in a program language can save the writing of as many as twenty computer instructions.

Knowing this, it is easy to see how program languages work. Here is an example from the COBOL language:

WRITE PRINT-LINE FROM NET-PAY.

This statement tells the computer to print an amount equal to an employee's net pay. PRINT-LINE indirectly names the printer. NET-PAY names a location in memory that stores a net pay amount. WRITE is a verb in English, but to the computer it is simply the name of a set of instructions. To find the memory location designated by NET-PAY and to move the contents of that memory location to PRINT-LINE might require as many as fourteen separate computer instructions. All these instructions are summoned simply by the verb, WRITE.

From this example it can be seen that programmers who use a programming language like COBOL don't have to concern themselves with such things as memory addresses or other internals of the computer. Their concern is primarily the proper use of the rules that go to make up the language. This suggests another important advantage of program languages: machine independence. A program written for one machine can be run on a completely different machine if they both speak the same language. In theory. As a practical matter, some modification is usually required but, in any case, the situation is a big improvement over programming in the computer's own instruction set, or machine language, as it is called. Machine independence of a program is also referred to as *transportability*. Transportability is something you will be concerned with if you find, as most users do, that you have outgrown one computer and want to move up to a more powerful model. You will save a lot of time and money if you can adapt the programs you have been using to your new computer. Program languages make this possible.

It should not be concluded from the above comments that high-level program languages make programming an easy task. Programming remains difficult, time-consuming and costly, but less so than without program languages.

PROGRAM LANGUAGES

There are many program languages, each one with some distinguishing features that earn it a place in the market and generate enthusiasm in its champions. Some are widely used languages, such as COBOL and FORTRAN. Others are applied to special areas, such as simulation or processing long strings of data. Of all these, you need to know something of only the four or five more widely used languages to get a feel for what might be right or wrong when you go shopping for a program or when you are considering investing time in learning a programming language. Professionals might want to look deeper if their work involves complex processing. The major programming languages in use today are:

- FORTRAN
- COBOL
- PL/I
- BASIC
- RPG
- PASCAL

Some might want to add to this list, but few would dispute those that are included.

FORTRAN and COBOL

FORTRAN was the first widely-used program language. It is intended for use primarily in scientific, engineering and mathematical applications. Its strengths lie in working with large numbers and performing complex calculations. At the same time, it is fairly easy to learn and to use. For the type of computation one might do in financial analysis or marketing studies, FORTRAN serves the purpose.

FORTRAN's weakness lies in data handling and input/output, the areas of prime importance to business. The need for a business-oriented language became apparent and the result was COBOL. COBOL is strong where FORTRAN is weak and vice versa, although COBOL is probably the more evenly balanced language.

Both FORTRAN and COBOL have been very successful in terms of the number of written programs and number of users. Most large businesses require COBOL for their major applications. They will also use FORTRAN for engineering or management science, and FORTRAN is widely used by professionals in science and engineering.

Since learning a language takes a good deal of study and practice, FORTRAN and COBOL's head start give them an almost overpowering advantage. Although they have a number of recognized weaknesses, any new language, no matter how improved, has an uphill fight.

PL/I

One such language that has had a fair amount of acceptance is PL/I. PL/I was designed to combine the capabilities of FORTRAN and COBOL, so that one language could be used in both business and technical applications. This feature makes it relatively easy to learn by those already knowledgeable in COBOL, smoothing its path to acceptance.

BASIC

BASIC is, indeed, a basic language. It carries simplification of programming several steps beyond that of FORTRAN and COBOL. The latter two are roughly of the same order of difficulty. To use them takes several months' practice. A novice can do simple calculations in BASIC in a few minutes and can write useful programs in a few days.

The advantage BASIC has in ease of learning and ease of use is paid for by its limited capability and poor performance. Even at today's low prices of computers, one would hesitate to program in BASIC unless ease of use was deemed an overriding consideration or one of the more advanced versions was used.

RPG

RPG is a very high-level language. In all the languages discussed so far the programmer had to tell the computer *how* to do a job. With RPG the programmer tells the computer *what* must be done—the computer then figures out how to do it. This type of language is sometimes referred to as *nonprocedural*, to indicate that the procedure for performing a job does not have to be specified. In practice, some procedures may have to be spelled out, but with RPG much of the programming can be simplified.

This is accomplished by the use of forms with headings and blank spaces. The programmer tells the computer what he or she wants it to do by filling in the blank spaces on these forms. The result is that less program time and skill is required to get a job done.

Despite these advantages, RPG is used much less frequently with small computers than is BASIC. BASIC was designed for use with a keyboard and display in an interactive mode of operation, making it a natural for use in small computers. RPG, on the other hand, was designed as a report generator for use in batch-type operations. In older systems, such as the IBM System/3, which some readers may be familiar with, the RPG forms are filled in by the user and then keypunched onto punch cards. These are then fed into a card reader for entry into the computer. None of this is in keeping with the small computer as it is used today.

In order to adapt RPG to today's small computer, versions have been developed which allow the RPG forms to be presented on a display screen. Entries are keyed in, and the full screen of data is transmitted directly to the computer. With RPG adapted to the more powerful equipment and processing techniques now being applied in small computers, its use in this area can be expected to grow.

PASCAL

PASCAL came from nowhere to become a leading contender as a programming language. Originally designed as an aid for teaching programming techniques to students, in the last few years PASCAL has suddenly emerged as "everybody's" favorite language.

PASCAL owes its success to the increasing emphasis on making programming more productive. With prices of computers falling, programming has been absorbing an increasing percentage of total system cost. To make matters worse, many programs were poorly written. They were difficult to understand and even more difficult to change. When you changed one part of a program you would find that five or six other parts had to be changed.

As a result, strenuous attempts were made to improve matters by simplifying program structure and specifying rules and procedures for programming. These rules and techniques are usually referred to as *structured programming*, a high-sounding term that in essence stipulates rules and guidelines on how to design programs.

Into this programming reform movement stepped PASCAL. More than the older languages, PASCAL lends itself to structured programming. With PASCAL, it is easy to produce programs that can be understood and changed when needed. In addition, it is easy to learn.

One problem. Having been developed in an academic environment, it was not supplied with those features necessary for many business applications, such as moving data between the processor and disk. To remedy this, vendors of computers who want to capitalize on the PASCAL phenomenon have had to add this capability and additional features to make their PASCAL a practical language in the real world. The result is that there are now a number of versions of PASCAL, and you have to be careful about which features you're getting with the language.

Standards for Languages

Multiple versions of a language are a disadvantage because they reduce transportability. Programs created with a particular version for one machine may not work on another. Programmers familiar with one version will be strangers to another. For this reason there has always been an effort to standardize languages.

Standards may be the result of international standard groups or national standard groups. In the United States there is the American National Standard or ANS for FORTRAN, and the American National Standard Institute or ANSI for COBOL. International organizations, such as ISO, set international standards. Also of significance are industry de facto standards set by dominant firms, such as IBM. When IBM, for example, comes out with a new version of RPG for its own computers, the use of this version may become so widespread that, in effect, a new standard will be created.

There are standards for FORTRAN, COBOL and BASIC, although a vendor's version may depart in varying degrees from these standards.

BASIC, in its original version, was too basic for many applications. The result was a number of extensions. Now there are Business BASIC, Extended BASIC and others. With these extensions BASIC has become a fairly powerful language, although not equal to FORTRAN and COBOL. Any version except an extended version is too limited in its number and file handling capability to be used in a serious business application.

Standards are always in conflict with change. Standards specify exactly how something is to be done, or, in the case of programming languages, the features and rules of the language. Change implies new features and new rules. These may be merely improvements, or they may be additions required by technological advances. If nothing else, the computer industry is subject to change, so that standards are difficult to arrive at and even harder to maintain.

The result has been the proliferation of different versions of "standard" languages. Thus, you are likely to see COBOL 4, FORTRAN IV and FORTRAN V and RPG II and RPG III, the numbers indicating the version of the program language.

One source of new versions is ANSI itself, which periodically reviews and updates the standards. The committees responsible for standards and their revisions avoid eliminating previous standards and limit themselves to adding new features. This provides upward compatibility, so that previous versions are not obsolete. In practice, compatibility depends on how computer vendors implement the language on their machines, so you cannot automatically assume that compatibility will be maintained from one version to another unless this is stated explicitly.

It is advantageous, but not necessary, to use programs embodying the latest version of a language. Many programs are written in older versions and it wouldn't make sense to scrap these or rewrite them just because a new version is announced.

Change is not the only force working against standards. There is also self-interest of the vendors. Nothing will lock a user to a vendor like having a library of programs that work only on that vendor's equipment. If the programs are standard versions, the user can move them to any other vendor's product that supports the same version. However, if there are even very minor differences, the programs won't run on different equipment and users will be reluctant to risk opening up their programs to change. Thus, we find vendors with their own versions, or extensions, of standard languages. Sometimes these versions are wide departures with no attempt at compatibility, but which retain enough of the original so as to be easy to learn by those who already know the standard. At other times a vendor's version will be limited to some extra features, so that upward compatibility is maintained.

This departure from the standards is not all bad. There is plenty of room for improvement, and the changes provided by the vendors can satisfy a real need. But you should be aware that taking advantage of these improvements can result in reduced transportability of your programs.

Assembly Language

Assembly language is unique in several respects. Assembly is just one step up from machine language, the only language understood by the computer. Accordingly, it is referred to as a lower-level language, while those we have been discussing are referred to as higher-level languages. Assembly allows the programmer to write in terms of actual program instructions, whereas in higher-level languages, remember, only groups of instructions are used. Finally, there is zero transportability of assembly language programs, and no standardization. Assembly languages are always written for one specific computer, and are geared to that computer's design and no other.

Given these negatives, why would anyone program in such a difficult language? The answer is performance. Programs written in assembly language run faster and require less memory than those written in higher-level languages. This is because assembly language provides more flexibility with which to tailor a program to a specific computer for performing a specific function. It is important to realize that there are times when ease of programming should be sacrificed for performance and times when the reverse is true. Knowing *when* to do so is the job of the computer professional. But you should know of this possibility because a switch from a high-level language to assembly in critical parts of a program can make the difference between a successful or unsuccessful application. We will return to the use of assembly language in a later section of this chapter.

General-purpose Languages

The PL/I language is good for working with both numbers and data. That is, it is a suitable language for programs requiring extensive calculations and also for business programs that emphasize the movement and modification of data. This is in contrast to FORTRAN which is number-oriented and COBOL which is a data-oriented language.

Languages not oriented towards one type of processing are called general-purpose languages. PASCAL is also considered a general-purpose language.

With proper extensions, any language can be made more proficient in areas other than those for which it was originally designed. These kinds of extensions are commonly found in several versions of COBOL and BASIC. Therefore, readers are cautioned not to assume that COBOL or BASIC might not be adequate for their needs just because they plan to do a wide variety of processing. On the other hand, if you want to do some of your own programming, you should consider the advantages of a general-purpose language.

LANGUAGE TRANSLATORS

The programmer creates a program in a high-level language he or she understands, but this language is unintelligible to the computer. Therefore, the program must be translated into machine instructions and memory addresses, which are the only things the computer is designed to work with. A *translator* is a computer program written expressly to perform the translation function.

When writing a program in a higher-level language, the programmer uses statements to tell the computer what to do and which data to do it to. The translator must look at each of these statements and convert them into machine code, consisting of instructions and memory addresses. There are two methods for accomplishing this task: *compilers* and *interpreters*. Which of these you use makes a big difference in how you run a program and how much production work can be derived from your computer.

FORTRAN and COBOL are languages used primarily with compilers while BASIC is primarily used with interpreters.

Compilers

Programs written in higher-level languages, such as COBOL are called *source code*. The same program translated into machine instructions is called *object code*. With compiler languages the programmer first writes the complete program on standard preprinted coding forms. This source program is entered into the computer, which is then instructed to compile the program.

Figure 5–1(a) (page 130) illustrates the process. Stored in memory is the compiler, a program made up of instructions, like any other program, but whose function is to produce the object program. The compiler translates the source code into object code, consisting of computer instructions. The printer produces a listing of the source code, together with error messages if it detects any violation of the rules of the program language.

In ordinary language we can have dialects and make all kinds of errors and still be understood by the other person. Misspelled words, dropped letters, even whole words can be lost and yet it may be possible to make sense of a message. Computer languages don't allow this. Everything must be according to the rules. Since even very careful people rarely perform a long task like programming without producing some errors, programming of any complexity always requires corrections of the original version. Source listings and error messages from the compiler are important tools in this process.

When the programmer has compiled a source code without an error message

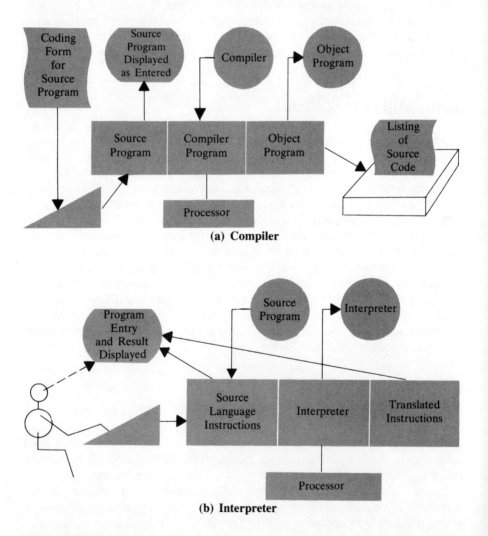

(a) Compiler

(b) Interpreter

Figure 5–1   Compilers and Interpreters

the object code is ready for a test run. Just because the compiler didn't detect any language error doesn't mean the program is error-free. All kinds of logical and arithmetic errors may still be lurking within the object code. The programmer will have developed test data expressly for the purpose of flushing out these kinds of errors. Not until tests are completed and corrections made—sometimes a lengthy and costly process—is the object program ready to be run against live data.

Interpreters

Interpreters work quite differently, as seen in Figure 5–1(b). Instead of translating the complete source program as compilers do, interpreters perform each instruction immediately after translation. Here is an example from BASIC.

```
10 LET A = 25
20 LET B = 4
30 LET C = A * B
40 PRINT "A TIMES B EQUALS" C
50 END
RUN
A TIMES B EQUALS 100
```

This simple example of multiplying two numbers illustrates both the ease of working with BASIC and the operation of an interpreter. Lines 10 through 50 comprise the BASIC program, each line being one statement in BASIC. The meanings of the statements are self-explanatory, once it is understood that the asterisk is used for the multiply operation.

After the program was entered, the operator keyed in a command to the computer: RUN. This was a signal to the computer to put the interpreter to work.

The interpreter translated each instruction. When it came to line 30 it calculated the result, so that when it came to line 40 it could display the result immediately on the display screen. Here is where the power of an interpreter lies: the quick presentation of results. If the operator wishes to make a change, this can be done and, again, the new results appear immediately for comparison with the old. This is interactive processing. If there had been errors in the program, the interpreter would have returned a message allowing the operator to make the appropriate corrections, and then immediately rerun the program.

The important points to note with respect to the two kinds of translators is that a compiler produces an object code that can be stored, called up and used over and over. After testing, translation—a complex and time-consuming process—is no longer necessary. Interpreters, in contrast, require some translation each time they are run. This consumes precious memory and computer time. Offsetting this is the immediacy of results that interpreters give.

Recognizing the need to increase the efficiency of operation of interpreters, more advanced versions have been developed which require less translation each time the program is run. Therefore, you should be aware that significant differences in performance might result from the use of different types of interpreters.

STRONG AND WEAK POINTS OF LANGUAGES

With the above descriptions of languages as background, you will be able to see why one language is selected for a particular task over another. Table 5–1 summarizes their relative strengths and weaknesses and where the languages are most often used. Some interesting points are made in the table that deserve elaboration.

Assembly languages are used where performance is important and there is no reason for modification by the user. A good example is word processing. Word processing takes lots of computer resources. Assembly language can hold this to a minimum. On the other hand, unlike business application programs, there is no good reason for a user to change a word processing program. If you aren't satisfied with what you have, you are much better off going to a more sophisticated program than trying to modify what you already have. Assembly language can also be used to increase performance on small sections

Table 5–1   Summary of Program Languages

Language	Strong Points	Weak Points	Where Used
Assembly	• Fast • Easy on storage	• Hard to learn • Hard to code • Hard to read • Easy to make errors	• Operating systems • Compilers • Programs not intended for change by user • At critical points in a program
COBOL & FORTRAN with compiler translator	• Only requires one translation no matter how many times the program is run • Fairly easy to use • Less mistake-prone than assembly	• Slower than assembly code • More storage than assembly code	• Operating systems • Compilers • Application programs to be run many times • Application programs intended for possible user modification
BASIC with interpreter translator	• Very easy to use • Gives results right away • Easy to read and change	• Slow • A glutton for memory	• Programs expected to run only once or a few times • Application programs intended for user modifications

of programs written in higher-level languages. For example, consider a program loop that may be repeated hundreds of times for each run of the program. Any speedup of the loop's processing will be magnified by the number of repetitions. This speedup can be achieved by exiting the higher-level language, hooking into assembly language for programming the loop and then returning to the higher-level language. This is obviously a job for a professional programmer, but under the right conditions the change in performance can be dramatic. You may hear or read that compiled programs are more or equally efficient to those written in assemblies. Don't you believe it. If you have performance problems, assembly language can be an out.

Note, in Table 5–1, that programs such as business applications, where modifications are often required, are written in higher-level languages, facilitating the job of program changes. For this, unless you plan to hire a professional programmer, BASIC is the way to go. Many nonprofessionals have learned and used BASIC. However, changing a program for a business application is not the same as programming a personal computer. Readers should proceed with caution in this area. We will deal with the important question of getting professional help for program selection and modification in later chapters.

Although COBOL and FORTRAN are traditionally compiler-type program languages, the heavy emphasis placed on interactive processing and on-line program development in today's small computer systems has resulted in the development of interpreters for modified COBOL and FORTRAN. BASIC has gone in the opposite direction—compilers have become available for this language.

Irrespective of whether a language is translated with an interpreter or a compiler, the resulting program can be on-line or batch—this is determined solely by the program statements, not the translator. Thus, many COBOL programs are compiled in batch mode and then run on-line.

HOW COMPUTERS MAKE DECISIONS

A computer can decide if it is time to reorder parts for inventory, how many parts to order, which suppliers to call first and whether to pay a premium for pretested parts. It is the ability to make decisions such as these that allows computers to mimic human capabilities and has led to the myth that computers can think. When the computer is deciding who will win an election, what stock to buy or what color boxes will sell the most cereal, it appears to be surpassing human mental abilities to make judgments. In fact, all such feats, no matter how impressive, are the result of one simple operation: the comparison of two items by a program. The items are usually numbers, but can also be words, phrases or sentences. After comparing two items the program has the ability to *branch* and to *loop*. Branching and looping are at the heart of what makes computers so effective in decision-making and other processing feats.

Branching

Suppose when you want your computer to decide when to reorder for inventory, you first supply it with a limit value. Then, each time there is an order, the number of units removed from inventory is entered into the computer. The computer has no problem in subtracting the amount withdrawn from stock on hand. The result is then compared to the limit value decided by *you*. Now there are two possible results: (1) the new on-hand amount is greater or equal to the limit, or (2) it is less than the limit. Depending on which of these results occurs, the computer takes one of two courses of action: call for a reorder, or not call for a reorder. This ability of the computer to do one of two things based on a comparison is called branching. All comparisons with limit values and branching are carried out under control of the machine's instructions, and are, therefore, determined by the programmer.

Figure 5–2(a) diagrams how branching is carried out. We have three routines which are three sets of instructions. The last instruction of routine 1 is a comparison. If the result of the comparison drops below the limit value, the

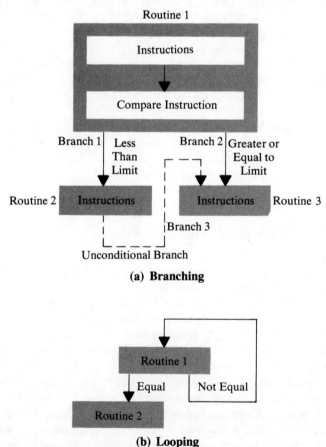

(a) Branching

(b) Looping

Figure 5–2   Branching and Looping

branch to routine 2 is performed. Otherwise, the computer branches to routine 3. In the inventory example, routine 2 would provide for indicating the need to reorder parts, either by printing out a report or by displaying this information to the operator. Routine 3 would bypass reorder processing while routine 2 when completed would probably go to routine 3, since this is the main line of inventory processing, required irrespective of reorder requirements. The branch from routine 2 to routine 3 is an *unconditional* branch that occurs in all cases. The branch from routine 1 to routine 2 or 3 is a *conditional* branch that requires a decision and depends on the outcome of a test. Note that either routine 2 or 3 can be considered a continuation of routine 1. It simply depends on how you want to define and label the routines.

Looping

In Figure 5–2(b) routine 3 has been removed and one of the branch paths loops back to routine 1. Here we have a slightly different criterion for branching than we used in the inventory example; we are asking the computer to branch one way—to routine 2—if equal and another way—to routine 1—if not equal. This creates a "loop."

The loop is repeated until a limit value is reached, at which time the program falls through to routine 2. There are so many uses for loops in computer applications it would be impractical to list them all. Looping, the ability of the computer to repeat operations rapidly at high speeds, is one key to their processing ability. The incorporation of decision points tells the computer when to leave the loop and proceed to other tasks.

A loop can encompass hundreds of instructions or just a few. However, all loops fall into about two types:

- Repeat the loop *until* a comparison test is satisfied.
- Repeat the loop *while* a comparison test is satisfied.

Here are two examples of statements actually used in program languages for conditional branching:

FORTRAN

10 IF (STOCK.LT.LIMIT) GO TO 65

11 CONTINUE

·

·

·

65 CONTINUE

COBOL

IF INVENTORY IS LESS THAN LIMIT PERFORM REORDER.

In the FORTRAN statement ".LT." stands for "less than." If the stock on hand is less than the limit value, the program branches to a statement numbered 65. Otherwise, the program continues with statement number 11. In this way the program can take one of two possible paths.

Note how closely the COBOL language corresponds to English, making it easy to read. If inventory drops below the limit, the computer performs a routine conveniently named REORDER. Otherwise it just falls through to the next statement, bypassing the reorder process.

Example: Cutting Costs of Inventory

A decision such as when to reorder for inventory is seen to be a rather simple process when the limit value is supplied from outside. How about more sophisticated decision-making, such as the number of parts to reorder?

Suppose, for example, a business found that the number of parts to be ordered should correspond to the rate at which parts are withdrawn from inventory. Then, when the reorder branch is taken, the computer is instructed to compute the number of days since the last order. This is divided into a standard elapsed time between orders for that part, giving the proportion by which the new order is increased or decreased relative to the previous quantity. Now any fractional part of the result is dropped, giving the number of parts to reorder.

The process requires (1), that the computer store the date of last reorder, the standard time between orders and the quantity previously ordered and (2), that the computer update the quantity and date of the last reorder with the current data and new quantity. From our previous discussion of how computers store and update information, you should be able to see in a general way how these two functions are performed by the computer.

It should also be clear that similar procedures could be used to vary the quantity reordered to accommodate seasonal and other variations in demand. Each type of business has its own patterns of buying and criteria for reordering. The computer is versatile enough to provide for these different requirements. Use it to cut costs of inventory.

We have described one important application of computer decision making, the reordering for inventory. Other cases abound in business applications, word processing and computational processing. In fact, a good part of all computer processing consists of deciding which of two paths to take, in other words, conditional branching. This is where the power of the computer lies. As you gain experience with computers, you will learn how best to use this power to advantage in your area of interest.

Tables

An alternate approach could employ a table instead of calculations. A table is a group of related items that can be listed in rows or columns. In the inventory example, a table might consist of two columns: elapsed time and reorder quan-

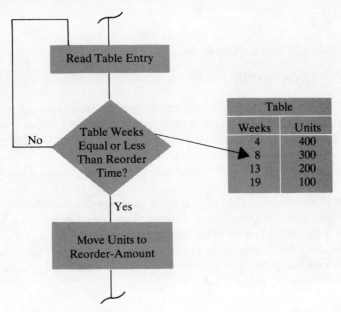

Figure 5–3   Searching a Table

tity. For various intervals of elapsed time between reorders you could supply a corresponding reorder quantity. The computer's task would be to scan the table looking for the reorder time that most closely equals the one currently applicable. Once found, the corresponding order quantity is easily retrieved. Figure 5–3 shows this process.

Often calculations of values can be replaced by a table of values. A table has several advantages. It can easily contain functional relationships that would be very difficult to calculate. Thus, in Figure 5–3 the relationships are not constrained by proportionality or any other simple formula, allowing you to enter values that better correspond to what you intuitively feel is "right" in the situation.

Another advantage of tables is that you can make the quantity values correspond to outside influences, such as quantity price breaks given by vendors. Finally, tables give you an easy way to provide for changes which are always occurring in a business environment. There is much less chance for error and cascading effects when changes are limited to table entries rather than program statements.

With these advantages why aren't tables used in all cases? The fact is that they are probably not used as often as they should be. However, there are many cases where tables are impractical. Tables eat up memory space and require somebody to determine the table entries. When the number of entries is large it makes more sense to use calculations than to search a table. In other cases it may not be possible to know the table entries before processing starts. Calculations may be based on several values entered at processing time, again making any equivalent table impossibly large.

The upshot is that in computers both tables and computations each have their place. Tables should be used whenever the number of entries is small and relationships are subject to changes that would require the reprogramming of the calculations.

TYPES OF PROGRAMS

To do useful work a computer requires a number of supporting programs in addition to those that do the actual job in hand. Those who plan to work with computers should know the roles played by these supporting programs and the major types of programs used to do the job.

The first major division of programs is between *application programs* and *system software*.

The term "software" originally referred to programs provided by the computer vendor. It was a part of the product that, together with the hardware, comprised a workable system. The user then added application programs written for specific jobs. Today, with application programs often supplied by vendors, "software" and "program" may be used interchangeably, irrespective of the program's source and function.

Application Programs

Application programs are written to perform specific jobs, such as order entry, payroll or general ledger. They must be matched to the specific job's requirements. Since these job requirements are similar from one business to another, it is possible to write programs that can be used by more than one business or organization. However, as the job requirements diverge, the programs must change accordingly. Thus, we find application programs that provide varying degrees of fit to a job, depending on the circumstances.

Examples of application programs were given in Chapter 1, Table 1–1, where for most of the items listed there is a corresponding application program.

System Software

System software differs in almost every respect from application software. System software is not job specific. It is designed to work with a wide range of applications. It is rarely supplied by anyone but the computer vendor and must be matched to the system hardware, rather than to a specific application. While the operations of application software are very much in evidence during data entry, processing and output, system software for the most part remains quietly in the background. If everything is working right, you should not be aware of it. However, this does not mean you don't have to know something about it.

System software consists of several types of programs and groups of programs. The following sections describe those you should know about.

The Operating System

The operating system is a set of programs that manage and allocate the resources of a computer system. Where performance is important, the quality of the operating system can make a big difference. Readers should understand what an operating system does and where potential problems lie. In this section we will describe what operating systems do. Later in Chapter 10 we will talk about selection.

Some of the functions performed by operating system programs include the following:

• Transfer data between memory and peripheral units, such as disk, keyboard, display and printer.
• Keep track of where data is on disk and in memory. Allocate space, as required.
• Load and link programs for execution.
• In multi-user systems or multi-program systems, they schedule jobs, allocate system resources, allocate time slots to users and supervise flow of tasks through the system.
• Provide for shutdown and start-up under both normal and abnormal conditions.

Each of the above functions will require one or several programs. Some alternative names for operating systems are "executive," "processor" and "controller" systems.

There are different types of operating systems depending on the type of work to be done and the equipment used. All operating systems designed to work with today's small computers will provide for the transfer of data between memory and disk. With this capability as the starting point, the following types of operating systems are available:

(1) Single user, single program.   This is the simplest type of operating system and the one that most readers will be using. It allows one person access to the computer at a time. That person can choose one of many programs to run, but only one program can be operating at a time.

All the following types of operating systems require a big jump in complexity. They require more equipment, more planning and more money. However, applied correctly, they can be highly productive. A number of readers can greatly benefit from their use.

(2) Single user, multi-program.   A multi-programming operating system can have more than one program in process at a time. The programs are not processed simultaneously, since there is only one processor in the computer. However, when the computer is waiting for the completion of a function for one program that does not require the use of the processor, it allows another program access. A processor is free for other functions when, for example, it is waiting for input from the keyboard, waiting for a line to print or waiting for access to a disk address. In each of these cases the computer can perform thousands of operations during the wait time. Multi-programming uses these slack periods to switch from processing one program to another.

Multi-programming is used extensively in large computers operating in batch mode. However, the situation is somewhat different for small computers, where only one user has access to the system. Here, one on-line, interactive program is all that any single operator can handle at a time. But there will be plenty of time available for the processor to work on a second program in batch mode.

The operator's program runs in what is called *foreground mode* and is given priority when the processor is needed. The batch program runs in *background mode* and does not require attention by the operator once it is started. Thus, when you see a statement in promotional material that the system can run background jobs, it indicates multi-programming capability.

(3) <u>Multi-user, multi-tasking.</u>   Multi-user operating systems are necessary whenever more than one terminal has simultaneous access to the computer. Multi-tasking allows several users access to the same program. One user may be at one point in the program, another user may be at a different point. The operating system keeps track of all this activity through its multi-tasking facility. When you read of multi-tasking capability of an operating system, think of several users sharing one program.

(4) <u>Multi-user, multi-program.</u>   This operating system simply combines the capabilities of the two previously discussed operating systems. It is the ultimate in operating system sophistication for today's small computers.

To provide the capabilities described above, operating systems require large programs. Some part of the operating system must always reside in memory, and for efficient operation a large chunk of memory may be required. The rest of the operating system is stored on disk and brought in as needed. Thus, in planning your computer system, you will have to provide memory and disk storage for system software as well as for application programs. Obviously, you will want to avoid operating systems that would only be overkill for your type of application.

Utilities

Utilities are system programs that perform important miscellaneous functions required in everyday processing. Examples of commonly used utilities are:

(1) <u>Sort and merge.</u>   Things to look for here are the maximum number of sort keys, the length of the sort keys and ability to specify ascending or descending order of the sorted items.

(2) <u>File management.</u>   Utilities that provide file management enable you to copy or move files and programs from one disk to another, an essential operation for backup purposes. Additional functions allow you to delete, create or modify files.

(3) <u>Edit.</u>   Edit performs some of the functions found in word processing for manipulating text. Its use as a utility is concerned mainly with providing the ability to write and modify programs using the display and keyboard.

(4) <u>Mathematical routines.</u>   This is a most important consideration for professionals who do a lot of computing. Computers, by themselves, have very limited computing capability, much less than desk or hand-held calculators. To perform calculations with a computer requires programs expressly written to perform mathematical functions. These can range from simple calculator-type operations to complex operations involving matrices, statistics, calculus, Fourier analysis, and so on. However, as a rule, only the simpler calculator-type functions are furnished with system software. For complex calculating, additional programs will be needed.

In this and the previous chapters we have described what small computers are, how they work and what they can do. Now it is time to discuss how to plan for a small computer system.

PART 2
The Planning and Selection of Small Computers

Where to Get Products and Services – A Profile of the Small Computer Industry

The purchaser of a small computer wants to know what to buy, the best place to get it and what kind of help is available. In this the purchaser is faced with a bewildering diversity of choices. The small computer industry is composed of a large number of vendors, different types of outlets and a broad range of sources for information and assistance.

In this chapter we will describe what the various segments of the industry have to offer and how you can find products and services.

THE SCOPE OF THE SMALL COMPUTER MARKET

We have mentioned previously that small computers cover a broad range of capabilities, from those designed for use as a personal computer to those that are almost as powerful as the big computers found in business and government. The attribute that we have chosen to single out as qualifying a computer as "small" is the ability to operate in an office environment without the need of a full-time staff of computer professionals. This is the unifying characteristic that results in common concerns of prospective users irrespective of the actual size of the small computer he or she will purchase.

The same characteristic has resulted in a split in the computer industry between large and small computers. Now small computers have their own periodicals, trade shows and sales outlets. Hence, we speak of the "small computer industry." We are, in fact, talking about a new, but distinct type of business. Small computers should no longer be thought of as just a small, secondary part of *the* computer industry.

In discussing the scope of the market and where in the range of small computers your needs may lie, it is convenient to use the broad division of the market into microcomputers and minicomputers.

Table 6–1 (page 146) gives an indication of the different areas of application for minis and micros. Figures are approximate and subject to change, and are presented primarily for getting a feel of the relative values for the two classes of small computers. From the table you should be able to determine quickly the class of small computer for which you will be looking.

145

Table 6–1   Minis and Micros Compared

	Microcomputers	*Minicomputers*
1. Price range	$1,000–$20,000	$15,000–$99,000
2. Number of people in organization	1–20	15–500
3. Possible users	Very small businesses Managers Project teams Professionals Schools	Small businesses; divisions, departments or branches of large organizations Professional organizations, school and hospital administrations Government units
4. Scope of user group	Personal computers or very small working groups	Organizations of various sizes

Point 4 in Table 6–1 indicates another way of classifying small computers: those intended for personal use and those intended for use only by organizations. Until recently, all computers were owned and operated by organizations, whether in business, government, education or other activity. The personal computer is a new and exciting phenomenon whose potential is just now being tested by numerous individuals. It is being applied both in the home and business, in many cases by those with no previous experience in computers. However, in this book we will be concerned with the personal computer only so far as it is applied in a business or professional environment. We will take note of the differences in the selection process between a computer intended for personal use and one intended for use by an organization.

VENDORS

The broad scope of the small computer industry, the large number of vendors and the variety of their products, while making the selection process somewhat overwhelming, increase the chances of finding a reasonable match to your requirements. The vendors offering products in the small computer market are as follows:

- Manufacturers
- OEMs
- Turnkeys
- Software firms
- Information utilities
- Others

This is quite a list for a first-time user to be confronted with. Some of the terms may look strange, but each type of vendor provides a valuable function, and the most unlikely may turn out to offer just what you are looking for. Here is a description of each type of vendor.

Manufacturers

Manufacturers produce some major part of the product themselves; the rest they buy from other manufacturers. The larger they are the more components they are likely to produce themselves. The important thing for you to realize is that equipment being sold under different names may have many parts in common. The computer system offered by a small company *can* be as good as that of a large company because they use the same or equivalent components. Whether it is or not as good is another question, one which depends on many factors.

Sitting on top of the heap is, of course, IBM. Their position is dominant, and their actions influence the rest of the industry. For this reason it is appropriate to single out IBM for special attention in order to provide some background on the company and its relation to other firms in the industry.

IBM rose to dominance in large computers by providing more customer service than other manufacturers. Instead of merely dumping hardware in the laps of inexperienced users, IBM provided service, programs, instruction and documentation. This should say something to first-time users about the importance of customer support.

There are three aspects of IBM's business that are significant to the industry and to potential buyers of computers. (1) IBM maintains unusually high margins; they have one of the highest rates of return of any company. (2) They can be slow in introducing new technologies and accommodating their designs to technological change. (3) The demand for their products is greater than they can handle, requiring some fairly long waiting periods for anxious customers. All this has allowed a number of smaller companies to operate under the IBM "umbrella" by either providing equivalent products at a lower price, providing products with greater capability or providing shorter delivery times. Within this group are some very small and some very large companies. Most live a precarious existence, constantly looking over their shoulder to see if IBM is going to lower the boom. This has not prevented some from prospering and growing rich because they have filled a very definite need. Buyers have benefited through cheaper products, faster delivery and enhanced features. In some cases, the more advanced products offered by competitors, notably in communications and small computers, have forced IBM's hand.

What has all this got to do with the small computer buyer? Well, IBM is in the small computer market with both feet.

They have several strong products in the small computer market. Of particular interest to readers of this book are their low-cost microcomputer products. This includes the Datamaster, System /23, a small business computer that can also do word processing. It provides for up to four work stations that share a common disk system.

As a complement product to the Datamaster, IBM offers the Displaywriter, a word processor that can double as a business computer. However, the most interesting of IBM's micros is its Personal Computer, a professional and business computer priced to compete with the likes of Apple and Radio Shack. IBM's Personal Computer is expected to find its way into networks of IBM equipment where it will sit on executive desks and communicate with data bases maintained by much larger computers.

IBM has adopted a new—for them—marketing strategy for their Personal Computer. They have gone to outside vendors for major components such as disks and printers. And they have invited independent manufacturers and program firms to develop products for the system. Thus, IBM's PC, like the rest of the industry, is the product of many hands. Result: a computer that is being applied in many areas and is growing in many directions.

At this point the reader may ask: Why should I look any further, why not go with IBM, save myself some trouble and get the support of number one? Several reasons. The IBM umbrella is still up. Roughly equivalent computers can be had more cheaply elsewhere. You may have a long wait for delivery. And IBM's line, while good from an overall standpoint, may not be as good in specific features as less expensive products. Last but not least, in the small computer industry there is a new umbrella: diversity. The number of different applications and the number of different features consequently required, is just too great for even IBM to come close to covering. This leaves the field open for any firm that can satisfy needs unmet by IBM and the other giants. One of these firms may have just the system that meets *your* needs. As we will point out in a later chapter, equipment comes second to programs in the selection process. Whether the equipment comes from this vendor or that is not as important as the capabilities of the program you get.

What all this adds up to is that in the small computer market IBM is just one good vendor among many. Their products and services should be evaluated along with others and accepted or rejected based on how they stack up with the competition—not based on some abstract judgment, but on how they best fit *your* needs.

Other large firms have entered the personal computer market, notably Xerox, Digital Equipment, and Hewlett-Packard. Some are packaging their own systems targeted at small business applications. But, like IBM, they generally rely on others to produce application programs for their machines. What the manufacturers contribute in this area is system software that makes the computer easy to use, easy to program and easy to maintain, or so they claim.

A sizable portion of manufacturers' products are not sold by them as end products. You will find them buried in the products of other vendors who sell them as components of their systems with their own labels.

OEMs

OEM stands for "original equipment manufacturer." However, the term has evolved from its original meaning to cover any vendor who purchases at wholesale, adds value, and resells at retail. In the small computer industry, the term OEM is frequently applied to a vendor who buys a computer from a manufacturer such as Digital Equipment, Data General or Datapoint at wholesale, adds programs that have been developed for *specific* applications and sells the hardware and programs as a package to the user. The vendor has *added value* and in that sense is a manufacturer.

If your ears didn't prick up on reading this, they should. OEMs are targeting their products to a specific market. That market could be you. When this happens consider yourself lucky, assuming that the OEM knows what he is doing. Finding a system that is designed specifically for the area in which you are looking to apply a computer is half the battle. You are now way ahead. The chances are good that the OEMs product will perform for you much better than a general-purpose program, and possibly as good or better than if you subcontracted for a custom job. The OEM is specializing. He's been around, knows what works in this application and what doesn't. Never mind that the OEM is going to make a bundle on the sale. Chances are excellent that it is far and away the best deal you can get if the OEM's product is a good fit to your needs.

Who are the OEMs? They can be anything from one-person outfits to major software companies. However, we will reserve the term for small firms because there are alternative designations for the large ones.

Turnkeys

A turnkey system is a complete system. You order it, it gets delivered, you plug it in, turn the key and go. (Well, almost. First you do some conversion.) An OEM, as described above, might not deliver a turnkey system. Possibly, you might order additional programs or equipment from other sources. Or you might order some customization yourself. However, these cases would be rare. Typically, OEMs will deliver a turnkey system, or they could very well put together a system that is not customized but promote it as a turnkey system because all the programs and equipment are provided that match some theoretical user. However, you might find that your requirements might differ in some important way from the theoretical user so that for you the system would not be a turnkey.

It would be futile to try to define these terms too precisely. The terms, OEM and turnkey are used extensively in the industry, they are important vendors to consider in the selection process, and it is well that you understand their roles.

Software Firms

Software firms complement the hardware firms, i.e., the manufacturers of computers. They provide the programs that make the computers go.

Why don't the manufacturers write and sell their own programs to go with their own computers? They do, to some extent. But the amount of programming required is so vast that even IBM can't begin to furnish all that is required of its machines. Manufacturers prefer to allocate resources to hardware and system software, leaving application program development to others.

To fill an ever increasing need for programs, numerous firms have come into existence, ranging from one-person operations to huge software houses employing hundreds of programmers. The more successful, widely used computers have a number of software firms that specialize in writing programs specifically for these machines. But supply and demand being what it is, even the less successful or newer computers are likely to have one or more software firms writing programs for that computer. However, the quality of the programs will have absolutely nothing to do with the machine that they are written for; the quality will be based only on the programmers who wrote them.

Software houses sell or license their programs to OEMs and small users through computer stores or by mail order. There is no way of knowing in advance where you will locate a program that meets your needs. It could come from a manufacturer, a systems house, or a small software firm that has decided to specialize in your industry.

The New Time-sharing and Information Utilities

A new type of vendor has appeared recently to sell communication, time-sharing and information facilities to owners of small computers. Any small computer with the appropriate software can use these facilities by attaching a dial-up modem, described in Chapter 4. With this inexpensive device the communications network becomes available to the small computer user who thus obtains access to the vendor's big computers and their extensive services.

Here are some of the facilities you can access through these vendors:

- Wire news services
- Major stock exchanges
- Data bases, such as the New York Times Consumer Data Base, and the Dow Jones News/Retrieval Service
- Business application programs
- Electronic bulletin boards for placing ads and notices that can be read by any user of the system
- Electronic mailboxes for communication between individuals. Consider how you might use such a facility in working with steady customers, suppliers or clients.
- Powerful computers to extend the capabilities of your own small computer

Clearly, these facilities expand the power of a small computer and its usefulness to you.

Rates are $2.75 per hour to $15 per hour, depending on time of day and service offered.

Two such services and their vendors are:

The SOURCE Information Utility
   Telecomputing Corporation of America
   1616 Anderson Rd.
   McLean, VA 22102

Micro NET
CompuServe
5000 Arlington Centre Blvd.
Columbus, OH 43220

SERVICES

There are a number of services available to assist in planning, selecting and implementing a small computer system. They can be of invaluable help to both the first-time computer buyer and the experienced user.

Systems Houses

A systems house works to your specifications. You tell them what you want and they deliver it. You can use a systems house to deliver a total, turnkey system or any part of a system. You get flexibility in what you can request from them, and a very customized system that can be tailored to fit your special needs. You are freed from having to select equipment and programs, relying on the expertise of the systems house for this. Instead, you devote your efforts to selecting a dependable systems house, specifying your requirements fully and unambiguously, and ensuring that your specs are met.

Systems houses often wear more than one hat. They may also be OEMs, consulting firms, of software houses. How they are listed in a phone book or business directory will depend on what their principal line of business is. Thus, custom systems work can be found under various guises, requiring some minor detective work to locate what you want.

OEMs are a good source for systems work if you are short of cash or looking for a business deal. Here's how it works.

OEMs sell computers and application programs as a package. How do OEMs learn the application and support themselves during the time they are developing the programs? Possibly he has an uncle in the business who is willing to give/lend financial support. More likely, a contract is obtained as a systems house to develop a turnkey system for a businessperson who can't find what he or she needs on the market. It's a beautiful arrangement. The OEM gets on-the-job training. What do you get if you enter this kind of deal? Why should you be the guinea pig for an OEM? Well, there are several possibilities. You can get a customized system together with the OEM's expertise in planning and other areas of data processing for bargain basement prices. You can use the OEM to teach you a good deal about data processing. You also know that the OEM plans to take the programs developed for you and market them to others in your line of business. It could be profitable. Why shouldn't you share in some of this since you taught the OEM the business and supported his or her development? Such deals are not uncommon. See what you can negotiate with the OEM when he or she is working for you as a systems house.

An OEM will tend to work mostly with minicomputers. However, in the micro area, many programmers are anxious to develop programs they can market. If you are someone wanting to use a micro, you can work with programmers in a similar manner.

Consultants

A consultant is a generalist in an age of specialists. Nobody today can be an expert in all areas of the small computer industry. Each person specializes in one or two machines and programming languages. Consultants, while usually having their own specialty, keep abreast of developments in all major areas and know the strong and weak points of many products. Most important, they know their way around, and what works and what doesn't.

There is a strong tendency for users and data processing professionals alike to fall in love with the products they know. It is not uncommon to hear people extolling one produce at the expense of another. On a close look, it turns out that the "expert" has been working with the product he or she is extolling and only recently started working with the "deficient" product. Usually, the supposed deficiency is nothing more than the result of not knowing all the tricks that come only with repeated usage and familiarity. It takes a year or more to become intimately familiar with a computer or a program language. With this kind of investment it is not easy to take an unbiased view of unfamiliar products.

Good consultants can rise above this kind of thinking. They can put themselves in your place and try to point you in the direction that is best for you. If their knowledge and enthusiasm are limited to one or two products, look out! They will point you in their direction, not the one necessarily best for you. Chances are they are more interested in a follow-up contract than helping you in the selection process. For this, of course, they have to get you to select the products that they are expert in. He or she may even be an OEM in disguise.

Independent Program Contractors

Independent contractors write programs on assignment. Unlike the systems house, they don't provide equipment. They are individual programmers who may work as independent contractors full time, part time, or they may just be moonlighting.

The independent contractor, by providing custom programs, can enlarge the scope of acceptable hardware for you. Knowing that his or her service is available increases your options with respect to the selection process.

As with the OEM, the independent contractor may plan to market the programs that he develops for you. The comments made with respect to working out business deals with the systems house apply also to independent contractors.

Software Firms and Other Vendors

Software firms were listed previously as vendors. They also provide various services—from consulting to customized programs or complete systems. The big software firms are not usually interested in small jobs. Readers will find that the small and very small firms will better suit their needs. These, together with the independent program contractors, form an essential segment of the industry in which programs are so important to success.

Manufacturers and OEMs also provide services, although limited, of course, to their own products. Typically, they provide forms or questionnaires that ask questions about your operations and needs. From these they can find the best combination of their own products that meets your requirements. The result is a system design of sorts. How well that design fits your requirements is another question. This is because you will probably be dealing with the sales department whose primary objective is to make a sale. Salespersons have neither the time nor the inclination to do a thorough design job.

OUTLETS

Besides ordering equipment directly from vendors, there are four major outlets where you can buy small computer products.

Computer Stores

Until recently, if you wanted a computer you went to the manufacturer. No longer. Small computers are now being marketed in ways that correspond to their new status as office machines.

Computer stores have sprung up in just about every metropolitan area. If you have decided that a microcomputer is what you are looking for, the computer store is an excellent place to start. They specialize in the low end of the market and sell both the computers and the programs to go with them. Their people can be very helpful in answering your questions and showing you what's available. You can examine the merchandise, touch it and get demonstrations of working systems using the available business program packages. Some computer stores specialize in only one line of computers. Most have several. Probably no store carries all lines. Conclusion: If you don't find what's right for you, shop around and see if you can do better. Look in the Yellow Pages under computers or data processing.

If you are a professional, or if you are looking for a personal computer, a computer store will suit your needs particularly well. The use of OEMs and consultants would probably be overkill for the kind of applications you will be considering. The computer store, on the other hand, is a place to meet people, find out what's going on in the area in the way of user groups and computer clubs. Computer store people tend to be knowledgeable, friendly and anxious to be helpful. Many are also genuinely interested in computing and get a charge out of working with others to help solve their problems. (Up to a point. Don't expect them to hold your hand like a consultant for nothing. They like to keep some time open to make sales and for other business activities.) On the other hand, those working in computer stores may be hobbyists without much actual experience with business applications of computers. Consequently, they may seriously underestimate the problems of using computers in a business environment.

Computer stores are not necessarily limited to low-end systems. They may also be dealers for one of the major business system vendors.

Dealers

Dealers sell both the minis and the micros. However, they usually handle only one product, but will know that product line thoroughly. The systems they sell will tend to include programs carefully designed to accommodate a wide range of users. If your application can be classified as "typical," you might find what you are looking for through a dealer.

Besides the Yellow Pages, dealers can be located in the usual way, directly through the manufacturer or in their advertisements. They may be associated with computer stores, office equipment suppliers or large to small dealer firms and systems houses.

Retail Outlets Other Than Computer Stores

Radio Shack, the giant electronics marketer, is the most prominent retail outlet. They sell only their own systems. These have been very successful in terms of the number sold. They are low-cost microcomputer systems with as much program support as any small computer in this class. Programs for the Radio Shack systems are sold through Radio Shack and independent software firms. Now Digital Equipment, the giant mini manufacturer, has opened its own retail outlets, and IBM is selling its personal computer through its own product centers and Sears Business System Centers. Office equipment stores are also being tried as retail outlets.

Mail Order

Software firms rely heavily on mail order. Also, vendors and middlemen sell via mail order. The two old standbys of the mail order business are used: direct mail and advertising in industry magazines and related publications. The risks here are obvious: Know who you're dealing with.

The Used Computer Market

There is a large, brisk market in second-hand minicomputers, printers, terminals and so on. If you're on a tight budget, this is a source you might consider. Except for printers, most computer equipment holds up very well. It will be replaced and sold to get more powerful equipment, not because it is worn out. The old models have a raft of programs that have been written for them over the years. Many have had years of use and are virtually bug-free.

The danger here is finding yourself in a dead end with a discontinued or soon-to-be replaced model. Project your future needs and determine how you will meet them before going this route. Also, find out how the computer will be maintained. For printers, you can get a new one or most of the dealers will provide reconditioning on used units.

The used computer market is a two-way street: you can sell your equipment there as well as buy it, something to keep in mind when you are adding up the cost of your system and trying to justify it on economic grounds. Prices vary all over the lot depending on supply and demand. Popular items may even sell at a premium over their retail price if there is a delivery problem from the manufacturer.

SOURCES OF INFORMATION

Knowing how and where to get information is the first step in becoming knowledgeable in a new field. The small computer industry has the usual assortment of papers, periodicals and trade shows found in other industries. Here is a rundown of what's available.

Publications

There are several publications directed at the small computer user: magazines, catalogs and newsletters. Magazine articles provide advice and relate the experiences of others. The advertising provides a wealth of information on what's currently available: computers, system components and programs. You will also find dealers listed and announcements by users groups and trade shows. Magazines are an indispensable source of information if you want to learn about the latest hardware, software and related developments in this rapidly changing industry.

Table 6–2 (page 156) gives information on some leading periodicals. You can find what other publications are available from ads in those listed. New ones are popping up all the time.

User Groups

It is said that if you put two users of the same computer in a room together they will form a users group. Misery loves company? At any rate, it is a fact that user groups tend to form around specific products, both computers and program packages, from the largest IBM systems to the smallest microcomputer system. Besides providing a forum for exchanging information, user groups can be useful in lobbying software vendors to make improvements in their products. If there is a users group for the product you are planning to buy, by all means contact them. What they have to say can save you valuable time and money, to say nothing of frustration, headaches and sleepless nights.

Trade Shows

Trade shows allow you to see all the major products under one roof. This is where the vendors put their best foot forward and introduce their new products. You will be viewing the most up-to-date equipment demonstrated by a group of people, so that if one person can't answer your questions usually someone else can. Depending on your attention span and how your feet hold out, there is no faster way to find out what's on the market.

Generally, in addition to exhibits, trade shows provide seminars covering all ranges of subjects and quality of presentation. Table 6–5 (page 159) lists trade shows and conferences.

It is one thing to know that a type of vendor or service exists. It is something else to locate the products and services you want. Table 6–3 (page 158) provides some guidance for this. The sources of information are arranged, roughly, from the general to the specific. You can imagine your search as starting at the appropriate point, and moving down to locate the specific product or service you are looking for.

With respect to equipment, Table 6–4 (page 159) provides a rough indication based on price of where to obtain equipment.

In this survey of the small computer industry only brief mention was made of how to use the services of computer professionals. This important point will be dealt with more fully in the next chapter.

Table 6–2   Publications

Periodicals on Small Computers

INTERFACE AGE
16704 Marquardt Ave.
Cerritos, CA   90701

A good choice for those interested in business and professional applications of small computers. The magazine bills itself as being for home and business applications, but the emphasis seems to be moving towards business applications. Available monthly from computer stores or by subscription.

KILOBAUD MICROCOMPUTING
Pine St.
Peterborough, NH   03458

Has some articles on business applications, but generally is more technically oriented than Interface Age and slanted more towards hobbyists and students. Available monthly from computer stores and by subscription.

Table 6–2   Publications *(Continued)*

BUSINESS COMPUTER SYSTEMS
Chaners Publishing Co.
221 Columbus Avenue
Boston, MA   02116

Targetted directly at users of computers in business systems. Treats the selection, use, and expansion of computer systems. Free to those who use computers in day-to-day business operations.

ICP INTERFACE SMALL BUSINESS MANAGEMENT
9000 Keystone Crossing
Indianapolis, IN   46420

A must. Information on what's available in software. Programs are described, equipment requirements specified and prices given. Also, articles on what's happening and how to use small computers. Available quarterly by subscription or free to qualified individuals, i.e., those involved in purchasing the software products described.

BYTE
70 Main St.
Peterborough, NH   03458

Probably the oldest and most successful of the small computer magazines. But mentioned here only to prove to readers that computers are not all work and no play. This magazine is strictly for the hobbyist, student and computer professional. If you happen to get hooked on computers, you will want to check this magazine out. Users may be able to locate consultants here. Available monthly in libraries, computer stores and by subscription.

DATAMATION
35 Mason St.
Greenwich, CT   06830

The magazine of the computer industry. Directed towards computer professionals, but managers in large organizations will find it of interest. Publishes articles and news on all phases of the computer industry—large, small and otherwise. Good editorial content and lively writing. Available monthly in libraries, by subscription and free to qualified individuals, i.e., anyone who is involved in the purchase of the advertised products.

on COMPUTING
70 Main Street
Peterborough, NH

Directed towards the personal computer user and low-end business systems. Articles on why and how to use small computers. Available by subscription.

Creative Computing
Box 879-M
Morristown, NJ   07312

Application and software for personal computers. Emphasis on education, small business and home applications.

SMALL BUSINESS COMPUTERS
Charles Moore Assoc.
Box 6
Southampton, PA   18966

Case studies on the application of small computers to business.

Directories and Catalogs

ADAPSO (Association of Data Processing Organizations)
Membership Directory
210 Summit Ave.
Montvale, NJ   07645

A large list of vendors and services. Includes the whole computer industry, large and small.

Table 6-2   Publications *(Continued)*

COMPUTER DATA DIRECTORY
Computer Data Publishing Co. P.O. Box 598
Cleveland, OH   44107

Lists computer companies, stores, products, clubs, etc. Available in computer stores for about $5.00.

MINICOMPUTER REVIEW
GML Corporation
594 Marrett Road
Lexington, MA   02173

Facts on minis and micros. 750 pages arranged for comparison of systems.

Minicomputer Software Directory
Minicomputer Data Services
20 Coventry Lane
Riverside, CT   06878

Software and software development for microcomputers.

THOMAS REGISTER
Thomas Publishing Co.
1 Penn Plaza
New York, NY   10001

A prime source, listing U.S. manufacturing firms of all types. Available in most libraries. For readers who are looking for special equipment not usually handled by vendors, this is the place to get leads on where you might obtain what you need—optical recorders, special printers, weighing devices, and so on.

Table 6-3   A Guide to Locating Vendors and Services

Source of Information	Comments
1. Trade shows	A good place to find manufacturers, OEMs, turnkeys, publications and software firms. Consultants may place their cards on bulletin boards or participate in seminars.
2. Publications and directories	An excellent place to locate turnkey systems, software products and manufacturers of equipment. Also a good source for finding other publications of interest. Notices of trade shows are provided and information on how to contact user groups can sometimes be found. Manufacturers, mostly the larger, well-established firms, can be found in *Thomas Register*. Periodicals can be used to locate consultants. Few advertise, but many write articles for industry journals. You will find a blurb at the beginning or end of the article stating that the author is a consultant and other pertinent information. Those consultants who do advertise will usually be found in classified ads or special sections of journals reserved for consultants and contractors.
3. Manufacturers	Equipment manufacturers can refer you to OEMs, programmers and consultants who utilize or specialize in their products, and to user groups.
4. Telephone book Yellow Pages	The best source for locating your neighborhood computer store. Suitable for locating service bureaus, time-sharing, consultants and programmers. Large city directories can be a source of OEMs, manufacturers, software firms, dealers and used equipment dealers. Look under: Computers, Electronic Products, Data Processing, Automatic Data Processing, Electronic Data Processing, Office Machines, as well as the above specific categories.

Table 6–3   A Guide to Locating Vendors and Services *(Continued)*

5. Computer and software stores	Retail stores may be able to refer you to consultants and programmers. They are the best single source for publications, and should be able to steer you in the direction of trade shows, user groups and computer clubs.
6. Computer clubs and user groups	These can be a prime source for finding consultants and contract programmers. They will often be members of a computer club. User group members may have employed professionals. They can be a source of leads, together with an assessment of the professional's competence.

Table 6–4   Where to Obtain Equipment

Price Range	Outlet
Under $1,000	Computer stores and mail order
$1,000–3,000	Computer stores, retailer and mail order
$3,000–10,000	Manufacturers, dealers, OEMs, and computer stores
$10,000 and up	Manufacturers, dealers, OEMs, system houses, time-sharing firms and used equipment dealers

Table 6–5   Trade Shows and Conferences

NATIONAL SMALL BUSINESS COMPUTER SHOW
New York City
Usually in the fall.

H. A. Bruno & Associates
110 Charrolette Place
Englewood Cliffs, NJ   07632
201 569-8542

INTERFACE WEST
Usually in the fall.

The Interface Group
160 Speen St.
Framingham, MA   01701
800 225-4620
617 879-4502

CALIFORNIA COMPUTER SHOW
95 Main St.
Los Altos, CA   94022
415 941-8440

WEST COAST COMPUTER FAIR
415 851-7075

NATIONAL COMPUTER CONFERENCE
Bormmer Elliott, Inc.
203 356-9411

How to Get Help
from Professionals

In many cases the product supplied by small computer vendors is incomplete. The product consists of a powerful computer and the necessary software. What is lacking are application programs or, at least, application programs that you can use without some customizing. This is true of both large and small vendors who can't afford to perform customized programming for each customer. The situation is complemented and aggravated by a lack of experience by first-time users who may not find a turnkey system that fits their needs, yet don't want to forego the benefits of a computer.

Into this impasse steps the computer professional who can serve the important function of bridging the gap between the user and the vendor's product. Computer professionals have successfully played this role in the past, and they are likely to do so to an increasing extent in the future as more and more businesspersons computerize.

Obviously, not everyone will have to seek professional services. Certainly many of those contemplating professional applications will not. But for those who do, this chapter presents some guidance on how to utilize their services effectively.

SHOULD YOU SEEK THE HELP OF PROFESSIONALS?

Large corporations and government use consultants and contract programmers extensively. They have no hesitation in calling on their services to provide expertise in areas in which they are lacking, and to smooth out peaks and valleys in their demand for data processing people.

Medium and small businesses are less willing to go for outside help. They are not used to doing so, and they often feel that the rates are too high. Yet these same people do not hesitate to bring in CPAs or lawyers as the need arises. They should have the same willingness to bring in computer professionals if circumstances require it.

In order to determine whether you should engage the services of a computer professional, ask yourself these questions:

- How much time am I willing to devote to computerizing an operation?
- Is this amount of time realistic in the light of how I want to use the computer?

- Is the application I am considering typical, or is it special, probably requiring a good deal of customizing?
- Am I considering one isolated application or will there be a need for relating applications that are interdependent?
- Is my application unusually complex? Do I need communication or multiple work stations?
- What are the risks? If my computer system doesn't work, could I continue to operate or would everything come to a dead halt?
- Am I able to pay and justify the high rates that good computer professionals receive?
- Are there satisfactory alternatives open to me? Your colleagues, associates, business and professional organizations may have all the information you really need. Some CPAs and tax people are becoming quite knowledgeable in the application of small computers.

The direction of your answers to the above questions should help you judge whether or not to go for outside help.

The specific areas in which you are likely to require assistance might be in any of the major phases of a computer project, that is, in the planning, selection, programming or conversion of your system.

HOW TO USE A CONSULTANT

Unfortunately, users often let the vendors do their planning for them. This is like sending the fox to guard the chickens. Good consultants try to place your immediate goals in the context of your evolving needs, so that you don't get locked into a computer system that won't adapt to what you will want next year and the year after that. They will have a broad knowledge of the industry, so that they can point you in the right direction with respect to vendors and approaches to computerization. They can assist you in the detailed aspects of planning, such as data gathering. Finally, they can help you select the right computer system from the wide array of possibilities.

For these services you can expect to pay $200 per day and up, with $400 to $500 per day more likely. At these rates, costs can add up pretty fast. A few pointers on how to keep these costs down follow.

How to Keep Consulting Costs Down

Consultants usually charge by the day. Accordingly, your aim will be to keep the number of days to a minimum. But you should realize that consultants will probably raise their rates if the time you employ their services is short. From their point of view, this is only fair, since they reason that their non-working time between jobs increases when they take short assignments. In any case, you will still come out ahead if you can reduce the consulting time as much as possible. Here are some ways to do that.

- Determine as precisely as possible what you want the consultant to accomplish. Don't use the consultant's time to go on a "fishing expedition." He or she can't help you if you don't specify what you want done.
- Don't hesitate to limit the consultant's time to as little as one or two days. Maybe all you need is to be pointed in the right direction, with some additional guidance from time to time. A one-day consulting fee may seem awfully high, but it will be less than two or three days combined.
- Don't use the consultant to gather data about your own operations. You can get this done faster and cheaper with your own people. If necessary, use the consultant to tell you what data to collect and perhaps to analyze the data, but the actual gathering of data should be left to others.
- Try to have the facts ready. Don't make the consultant keep coming back because you can't provide the needed information. When the consultant takes the assignment, find out right away what information will be needed and then get it before he or she starts to work. The data gathering forms presented in Chapter 9 will help in this. Review these forms with the consultant to see if further data is necessary—each project is in some respects unique. If the consultant has his or her own data gathering forms use them. Consultants work fastest with what they are familiar and feel comfortable with.
- Designate one person to be the liaison man with the consultant during the assignment. Preferably, this should be you or, at least, someone who knows your business well enough to quickly get missing data and answer questions on the spot.
- Try to provide a good on-site location where the consultant can get the work done. Consultants don't have to work on-site to do a good job, but when questions come up they can be handled quicker when the consultant is right there. It also allows him or her an opportunity to get a "feel" for your operations and style of doing things.

How to Find and Select a Consultant

Good consultants are hard to find. Often they don't advertise, getting their work mostly by word of mouth through a network of professional and business contacts. Vendors sometimes maintain a list of consultants who they know have developed an expertise in their products and who they believe will enhance the reputation of their products. Thus, vendors can be a good source *after* the computer has been selected. To get an unbiased view in the planning and selection phases, you will have to look elsewhere.

In the previous chapter, and specifically in Table 6–4, we described how to locate consultants. At this point we need only suggest that you start with your acquaintances and colleagues.

When you find a candidate for a consulting job you must, of course, qualify him or her. This is done with the usual resume, references and interview. The first two have limited value. The art of writing an impressive resume is not hard to acquire (or pay for). References, unless you have reason to know otherwise, can be deceiving. They will include only the successes, and these are hard to evaluate from afar. This means you should rely heavily on the interview. Here is what you should look for:

- A good understanding of *business* as well as computers. Avoid child geniuses, hobbyists and recent graduates in computer science. They may be whizzes at computer technology, but are unlikely to have experience in applying computers to real-life business problems.
- An interest in finding out what your goals are and what problems you hope to solve with a computer. A good consultant will want to hear what you have to say and get an accurate picture of the project as rapidly as possible. And he or she will be sizing you up as well. If you don't seem serious or it appears that the two of you will not work well together, there are plenty of other places he or she can go. On the other hand, if all he talks about is himself and how much he knows, showing no real interest in the prospective assignment, drop him.
- Try to find out if he has a broad knowledge of the industry or if he is a one-computer person, who will try to lead you towards the one thing he knows about. The resume will give you some clues and some talking points. Other talking points can be taken from articles on computers in business magazines. A remark such as, "I understand TI is planning to introduce a new small business computer," can be used to test his or her knowledge of the field and attitudes to different types of products and vendors. Consultants will use such openings to let you know that they are knowledgeable, even if not familiar with the specific issue you raise. Nobody can know everything, and your aim is not to trip them up, but to draw them out, to see if they have a broad knowledge of the industry.
- Has he or she ever installed a computer in your type of business? If so, this is a big plus. However, don't make this a necessary condition. Direct experience in your line of business shouldn't be necessary for the consultant to do a good job. If you have to go to a consultant in the first place, chances are your application is not "typical" and, therefore, that finding a consultant with that expertise is not going to be easy.
- Is he or she trying to snow you? Using lots of buzzwords to impress you? Right at the outset of the interview make it clear that you are going to insist on understanding everything said. The first time a buzzword sails by you, ask for an explanation. And keep doing it. It is perfectly natural for any professional to use some jargon, because the words become so familiar they are used automatically. But the consultant's job is to explain things to you and help you make decisions, not confuse you with technical details and the latest buzzwords. If he or she can't do this, look elsewhere. You are not in a position to judge technical competence, but if a consultant can give you clear answers to your questions and explain buzzwords in a way that makes sense, chances are he or she knows the business. This, and references, are what you will have to rely on.
- There is a fine line between what information you can expect the consultant to freely give you in an interview and what information you should expect to

pay for. On the one hand, you will be trying to find out how well the consultant understands your goals and whether he or she is capable of helping you to achieve them. At the same time, the consultant will be trying to convince you that he is capable, without providing information that might make his further presence unnecessary. Therefore, you should not expect specific answers to questions that cross the dividing line of what it is in the consultant's interest to tell you. It is his job to convince you of his capability without such specifics.

What a Consultant Can Do for You

Here are the main areas where a consultant can provide assistance.

- Deciding what functions should be computerized
- Determining in what order these functions should be computerized
- Preparing a plan for computerization
- Selecting the best route to computerization—off-the-shelf or custom programs
- Selecting a program
- Selecting programmers
- Selecting type of vendor—turnkey, computer store, dealer, systems house or software house
- Reviewing the terms, details, and specifications of a vendor's contract or proposal
- Approval of final "delivery in accordance with specifications"
- Preparation for testing the system
- Conversion
- Fine tuning the system

If detailed system design is required, this should be done by someone with previous experience in the same type of application. This role can more appropriately be filled by a programmer than a consultant. The latter should be used for guidance, the former for specific, detailed tasks.

HOW TO GET PROGRAMMING HELP

The situation with respect to programmers is almost the exact opposite of that for consultants. Good programmers are easier to find—there are more of them. And to be most effective, programmers should be highly specialized in the program language, equipment and type of application that you are hiring them to program.

Program language should be no problem if you stick to the most popular, and there is no reason not to. However, the equipment and the type of application, particularly the latter, are less subject to your control. For special reasons you may want to buy equipment that is not widely used. And, since the more custom programming your application requires the less typical it is likely to be, finding a programmer with the right background may not be easy. Nevertheless, the effort should be made to get as close a match as possible.

As pointed out before, new programs are seldom right the first time around. Many of the successful programs running today were failures when first completed. It took time and money to work out the bugs and make it right for the intended application.

All this should tell you how important application-related experience is in programming. A programmer who comes with experience in your application area is one of the best ways to smooth your path to a successful computer system. Even if the rates seem high you will find yourself amply repaid by his or her expertise.

Whenever possible, the vendor of the computer system or program should make any necessary changes in the program. There are two good reasons for this. First, the vendor has people familiar with the application and the programs in question, a big plus for the reasons stated above. Second, unauthorized changing of programs can result in loss of warranties, assuming there are any. Unfortunately, the vendor often does not provide customizing and it may be necessary to go to third parties for this service.

If you are not able to find a programmer with the right experience you should expect to get a reduced rate from any programmer who receives on-the-job training at your expense. Even if you get a low rate, you won't offset all the extra time an inexperienced programmer will cost you. But at least you will be compensating somewhat for the longer time you will have to pay him or her.

Using Consultants for Programming

In the small computer industry, most consultants will do programming and vice versa. Although the roles are quite distinct, the people who perform them are not. Thus, it is common for the same person to help plan, select, program and install a computer, acting pretty much as a one-person systems house.

Is it a good idea to take this route? When the roles are combined, it is impossible for the contractor to give as broad and objective advice. As noted above, the consultant should be a generalist, the programmer a specialist. If the consultant is going to do programming, it wouldn't make sense for him or her to select an unfamiliar language and equipment, and it is not humanly possible to be expert in more than a small part of what is available on the market. Also, when the roles are separate, the consultant can be used to monitor the programming effort, and the programmer may usefully supplement the knowledge of the consultant. If you put all your eggs in one basket, your risks are increased.

On the other hand, using one contractor simplifies the whole process of using outside help and your overall costs for this help should be lower. The project can proceed more smoothly and faster when one person follows through from start to finish.

The following points should help you decide which route to take:

- If you are considering a single, isolated system and a minimum amount of programming, use one contractor.
- If you are interested in planning an ongoing program of computerization over several years, use separate contractors.
- If you have several applications that could be computerized, use separate contractors.
- If you think you may need a multi-user or communication system, use separate contractors.
- If you can find a consultant who has programmed the same type of applications you are considering, use one contractor. Unless you are set on going all out, *the right kind of programming experience should dominate all other considerations.*

Programmers often call themselves consultants, and firms that provide programmers and system analysts often call themselves consulting firms. This confuses the issue, but the reader, knowing this, should have no trouble separating these functions in his or her own mind.

INDEPENDENT CONTRACTORS VS. OTHER SOURCES

We have been discussing the use of consultants and programmers under the assumption that they are independents, not affiliated with a firm of any size. There is also the possibility of using systems houses, consulting firms and software firms to perform the same functions. What are the pros and cons?

First, it must be recognized that it is the *ability* of the person who does your job that will be decisive, not whether he or she is independent or is employed by someone else. Bearing this in mind, the advantages of using a systems house or a software firm are:

- They are likely to have a diverse pool of talent which can be drawn on as the need arises.
- They may have facilities for testing, which can cut programming time significantly.
- You have more assurance they will be around during and after your computer project, providing continuity across projects.
- They are easier to locate.

The disadvantages are:

- Their rates are likely to be even higher than those of the independents.
- The person assigned to your project may be pulled off to work for what the firm believes to be a more valuable client.

- The person assigned to your project may quit. He or she is an employee and, like many computer professionals, is probably not averse to job-hopping.
- It will be harder to get help for short periods on an "as required" basis.
- The employees of a systems house or software firm will generally not be on as high a professional level as an independent who has to make it without a firm's backup.

Taking all these pros and cons into account, your overriding consideration should still be to get programming help from those with experience in your area of application.

THE ROLE OF A PROPOSAL

You should request a proposal from any and all candidates offering to perform computer work for you. The proposal puts in writing *what*, *when* and *how* the candidate expects to do the job, and becomes the basis for evaluating competing candidates and for any contract that is ultimately agreed to.

There is no set rule about how a proposal should be written. The size of the proposal should correspond to the complexity and duration of the project under consideration. For simple projects, a letter is sufficient. Otherwise, a formal proposal should be drawn up, but need not be lengthy or elaborate. It is common practice to include some boiler-plate information about the firm, what it has done in the past and resumes of its principals. Overreliance on boiler-plate and expensive format should be taken as a warning sign.

What to Look for in a Proposal

Here are the things you should look for. Their presentation and names might be different, but they all should be present in a good proposal.

- A project or job definition. This is where the candidate for the job demonstrates that your job requirements are understood. It should be stated clearly and concisely.
- A plan of attack. This describes how the "mission" will be accomplished. Depending on the complexity of the project, it could be subdivided. Thus, a complex project might be broken down into phases, tasks and steps.
- Deliverables. This tells you what to expect for your money. Deliverables can include progress reports, interim reports, equipment, program or functional specifications, actual programs or actual equipment and documentation.
- A schedule. The schedule should be subdivided to correspond to the plan of attack. For each subdivision, the time required and number of personnel to be used should be given, together with totals for the project. The time that deliverables will be available should be indicated.

The above items are minimum requirements to avoid open-endedness and ensure that you know what to expect and can monitor progress. There is nothing worse than being well into a project and finding you don't know what has been accomplished or when you can reasonably expect completion, and then to get into a dispute with the contractor over what was intended in the first place. Avoiding such situations is one of the major functions of the written proposal.

Other items that might be included in a proposal are:

- <u>Scope.</u>   A precise statement of what areas will and will not be covered. Useful whenever there is ambiguity about the limits of a project.
- <u>Personnel.</u>   Those who will be assigned to the project, their qualifications and resumes.
- <u>Dependencies.</u>   Information, data, personnel or equipment without which the project can not be successfully completed. Useful for specifying what is necessary but *outside* the contractor's control.
- <u>Costs.</u>   A breakdown and schedule of payments for services rendered, usually keyed to certain deliverables. This item is better left out of the proposal and presented in the form of a covering letter or separate document. This allows the proposal to circulate freely without everyone knowing the cost picture.

How to Evaluate
Computer Applications

In previous chapters we described what a small computer can do. After a first-time user learns what a computer can do, the most frequently asked questions are: Should I get one? What will it cost? In this chapter we will describe how to answer these questions.

It should be obvious that the evaluation of a computer application must go hand in hand with the planning of an application. It is impossible to estimate costs if you haven't reached the point in the planning process where you know what equipment you need. However, when describing evaluation and planning it is easier for the reader to first approach these subjects separately. Accordingly, in this chapter we discuss the evaluation process while the next chapter treats the planning process. But the reader should never lose sight of the fact that these processes are related.

The degree of planning and evaluation necessary varies widely. As an example of an application that requires very little of either, consider the professional writer who simply wants a low-cost word processing system. She goes to her local computer store, which she found in the Yellow Pages, and tells the salesclerk what she is looking for. The salesclerk shows her the best system in the store and demonstrates what it can do.

"How much?" she asks.

"Only eight thousand," the clerk replies.

"Oh, I was afraid of that. Anything for less?"

The clerk demonstrates a simpler system. Reluctantly the writer decides to settle for less capability and stay within her budget. The clerk then loads three cartons into her car and she drives home the owner of a small computer.

The above example is not intended to imply that all purchases of word processing systems do, or should, take such a short route to the purchase of a computer. Professional writers have been known to shop around as long as a year before making a decision. But the point of the example is that such a short route is feasible and can be justified on the basis of what a user must do to evaluate a small computer in this particular application.

The example illustrates some very important points. Readers should be clear on precisely why, in this case, the buyer could, with some justification, make such a quick decision because the same considerations should determine the extent of the evaluation and planning process in other situations.

The simplicity of the planning and evaluation process in this example is based on the following facts:

- There was never any question of whether the word processing programs could be used right off the shelf without modification.
- The decision to buy or not to buy could be made without the need to gather information about how the writer carried out her professional activities.
- The functioning of the word processing system did not depend on the data entered. Whether it received Shakespeare or gibberish, it could correctly perform its functions.
- There was no need to convert existing files or build new files.
- In this writer's case, system failure was not a big problem. She could go back to her old methods until her computer was repaired. Not all users of word processing systems could afford this simple a response to system failure.
- Only one person will be involved in operating and using the computer.
- Growth can be provided for by simply selling the system and buying a more powerful one.

The more the above points fail to be satisfied the more planning and evaluation will be required by the purchaser of a small computer.

As an example of the other extreme in planning and evaluation requirements, consider a distributor of industrial parts. He would like to handle phone orders quickly. For this he will have to provide each salesperson with a keyboard and display for immediate information on inventory and immediate entry of orders. Later he looks forward to expanding the order-entry and inventory system into an accounts receivable system, a purchasing system and an accounts payable system. Finally, the distributor is planning on a substantial expansion of his business by taking on some important new lines.

Clearly, the distributor in this example has his planning and evaluation work cut out for him.

The applications under consideration by readers will fall somewhere between these examples.

How much effort should you put into planning and evaluation? If too much, there will be lost time and missed opportunities. If too little, costly oversights and delays may result. However, experience shows that from the largest to the smallest applications, generally not enough attention is given to planning. This may be due to a natural desire to "get on with the job" and to assume that things will work themselves out. But another factor seems to be the tendency to consistantly underestimate the complexity of the job. Both computer professionals and neophytes fall into this trap. The many details that determine the success or failure of a computer system seem to be too far below the surface to be readily visible in advance. Readers are urged to plan carefully and resist the temptation to rush ahead. The likelihood of overplanning or wasting time is much smaller than that of not planning sufficiently.

There are two viewpoints on the proper way to evaluate a computer application. For lack of better terms, we will refer to these viewpoints as the "financial approach" and the "non-financial approach" to evaluation.

The financial approach rests its case on money calculations. In answer to the question, "Should this application be computerized?" the financial approach looks for savings, benefits, profitability and payback.

The non-financial approach places emphasis on non-measurable benefits from the computer. In answer to the same question, the non-financial approach looks for how the computer can increase sales and improve operations through better handling of information.

We will discuss both of these approaches to computer evaluation, presenting the case for each. Included in our discussion of the financial approach will be the important subject of the costs of computerization and how to estimate them.

THE FINANCIAL APPROACH

The financial school advocates reducing all costs and benefits to dollars and cents. Then the computer system is evaluated just like any other capital investment. A simple and widely used technique is that of cost comparison. It is probably the most widely used method for determining whether or not to computerize an application.

Cost Comparison

This method compares current costs to the costs of using a computer. If computer-related costs are lower, the computer is considered justified and a purchase decision may be made on this basis alone.

Since computer systems entail both one-time costs and recurring costs, both must be accounted for. Recurring costs should be no problem, but the allocation of one-time costs introduces some arbitrariness into the calculations, as does the treatment of any equipment that will be replaced by the computer.

The simplest case to analyze is leasing a turnkey system. Here, all up-front costs are borne by the vendor. The user's one-time costs will be negligible, and recurring costs are known with reasonable accuracy.

Anything less than a turnkey system entails significant one-time costs, the amount depending on the up-front equipment, planning and programming expenses of the user. These one-time costs can be allocated over the estimated life of the system or some payback period can be designated in which the initial investment must be recovered.

Calculating Costs

The cost comparison method as well as methods to be explained later all require the determination of the costs of installing and operating a computer system. Here are the components of computer system costs that should be included, when applicable.

Up-front Costs

These are the obvious costs and many people mistakenly think they are the only ones.

- The computer and any additional equipment that may be necessary.
- The programs, if purchased separately. Programs may be sold with the equipment for one price, in which case they are said to be *bundled*.

Hidden Costs

These are the costs people tend to overlook. Vendors or their sales staff may not mention them and they are not easy to put a price tag on. Rules of thumb for hidden costs are from one to four times the up-front costs. The lower figure applies to the simpler, non-customized applications; the higher figure is used when main-line business applications are planned.

Here are some common sources of hidden costs:

- Program modifications, if required.
- Planning. Your time as well as any employee's time who is involved must be included. Include here data gathering and evaluation.
- Support costs. Include in this all outside services required to get the systems up and running—consultants, contract programming and vendor charges for services.
- Training. Include all time and materials, such as manuals and break-in period for the operators.
- Installation. Ordinarily not a major item.
- Conversion. Include the costs necessary to convert files, prepare test data, test and design and print new forms. This can be significant.
- Space. Small computers don't require much space, but small businesses don't usually have any to spare either.
- Equipment maintenance. A maintenance contract will give you a figure on maintenance costs even if you don't actually sign a contract. You should figure the contract rates as a reasonable guide to costs. Lacking this, assume 1 percent of total equipment costs per month for maintenance.
- Program maintenance. This covers program changes required to tune the system after cutover, to take care of unforeseen shortcomings in your programs, to provide for changes in business conditions and to accommodate business growth. Program maintenance is the big sleeper. Depending on the situation, it can be considerably larger than one would expect and by its very nature it is not readily subject to prediction. For unmodified, seasoned programs, figure 3–6 percent of program price.

- Operating Costs. Primarily, the time of the operator who runs and enters data in the computer, but this includes incidentals as well, such as supplies, electricity, and possibly air conditioning.
- Insurance.
- Cost of money.

Rules of Thumb for Costs

How much will it cost? The answer to this question, as is evident from the previous discussion, will vary widely and depends on a number of factors. Yet those contemplating the purchase of their first computer need to get their bearings. Rough estimates, which indicate what to expect are wanted. These estimates can be provided by rules of thumb.

A rule of thumb can be both a useful and a dangerous thing. With it, a few quick calculations on the back of an envelope can provide cost figures that otherwise might require weeks of work and still be off the mark.

On the other hand, rules of thumb can be wrong. They can be wrong in general or in a specific application. They appear in print and presumably give expected or average costs of the average user. How many cases are they based on? How representative are these cases? How valid are they in the first place? The fact that they often mix one-time and recurring costs doesn't lead one to have confidence in them. However, the fact that they appear in print gives them credibility and authority, and therein lies the danger. They become part of the conventional wisdom and are accepted uncritically.

Despite their shortcomings, rules of thumb are too useful to be dispensed with. But those who use them should do so with a good deal of skepticism, allowance for error and only for initial evaluation. Hard facts should replace the rules of thumb as the planning process becomes more advanced.

With all these caveats, we list, in Table 8–1, rules of thumb for estimating costs. Some, such as hidden costs and program modification costs have been given a broad range of values, reflecting the uncertainty involved. Others, such as maintenance and service can be estimated more precisely. Also, there are costs, such as down periods and time for repair, that can not even be stated in dollars. You will have to estimate these yourself, based on time lost and what this lost time will cost you. Finally, we have the rule of thumb for program modification costs, based on equipment costs whose validity appears doubtful, but which is used because of its simplicity and complete lack of ambiguity. It is included as an example of how simple-minded rules of thumb can get in pursuit of quick-and-dirty estimates.

Hidden costs are for one-time cost only. Operating costs will have to be estimated based mostly on data entry requirements. Estimates for this are given in Chapter 11.

Finally, bear in mind that as hardware costs drop relative to labor costs, the figures givein in Table 8–1 (page 174) have to be revised.

Table 8–1   Rules of Thumb for Estimating Costs (to be used with care)

HIDDEN COSTS (one-time costs only)

Low-end system (to $20,000): Hidden costs will be about equal to up-front costs (equipment and programs).

Medium system ($20,000–$50,000): Hidden costs may be one and half to two times up-front costs.

High-end system ($50,000 and up): Hidden costs can be two to four times up-front costs, or more.

PROGRAM MODIFICATION COSTS

(a)   Based on how well the program fits the application
Good fit: up to $2,000
Fair fit: $2,000–$5,000
Poor fit: $5,000 and up

(b)   Based on equipment cost (not recommended):
Allow one fifth of equipment cost for program modifications.

MONTHLY MAINTENANCE

Allow an average of 0.6–1.0 percent of equipment costs per month for maintenance.

EVALUATION

Payback: Cost of equipment should be returned in three to four years.

Labor savings: Possibly one employee displaced per $20,000–$40,000 investment.

SERVICE CALLS AND TROUBLE SHOOTING

Equipment: $100–$140 per call
Programs: $200–$250 per day
Consulting: $300–$600 per day

DOWN PERIODS PER YEAR CAUSED BY EQUIPMENT FAILURE

Optimistic: 0–1
Careful: 2–4
Pessimistic: 5 or more

TIME TO REPAIR

One-site service: ½ to 1 day
While you wait service at a service center: 1 day
Leave and pick up at a service center: 2–7 days

EVALUATION AND PLANNING

Six months to a year. Even low-end users will spend six months or more to become familiar with what's on the market, analyzing their needs and evaluating vendors' offerings. High-end users, on the other hand, try to reach a decision within a year, irrespective of complexity.

CONVERSION

Time to convert: Two to four months to train and cut over to a typical business application, such as order entry or payroll, part of which should be parallel operation with the existing system. Simpler systems might cut this back to one to two months.

INSURANCE

1.3–1.5 percent of equipment cost per year

CONSULTING

Technical: $25 per hour and up
Technical, business and management: $40 per hour and up

PROGRAMMING

Average programmer: $15 per hour and up
Skilled Programmer: $30 per hour and up. $5,000 for a simple business application in BASIC.
Cost Allocation: Program design, coding, and testing. 20–50%
Updating programs and correcting errors: 50–80%

Benefits

The cost comparison method of evaluation is limited by the fact that the computer may provide benefits not reflected in the cost-saving calculations. Those who rely on this approach generally view the computer as simply a replacement for people and less efficient machines. They don't look for new avenues for profits. The computer system may cost about the same or even more than the current system, yet provide additional benefits which justify its purchase. Therefore, a more effective evaluation method is needed than simple cost comparison. Before describing this method, let's review examples of the kind of benefits we can expect from a computer.

Direct benefits
- Reduce personnel.
- Avoid hiring of additional personnel.
- Cut overtime.
- Cut inventory.

Indirect benefits
- Better customer service. This means not just faster delivery, but also faster replies to inquiries and more reliable servicing of orders.
- Better information. Computers can provide more information on more aspects of operations and in a more timely manner.
- Free yourself and others for more productive work.
- Increase the accuracy of records. Less paper shuffling and less copying of figures reduce chances of error.
- Establish and enforce well-defined procedures. The computer requires set procedures and in turn, it can enforce set procedures on those using it. The result is more efficient operations and better control.
- Assist in planning of operations. Examples are the planning of deliveries so as to reduce time and cost, planning of year-round inventories based on past performance and planning of pricing or rental strategies.

The reader will recognize the difficulty in placing dollar amounts on indirect benefits of the kind listed above. Nevertheless, the financial approach to evaluation requires that some estimate be made. Either that, or the benefit must be considered too negligible and left out of the calculations altogether.

Suppose you expect that the computer will enable you to provide better customer service. The financial approach requires translation of better customer service into increased sales before this benefit can be accounted for in a financial evaluation.

Or take the case of reduced errors. This benefit has to be translated into the labor saved in correcting the mistakes as well as increased sales as a result of better customer relations.

Advocates of the financial approach maintain that placing a dollar value on anticipated benefits forces users to think clearly and realistically about what they are doing and to analyze just what the expectations should be; and it provides a basis on which to measure the actual performance of the system when it is up and running. The underlying assumption is that if you probe deeply enough you can come up with dollar values that are meaningful.

Payback Evaluation

Payback evaluation is based on the idea that risk is reduced and profits increased if an investment is paid back within a given time frame. Three to five years are commonly used payback periods. Payback evaluation can accommodate both saving and other benefits in the same analysis.

Figure 8–1 illustrates the cases we will be working with. This figure is not drawn to any particular scale. Rather, it illustrates quite generally the concepts we will be discussing below.

Typically, an investment consists of a large initial outlay—one-time costs—followed by smaller, recurring costs associated with operating and maintaining the equipment. Offsetting the recurring costs are recurring savings, sometimes called displaced costs, which are the result of the new investment. The new investment can also result in increased sales and more efficient operations. All these contributions to increasing profits are called the *benefits* of the investment. If the new investment replaces old equipment that has a trade-in value, the one-time cost can also be offset. Readers with older data processing equipment will be in this position.

The net benefits per year from the investment are the difference between total benefits and recurring costs calculated or averaged on a yearly basis. As the net benefits accumulate the original investment is recovered. The time to full recovery is the payback period. It can be easily calculated by dividing one-time cost by net benefits per year.

Calculation of the payback period is key to the construction of Figure 8–1. Consider a $50,000 investment in a computer system. Recurring costs are estimated as $8,000 and saving from present operations as $20,000 per year. Then, net benefits are $12,000 per year, giving a payback period of $50,000/12,000 = 4.2$ years.

The picture changes if the equipment is rented or leased. However, the calculations are the same. Assume one-time costs for planning and installation are $20,000, recurring costs—including the lease—are $9,000 and benefits still $20,000. Then net benefits become $11,000 and the payback period is now $20,000/11,000 = 1.8$ years.

Figure 8–1 illustrates the two cases. Before cutover to the computer system there is negative cash flow as money is spent to get the system up and running. The curves show *accumulated* expenses which peak at cutover.

After cutover, benefits start accruing from use of the system. Although these benefits are offset by the recurring costs of the system, the difference, or net benefit, is positive. Now the curve reverses direction as the net benefits start offsetting the original investment, I, and the system is now in the payback period, PB.

When all of the original investment is recovered we hit the break-even point. The time from cutover to break-even is the payback period calculated above.

After break-even, profits start to accumulate. The profit line shows the *accumulated* profits at any time, T, from the start of the project.

As shown in (a), the purchase of equipment causes the curve to drop sharply, whereas equipment rental results in a more constant slope to cutover, shown in (b) somewhat idealistically as a straight line. Otherwise, the two curves are the same, differing only in the amount of investment and the length of the payback period.

As every businessperson knows, investment is less when renting or leasing, but total profits will eventually be greater when equipment is purchased. However, the graphs can be used to show by how much this is the case at various points in time. Knowing the investment, and the break-even point, a straight line through these points will give you your profit line. From this you can mark off the profit received over any elapsed time.

We have assumed that investments, recurring costs and benefits occur at a constant rate. This is certainly not the case in real life, but if we think of the graphs as averaging out fluctuations, we can get reasonable approximations.

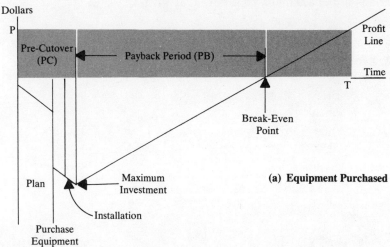

(a) **Equipment Purchased**

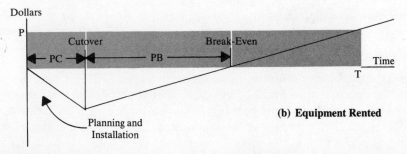

(b) **Equipment Rented**

Figure 8–1   Cost-Benefit Curves

Payback period as a measure of risk is based on the idea that the sooner an investment is returned the safer the investment. We know what is happening today and can make a reasonable guess as to what will happen in two or three years. After that, "anything can happen." Better get our money back as soon as possible. Thus, a fast payback is seen as the way to minimize financial risk. So important is the consideration of getting the investment back quickly that payback period is often the only criterion used to evaluate computer applications and other types of investments.

But this leaves out the question of profitability. Any investment analysis should weigh risk against profitability before coming to a decision. What is the relation of profitability to payback period?

Evaluating Profitability

Notice how the slope of the benefit line in Figure 8–1 indicates profitability. The steeper the slope the shorter the payback period and the greater the profits after break-even. It is also clear from the figure that the slope of the profit line depends on only two things: the initial investment and the payback period. Increasing the former and decreasing the latter result in a steeper slope and more profit.

The amount of accumulated profit, P, at any time, T, will be

$$P = \frac{I}{PB}(T - PB - PC)$$

where, as before:

T = elapsed time

I = investment

PB = payback period

PC = pre-cutover period

If you draw a graph such as that shown in Figure 8–1 you don't need the above formula. You can read P directly off the graph where T intersects the benefit line.

Total accumulated profits are not the same as profitability. Profitability is measured by return on investment, commonly called ROI. ROI relates total profits to investment and time. Obviously, $200 of profit from a $1,000 investment in one year is quite different from the same profit on $2,000 in two years.

We can easily calculate return on investment from the above formula for the total accumulated profits. We simply divide by the investment and time measured in years, or,

$$\text{ROI} = \frac{1}{\text{PB}} - \frac{1}{\text{T}} (1 + \frac{\text{PC}}{\text{PB}})$$

This gives the *average* return on investment per year from a computer system from the start of the project to any later time, T. In the first years, the ROI will be negative, indicating investment and recovery of investment. After the payback period, ROI becomes positive and increases towards the limit of 1/PB. Bear in mind that the ROI is on a per year basis averaged over a number of years equal to T.

From the formula it can be seen that a high return on investment is the result of a fast payback (small PB) and a long useful life (large T).

Table 8–2 gives the return on investment, various payback periods and system lifetimes. The first three columns apply to cases where the pre-cutover period is short enough to be negligible. The other two groups apply to pre-cutover periods in the neighborhood of a half and a full year. Since your calculations will be based on rough estimates of benefits, costs and time periods, you should be able to get sufficient accuracy for equivalent estimates of ROI from the table—you're not looking for pinpoint accuracy.

Table 8–2 brings out some interesting points. Consider a computer application having a negligible pre-cutover period—say three months or less. If the payback period is as short as one year and the life of the system is only two years, you can expect an average return on investment as high as 50 percent per year. However, an increase in the payback period of only six months causes the ROI to drop to 17 percent illustrating how fast payback affects profitability.

As the life of the system in the above example is increased from two to two and a half years and from two and a half to three years, ROI increases, but it approaches a limit given in the table as 100 percent. This means that longer useful life always results in a higher average ROI, but this average will never exceed the limit of 100 percent. The limit values are seen to depend only on payback periods, not on the pre-cutover period.

Table 8–2 can be used in several ways. Thus you might ask: How long must I keep a system if I want an ROI of around 20 percent and my pre-cutover time is expected to be about one year?

From the table, you will find the answer to be five years if your payback period is around two years. However, this drops to two and a half years for a payback period of one year.

Other questions can be formulated and answered by the table. Any three of the four quantities can be specified and the fourth read from the table. If you are interested in values outside the range of the table, they can be easily calculated from the above formula.

Readers may wonder why the amount of investment, I, and the net benefits, NB, don't appear either in the formula for ROI or Table 8–2. Surely, these quantities must have an effect on profitability. They do, but they have both been absorbed into payback period. Remember we originally calculated pay-

Table 8–2   Return on Investment

	Precutover Period Negligible			Precutover Period Equal to Six Months			Precutover Period Equal to One Year	
PB	*LIFE*	*ROI*	*PB*	*LIFE*	*ROI*	*PB*	*LIFE*	*ROI*
1	1.5	33	1	2.0	25	1	2.5	20
	2.0	50		2.5	40		3.0	33
	2.5	60		3.0	50		3.5	43
	3.0	67		3.5	57		4.0	50
	Limit	100		Limit	100		Limit	100
1.5	2.0	17	1.5	2.5	14	1.5	3.0	17
	2.5	27		3.0	23		3.5	20
	3.0	34		3.5	29		4.0	26
	3.5	38		4.0	34		4.5	30
	Limit	67		Limit	67		Limit	67
2.0	2.5	10	2.0	3.0	9	2.0	3.5	6
	3.0	17		3.5	14		4.0	12
	3.5	21		4.0	19		4.5	17
	4.0	25		4.5	22		5.0	20
	Limit	50		Limit	50		Limit	50
2.5	3.0	7	2.5	3.5	6	2.5	4.0	5
	3.5	11		4.0	10		4.5	9
	4.0	15		4.5	13		5.0	12
	4.5	18		5.0	16		5.5	15
	Limit	40		Limit	40		Limit	40

back as $PB = I/NB$. Thus, I/NB can always be substituted for PB. But note that it is not investment or net benefits by themselves which determine return on investment, but only their relationship as expressed by $PB = I/NB$.

So far, we have not taken into account the possibility of resale, trade-in or transfer to another application of the computer equipment. The resale value of a popular model can be substantial and should be accounted for when more accurate estimates of either total profits or ROI are wanted. However, at the time of planning and evaluation it is very hard to know what the resale value will be several years in the future. A conservative estimate might leave this out altogether. However, if you do want to use a resale or salvage value, it can be treated as an addition to accumulated profits. Then by dividing by total investment and equipment life you can obtain the additional return on investment.

Consider an ROI from Table 8–2 equal to 8 percent. You estimate resale value as $10,000. The original investment, I, will be $60,000 and the life, T, will be five years. Then, ROI with resale $= 8 + 10,000 (60,000 \times 5) \times 100 = 9.2$ percent.

Evaluating Alternatives

The previous analysis applied to only a one-alternative investment. Often, however, there are several choices. We may want to compare the profitability of different applications, different ways of computerizing, purchase-lease alternatives or even the purchase of a computer versus some other use of our money. In these cases it is sometimes necessary to take into account the *present value* of money in order to arrive at valid conclusions. This will be the case whenever there are significant differences in the times at which money is spent, saved or received.

Present-value analysis is based on the fact that money in hand can be reinvested. At some future date the dollar invested today will have more value than a dollar received at the same future date. The further into the future dollars are received, the less the present value of those dollars.

Present-value analysis requires some predictions about the future rate of interest or rate of return available, no mean task in today's money markets. Also, the relationships do not lend themselves to easy forms of presentation and calculation. This places present-value analysis beyond the scope of this book. Readers who wish to pursue the subject further can find detailed descriptions in books on capital investment.

Situations in which present-value analysis could make a difference are when a rental is being compared to a purchase or when resale value is a consideration. Otherwise, where the pattern of cash flow follows the curves shown in Figure 8–1, and most readers will find this to be the case, alternative investments can be evaluated by comparing payback periods and ROIs, as described in the previous section.

THE NON-FINANCIAL APPROACH

The non-financial approach to evaluation stresses business judgment in making a decision over straight dollar and cents arguments. It is the newer of the two approaches and has gained favor as the informational benefits from computers have become of increasing importance to users.

On the other hand, the financial approach has been around a long time. It is how computers were evaluated when first introduced into business applications for such tasks as accounting and the replacement of clerical functions. In the latter case especially, there was the possibility of easily identifiable cost saving on which it was not too hard to place a dollar value. The computer was viewed primarily as a means to replace labor. Computing the wages that would be saved gave a fairly solid estimate of benefits.

At least on paper, if not always in fact, the cost-benefit approach was a viable method for evaluating computerization. It had the added advantage that it fit people's idea of how hardheaded business decisions should be made.

However, as computers moved into new areas of application it became increasingly difficult to apply the cost-benefit evaluation in any meaningful way. Furthermore, people began to realize as the results of a good number of projects became known, that the cost-benefit approach broke down at least as often as it worked, even in those situations for which it is best suited—the direct replacement of people.

Here are some of the points that have been made against the financial approach.

Accuracy of Estimates

Costs and benefits in many cases cannot be estimated accurately enough to provide meaningful results. If an application is clearly beneficial or clearly not beneficial, cost-benefit analysis is not necessary. It is in those cases where the correct decision is not clear that cost-benefit is needed. But if costs and benefits can not be estimated with reasonable accuracy, we are only kidding ourselves if we rely on them.

Suppose the computer and programs will cost $15,000. Your inventory system is in a mess and you would be more than happy to pay twice as much to get some relief. You saw a demonstration at a dealer's and the programs did everything you want, and more. Do you need to do a cost-benefit analysis? Not likely!

Now, suppose, instead, that your inventory system could stand improvement, but it is not in that bad shape. You could, at present, afford to go as high as $19,000 or $20,000 for a computer. But the programs you saw at the dealer's demo are completely inadequate. The dealer, whom you have reason to know as knowledgeable and forthright, tells you that in his experience similarly situated businesses have saved anywhere between $4,000 and $6,000 a year. However, to get the kind of programs you need might add between $3,000 and $5,000 to the $15,000 price. But he suggests you do a detailed cost-benefit analysis to determine if you really can justify the purchase of the computer. At this point, you decide you've heard enough. You can make a business decision on what you already know, so you decide to look for better areas to invest your money.

If, instead, you had taken the dealer's advice about making a cost-benefit analysis you would have been faced with:

- Estimating inventory savings due to tighter controls and better information.
- Estimating increased business resulting from improved customer service.
- Accepting a programmer's estimates for the cost and customization of programs that meet your somewhat unique requirements.

Now you have to ask yourself if, with all the uncertainties in the above estimates, whether in the end you are any better off than if you had made a business decision based on the off-the-cuff figures provided by the dealer.

The Myth of Objectivity

Cost-benefit analysis appears to provide an objective criteria, free of personal bias and emotion.

In fact, experience shows that quite the opposite is true. Because there is so much room for the manipulation of figures in the estimating process, it is common to find that those who want a computer can find numbers to support their claims, and those who don't want a computer can do the same. Go back over the costs and benefits listed in the previous section and see how difficult it could be to make unbiased estimates. Whether the bias is conscious or unconscious is beside the point here. When a dollar value can not be known within wide limits, estimates will be made that support whatever conclusion the estimator wants to see.

Estimates of computer development time and costs are commonly underestimated by a factor of two or three. Who makes these estimates? Computer professionals and users, of course—exactly those people who stand to benefit from the project. If the same applications were estimated by a skinflint and computer-hater, guess what the numbers would look like.

In large computer systems, the underestimation of costs is so prevalent that it is more or less accepted as routine.

In the view of the non-financial approach, a hardheaded computer evaluation requires a recognition of the limitations of quantitative techniques and the need to use business judgment in assuming business risks.

Synergism

It is probable that if the true cost of many now successfully working applications had been known in the beginning they never would have been approved on the basis of a cost-benefit analysis. Yet at bottom, the business judgment that led to the implementation of these projects was correct, as proven by the fact that business continually wants more computerization, not less. The original analysis was off the mark on the benefits side of the equation as well as the cost side. Benefits were underestimated because the long-term trend toward lower costs and more powerful systems can not be factored into a cost-benefit analysis of a single application. This is no less true for a small business than for a large one. The introduction of a computer into your operations should be viewed as just the beginning of a continuing process of automation and not merely the application of the computer to a single area. When the computer is applied to several areas its worth is more than the sum of the individual contributions. The computer becomes more powerful as it takes in more applications. Consider, for example, how business applications might be combined with word processing to provide more than the sum of the parts. Synergism. Creating synergism requires business judgment. Although the result can sometimes be analyzed by a cost-benefit approach, more often business judgment is the more appropriate tool.

The non-financial approach has led large corporations to routinely budget a certain amount for computer systems and their expansions. The amount budgeted may expand and contract with general business conditions, and it may reflect the ongoing tug of war within the firm for allocation of funds, but by and large, the need to budget for expanded computer usage is a recognized necessity for doing business in today's world. What the large, experienced users look for primarily in the use of computers are ways to provide for the information needs of the organization. More and more business judgment is needed in place of dollar and cents calculations.

Small-businesspersons, or managers working on a tight budget, might think their situation is completely different. Yet, on a smaller scale, they proceed in a similar manner, that is purchases are made based on business judgment rather than detailed financial calculations.

When office equipment, such as typewriters and copiers, first appeared on the market, no doubt sales personnel had to convince customers that the purchase of these devices would save them money. Today we see the same thing in small computers. Sales representatives emphasize savings as a criterion for purchase. Customers are given work sheets on which to add up costs and calculate payback periods. This can be helpful, but there is the danger of the customer focusing attention on the wrong areas when deciding to buy or not to buy.

Undoubtedly, the small computer will soon be considered as essential for running a business as typewriters are today, and the questions asked will be similar. Not: How much will it cut costs? But: What special features does it have that I can use to advantage?

WHO IS RIGHT?

We have presented two points of view on the role of computers in business. While not completely irreconcilable, they do not have much in common in their approach to making the ultimate decision, to computerize or not to computerize. Here readers will have to exercise their own judgment.

If you feel that a cost-benefit analysis would be useful and that you have the facts to base it on, by all means you should make the most of it. On the other hand, if you can't justify a computer based on dollars and cents yet are convinced in your own mind that applying one would make good business sense, by all means follow through. The thing to avoid is the extreme positions you may hear and read, such as:

• Never buy a computer unless you can justify it financially.
• Know exactly how you will recover your investment in a computer.
• The power of the computer is wasted on cost displacement applications.

As you learn more about small computers, data processing and information processing, you will be in a better position to judge how best to evaluate computers for your area of interest.

Planning for a
Small Computer System

The most important point to recognize in planning for a small computer is that a computer can do more than one thing.

When we purchase a piece of equipment we are used to having only one use in mind. A copier copies. A typewriter types. And a desk calculator calculates. That is all. A computer is not like this. Put in one program and it's a data processor. Put in another and it's a word processor. Put in another and it's a communication terminal. By switching programs we can transform what we have into a completely different product.

This is something new. People are not conditioned for so much flexibility and therefore don't use it. A good many of the small computer installations are underutilized. Good planning consists not only in having the computer do a good job in one area, but do a good job in all the areas where it can be applied to advantage.

In the very small business it is hard to justify a computer over a calculator or magnetic ledger card system, if the computer is used for only one task. But as soon as we take advantage of the computer's ability to do more than one thing, even very small businesses can benefit.

It is important to understand that we are not talking here about using the computer in some sophisticated way or building complex systems requiring professional talent. Consider the different ways a small computer can be used, all of which we have discussed previously, but list again for emphasis:

- For business data processing
- For computational problems
- As a word processor
- As a communication terminal to information utilities
- As a personal computer in business-or profession-related activities

All these functions can be performed with the same equipment simply by switching programs. It doesn't make sense not to use this capability as much as possible.

In planning for a computer system, and when trying to justify it economically, you should keep asking yourself: Am I using the computer to its maximum advantage? What else might I do with it? How much idle time will there be?

Illustration 9–1 COMBINED FUNCTIONS IN A SMALL COMPUTER. Wang's Integrated Information System is an example of the trend to use the small computer for word processing, data processing, and communications. (Reprinted courtesy of Wang Laboratories, Inc. One Industrial Ave., Lowell, MA 08151.)

Planning a small computer system requires that you address three questions:

- What do I want to do?
- What can I do?
- How am I going to do it?

WHAT DO YOU WANT TO DO?

There are a number of reasons people want to install a computer. At the top of the list are cutting costs, improving customer service and reducing the work load. Other reasons, not usually mentioned by first-time users, might be improving accuracy, systemizing and enforcing discipline on the procedures of an organization, improving access to information and providing better controls. Further reasons, which are usually not discussed openly, are prestige, fear of being left back, pride and the desire to have a new gadget to play with. If any of these latter reasons apply to you, don't feel guilty; you have plenty of distinguished company. Some very big computers in industry and government have been bought, at least in part, for these reasons. However, these personal motivations need not exclude the reaping of material benefits.

The Right and Wrong Reasons for Installing a Computer

At a seminar on the business applications of small computers one of the speakers discussed the right and wrong reasons for installing a computer. The wrong reasons were:

• Just to try it out and see what it can do.
• Because the competition is using one.
• When there are no specific problems to apply it to.
• Just for the sake of change.

The right reasons were:

• You can show a definite cost saving.
• You have determined exactly how best to use it.
• Business is expanding and will require additional personnel that might be saved by the computer.

Although these points have some validity, exception can be taken to most of them, particularly the philosophy behind them. This is the old view that computers have to reduce costs to be justified. Worse, it turns the learning process upside down. The first-time user has no way of knowing exactly how best to use the computer. Getting to know a computer and how to use it requires time and experience. The first application of a computer, no matter how precisely defined, is often only a buy-in for the user. The really high payoff application comes later with a realization of what a computer can do, and may not even have been anticipated at the beginning.

It shouldn't be necessary to tell readers of this book that computers cost money, and money is scarce. This seems to be the lesson of those cautioning against an experimental approach. Evidently, they fear that without proper warning, you will run to the bank, cash in your bonds and fritter away your money on an expensive computer system. In fact, the opposite is true. You're going to do a lot of investigating and planning before you make a move. The point is that in doing your planning you must recognize that many of the potential benefits from computers are intangible and you can not cost justify them in advance; sometimes you must just "try out the computer to see what it can do." Even if your first choice of an application is off the mark, it would be very surprising if there weren't some aspect of your work that couldn't profit from a computer.

Computers have become so cheap they are being bought by individuals for home use and for hobbies. Most of these purchases are by people who have no specific use for them in mind—they just want to see what they can do. Often they end up by applying the computer to business applications or in their professional work.

There probably isn't one big business that doesn't have a lot of computing power today, and that doesn't wish it had more. In a few years computers will be as common in small businesses as they are in large ones today. If you can't think of any reason for a computer other than that your competitor has one, that itself is a pretty good reason. You just can't afford to get left back. Therefore, it is not so much a question of *whether* to get a computer as *when*, and how best to apply it.

Applying computers to your organization should be looked at as a long range commitment. Most readers probably have in mind one or more areas that they feel could use a computer, areas where there is a lot of paper shuffling, a scramble to get results out on time and drudgery so far as you or your employees are concerned. You may be tempted to jump right in and attack your immediate problems. But before settling on this area as your first application, please give careful attention to the following section. It could save you much time and effort.

Guidelines to Good Planning

Installing a computer has been compared to getting married. Both similes are apt. Once you settle on a certain approach and pick a computer, your course is set and it can be very hard to change it. Therefore, rather than jumping in in haste and repenting at leisure, it pays to give some thought to what you should do and the right way to do it.

Think for a while about your overall operations, trying to forget about your immediate problems. What are the vital areas of your business or organization? What direction are you going in and what do you expect to be doing two or three years from now? Answers to these questions should determine where you can most profitably employ a computer. You will also see how your immediate problems relate to the big picture. You can solve these immediate problems in such a way that your solutions fit into the big picture rather than clashing with it.

You would be amazed and shocked at how much money has been wasted by big business and government by poor planning. Major systems have been installed that can't accommodate the introduction of new products. Systems are installed in different areas of the same organization that can't communicate because they use incompatible equipment. Systems have been installed to solve some immediate, isolated problem, but contribute little, if anything, in benefits to the main line of business. These are not isolated instances; they are quite common. They are the result partly of a necessary learning process, and partly of the difficulty of planning in a large organization where conflicting interests pull in all directions and the needs of the organization as a whole get lost.

In this, your position is quite different. The need for seeing the big picture is now well established. The difficult lessons of planning each application in isolation have been learned. And finally, unless you happen to be a manager in a large organization, you are completely free to plan in any way that seems most appropriate to you. Take advantage of this. You may be impatient to get going and not at all inclined to speculate on what your needs may be tomorrow—you know what you want today. In this, a quick decision could be a costly one.

Here is a step-by-step approach to planning:

- Think about your overall operations. They may be related to business, government, your professional activities, or even an area of a large corporation. The approach is the same in each case.
- List the operations that could be placed on a computer. You can use Table 1–1 on p. 23 as a guide.
- Think about where you are going, and where you will be in three years. How does this affect your list? Are there new operations that should be added? When might they be ready for a computer? Will any operations be terminated or modified? When? Can you project your operations beyond three years?
- You now have a list of current operations and future changes with associated dates. Now comes the key step. Assign priorities to your list. Which computer application looks like it can contribute most? Which least? Give each application a number and rating. If you can calculate cost savings as a guide, fine. But remember that many computer benefits can not be reduced to dollars and cents in the planning stage. You know your operations and you have to use that knowledge to judge where the priorities should be. The more you work with computers, the better you will get at this.
- You may try assigning dates of implementation based on priority, thus giving you a scheduled computerization plan for the whole three years or more that your plan covers. This is a refinement, though a very useful one. Using it will place you in the select company of those who are trying to avoid the mistakes of the past by planning on a broad front, rather than isolated tasks.
- Look at the application having priority one. Does it look too ambitious? Should it be postponed until you have more experience, and a simpler project started first? In the following sections we will be discussing specifics that will help you decide this question.
- Now consider how you can take advantage of the computer's ability to do more than one type of processing. When, if at all, will you try to do word processing or communications?
- Once you have decided which applications you will tackle first, you are on your way. But you cannot forget the others while you are planning the first. Your strategy must be to make all your decisions consistent with the other members of your list. This may not always be possible, but this should be your goal.
- You now have a "master planning list." Use it. Refer to it as you proceed through the following steps, constantly reassessing your original choices in light of what you learn later.

Here are some guidelines on how to pick high payoff applications and set priorities in your master planning list:

- Pick areas that can benefit most by having greater and faster access to information.
- Try to free the best people for more important tasks.
- Choose applications that can show the greatest increase in sales and decrease in inventory.
- Pick areas that are related when planning successive stages of implementation. Related areas can benefit from one another's computerization, thereby enhancing the overall payoff.
- Try to eliminate data entry operations. That is, pass data through common files rather than printing the data in one application and then resubmitting it in another. Data entry consumes labor, is a source of errors, results in delay and is a waste of talent. Keep it to a minimum. Again, this is achieved best when related applications are used.
- Don't assume that major problem areas are always the best candidates for a computer. Problems may be the result of a rapidly.changing situation, personnel inadequacies, or basic business deficiencies, none of which invite the use of a computer.

WHAT CAN YOU DO?

What you want to do and what you can do are two different things. A small-business person or professional has limited resources which must be allocated carefully. You are contemplating an investment in your valuable time and money, and it is a good idea to assess realistically whether the intended application is possible.

First-time users are anxious to apply computers to accounting, inventory, and payroll. However, these are critical areas of your business. If major problems develop you could be in trouble. Unless you can afford professional help, a less critical area for your first application of a computer might be an area such as word processing, financial planning or sales analysis. Then you can familiarize yourself with the computer world, study the equipment and evaluate your vendor's product before committing to major projects. Finally, before committing yourself to any major application, check with your accountant and lawyer.

The Computer System's Biggest Enemy

The computer system's biggest enemy is change. This is somewhat surprising. Previously we have gone to some length to point out how versatile and flexible computers are. Now we are saying they are inflexible. Why?

The answer is that we must distinguish between computers and computer systems. Remember that the computer is just a piece of hardware looking for an assignment. A computer system is a computer loaded with programs and hooked up to input-output devices of various types. The computer system has been designed for a very specific assignment which must be performed according to very definite rules. Change those rules only a little and you're in trouble.

How important are changes to a computer system? The answer is that they are critical. Big companies provide for changes by maintaining large staffs of data processing professionals. A good percentage of their time is devoted to program maintenance and the planning for new equipment, not just to accommodate new applications but to respond to changes in business requirements. The smallest change in procedures has to be communicated to the computer. And what looks small in the rule book may reverberate through a program, requiring all manner of subsidiary changes.

What is normal for a big organization can be fatal for a small one. The resources devoted to the continual program and equipment modification that goes on in large organizations are not available in small ones, certainly not to the same extent in terms of percent of sales or net income. Look at it this way. The difference between a large and a small organization is mostly in how much is done, not in what is done. The small organization must accommodate to most of the same changes faced by the big organizations. If you have a small travel agency, a change in rates is as critical to you as for a major transportation company. Will your computer system be able to cope? Will you have the resources to make the required changes? Changes are something you can't afford to ignore. How do you plan for them?

Here are the points to consider in order to determine if you can cope with changes:

- Evaluate your organization, whether a business or otherwise, in terms of expected changes. Computer systems like unchanging environments. What environment will it get in your application? Are you adding product lines? New departments? New categories of personnel? Expanding into new territories? Are you subject to special regulations that could change? No activity is immune from change. The questions are: When? How fast? How often? How significant? The more stable the environment, the easier it is to maintain a computer system. A rapidly growing, changing environment should be a warning signal to you to proceed slowly and plan carefully. Make a "Planning for Change List" with appropriate comments of all anticipated changes.
- Examine your intended computer application in relation to your organization's environment. Is it subject to any changes identified in the Planning for Change List? Does it suggest additional changes not already listed?
- Check off those areas subject to change that are controlled by external forces—government agencies, industry boards, professional organizations and so on. Your exposure can actually be made less in these areas than those that result from your own activities. Here's why: Changes that affect a large number of users will be supported by the vendors supplying programs in that area. In these cases, your object should be to purchase your program from reliable vendors and avoid custom programs that you will have to maintain yourself. Expect to pay for any new version of your program. Whatever its

cost, it is bound to be substantially less than you could do in-house. For dealing with this problem you may want to get the help of a profressional. Chapter 11, "How to Select a Small Computer" describes the possible vendors and sources of assistance.
• Make an evaluation. Is the application you have chosen feasible for you? The more an application is subject to change the more unknowns you have to deal with and the greater your risks. Would you be better off with a less desirable, but less risky project? If you decide to minimize risk, review your Master Planning List and pick an application with suitable risk. Any decision you make at this point is provisional and subject to other considerations dealt with below.

Can You Tolerate Computer Failure?

Computer systems can fail. Either the equipment or the programs can cause a system to go down. No matter how rare an occurrence, you must be prepared. The feasibility of the application you are considering will depend on how failure will affect your operations and what you can do about it. Here you should be very specific; broad generalizations are useless. Draw up a set of specifications along these lines:

SPECIFICATIONS FOR RESPONSE TO FAILURE
(1) In this application the system can be down a maximum of_____minutes/hours/days.
(2) While the system is down, it will be necessary to continue operations manually, or by some other means._____ (yes or no)
    Comments:_____
(3) In order to reduce the probability of being "off the air" to a minimum, backup equipment will be required for the following units:
    Printer_____
    Disk_____
    Keyboard_____
    Display_____
    Computer_____
(4) The system will have the following shutdown, restart and recovery capabilities: _____
_____

Point (1) asks for a business judgment. Depending on the case in hand, the amount of tolerable down time may be critical or not, but in any case you should set a maximum figure you think is tolerable. When you get to the selection process, as described in Chapters 10 and 11, you will determine if the selected vendor can meet this requirement.

If the answer to point (2) is yes, you need to develop a set of procedures outlining how you will continue operations if the system goes down. This is the only way you can be sure that continued operations are really feasible. Here are the kind of questions you should ask:

- How will data normally entered into the computer be recorded? On what medium and in what format?
- How will I deal with situations in which data stored in the computer is needed? In this you will be aided if your system produces frequent printouts, in which case the most recent reports may be satisfactory. Another strategy is to run your files on another machine.
- How will I generate documents such as checks and government reports that can not be put off without a penalty?
- Which data processing functions will have to be performed while the system is down and which can be postponed until the system is back on the air?
- How many people will be needed to perform the above tasks? Who will do them? How will other work be rescheduled to allow for the added work load? Will overtime be needed?
- When and how will operations be resumed when the system is back on the air? How will the accumulated data be entered? By whom? What will be the schedule?

If you can't answer all the above questions, or if the answers look like a horrendous nightmare, maybe you should question the feasibility of this application.

Point (3) lists the most common units that go to make up a small computer system. If you have others, add them to the list. The units are listed in roughly the order of increasing reliability, or their MTBF. MTBF stands for "mean time between failure." It is simply the average time a unit can be operated before it fails. Not the minimum or maximum but the average, which of course means that your unit may perform better or worse. MTBF depends on lots of factors, not the least of which is the definition of "failure." When does a unit fail? When it stops working completely? When it delivers one error in 10 million? Or one error in 100 million? MTBF is a loose term unless the conditions it is meant to describe are known in detail by the user.

Ask your vendor for MTBF figures. Discount that claim by 15 to 20 percent to be safe. Then, depending on your reliability requirements take 100 to 50 percent of the discounted figure as a guide.

For example, if your vendor's salesrep says the MTBF for a unit is nine months, you might estimate about seven months MTBF. Now, if your reliability requirements are not more than one outage a year, clearly you better buy an extra unit for backup.

On the other hand, if two outages a year are tolerable, you're on the borderline. With a worse than average unit and bad luck, you could be looking at three outages a year. If three outages a year are tolerable, you can go without a backup unit and feel pretty safe.

MTBF is only half the story. There is also MTTR. MTTR is "mean time to repair." You can't make an intelligent assessment unless you take into consideration both MTTR and MTBF. Here's why. Consider two units, one called RELIABLE and the other called UNRELIABLE, with MTBF of one year and three months respectively. Now suppose the MTTR for the RELIABLE unit is a week and that for the UNRELIABLE one is one hour. The picture has changed! Now UNRELIABLE looks like the better choice. Clearly, MTTR makes a difference and you should take it into account.

Your analysis of MTTR is similar to MTBF. You get the figure for MTTR from the vendor, or whoever else you arrange to do the servicing. Strictly speaking, you are interested in the time to get your system back on the air, not MTTR. If the service technician plugs another unit in place of the failed unit and gets you up and running, the time to actually repair the unit is of no interest to you. Or you might be required to bring the unit to a service center and receive a replacement. In any case find out the time, for each unit of the system, that you will be off the air. Factor this information into your decision on whether you need a spare unit on location.

Table 9–1 is an attempt to give some indication of what you can expect to find in the way of equipment reliability and repair. The wide range of values for MTBF should be a warning to go slow when using such MTBF values. One is never sure how much difference in quoted MTBF values represent differences in quality of product and how much they are the result of differing attitudes on what MTBF should convey.

The rules of thumb are an attempt to translate all these numbers into something more meaningful to the nonexpert user. However, as with all rules of

Table 9–1   Data on Equipment Reliability and Repair

1. __MTBF__

Floppy disk	2,000–8,000 hrs.
Winchester disk	4,000–10,000 hrs.
Display	2,000–5,000 hrs.
Matrix printer—impact	800–2,000 hrs.
Matrix printer—non-impact	4,000–10,000 hrs.
Daisy Wheel Printer	2,500–3,500 hrs.
Processor and memory	2,000–5,000 hrs.

2. __Life Expectancy__

Keyboard—mechanical	10 million keystrokes
Keyboard—capacitive	100 million keystrokes

3. __Error Rates__

	Recoverable[1]	Non-recoverable[2]
Floppy disk	1 error out of 10^9	1 error out of 10^{11}
Hard disk	1 error out of 10^{10}	1 error out of 10^{12}

4. __Rules of Thumb__

   (a) Expect three to five failures per year.[3]

   (b) Assume 30 minutes to 3 hours to repair, with a 1-hour average.

   (c) Allow 4–6 hours for a technician to arrive if service is within 100 miles. Increase this to 10–12 hours if service center is 100–200 miles away.

   (d) Allow 3 days for repair if a unit is left at a service center.

[1]Can be detected and corrected.

[2]Can not be detected and corrected.

[3]These figures are for equipment failures only; program failures could make these much higher.

thumb, they can be off the mark in particular cases. For MTTR you must rely on your vendor, but try to check with other users on the quality of service they are getting.

The information asked for in point (4) will be supplied by the vendor. Shutdown and restart facilities provide for reducing the loss of data when there is a power failure, and allow you to restart the system at some convenient point in the operations that is consistent with the point of shutdown. You are not concerned with the particulars of shutdown and restart facilities except to make sure they are available, to provide for the needs of your application and to know how you will use them. If you are working with a professional, he or she is the one to look into this area.

Recovery is necessary whenever there is a failure (due to either hardware or software problems) that affects the files. Two cases in particular require discussion.

Suppose, in the process of updating a file, the system goes down. You can't just rerun the program because then you might update some records twice. On the other hand you can't start precisely where you left off, because you don't know exactly where you were when the system crashed. Large computers and some high-end small computer systems will store a copy of each record before it is updated. This, then, makes it possible to restore the file to its original state at some convenient starting point.

The second, more serious case, is when a file is damaged, because of a read/-write head crash or for other reasons. Now, the file must be replaced and brought up to date.

In small computer systems both these cases are provided for by periodically making copies of a file. The question of frequency thus arises. The answer should depend on the rate at which data is changed. Ordinarily, at the completion of a session or at the end of each day might be sufficient. Consider, however, the effect of the system going down near the end of the day. You will then have to reenter a whole day's work. Can you find time to do this? More frequent copying will reduce the reentry time but will require extra work to provide for an infrequent occurrence. There is a trade-off here, which you will have to evaluate in terms of your own operations.

If you plan to operate your computer on-line for, say, the entry of orders as they are received, how do you provide for system failure? A backup copy of the file is no longer sufficient, because the new orders entered since the last copy will have been lost. This situation can be provided for in two ways, both of which require that each new order be recorded in a separate file, that is, logged as soon as it is entered. Now, if there is a crash, these entries can be used to update the backup copy of your file automatically. This requires that your system have a special facility for doing this. If such a facility is absent, it will be necessary to print the log and then reenter the transactions at the keyboard, updating the backup copy manually.

Once a file is copied for backup the log file is usually expendable. However, it is good practice to always print the log, so as to have an audit trail and as a contingency if file problems surface at some later time.

Although the need for recovery procedures should be infrequent, they definitely must be considered in the planning stage. Too often this is ignored by small computer users. The above discussion should alert you to the nature of the problem and what solutions to look for when the time comes to select equipment and programs.

At this point you should again consider feasibility. Normally, the reliability will be adequate for your needs and you will be able to live with it. However if your operations, for some reason, require more than average reliability, at this point you might conclude that you can't get the up time you need without spare units. If this is too expensive, consider another application, with the idea of returning to this one at a later time.

We have now completed the easy part of the discussion of failures. That was concerned with equipment, where such things as MTBF and MTTR are measurable, available and can be used in the planning process. Now we enter the no-man's land of *program failure*. There is no such thing here as mean time of failure or repair. The only guidelines available here are a few generalities:

- The longer a program has been in use the less likely are failures. As a program is used, problems that develop are, hopefully, fixed by the vendor, thus decreasing the probability of errors.
- The more people using a program, the less likely are failures, unless the program is new. Again, problems are culled out more rapidly.
- The more a program is tested the less likely are failures. However, only very short programs are ever tested for all possible errors. Assume that any program you are going to use will have some errors.
- Fixing an error in a program can result in new errors. These errors might not show up for some time. They can make parts of the program that previously were error-free bomb out.

Program failure can cause the system to go down just the same as equipment failure. If the problem is isolated, you may be able to work around it and continue operations. But this can create more problems than it solves. It is better to be prepared for backup operation.

Fortunately, spare copies of software can be stored at your location for just such emergencies at a reasonable cost. (Check with your software vendor on this. He will have a policy on copying his software.) When this doesn't solve the problem, proper planning requires that you add to your Specifications for Response to Failure the following point:

Procedures that will be used in case of software failure (work with your vendor on this, but don't let him minimize the problem).

If you can't get back on the air, your procedures will be the same as for a hardware failure. In any event, you should try to stay with programs that have been used by many customers for a long time. These will be the most reliable. Remember, customized programs require the most care in planning for emergency situations.

Risk/Reward Trade-offs or, How to Obtain a Competitive Advantage

For those willing to assume the risks, a computer offers numerous possibilities to get a jump on the competition. As with anything else, getting an advantage through the use of computers requires you to stick your neck out a little. If you run with the pack you can't expect superior results.

The small computer industry, although (or because) still very young, is already a large industry with numerous vendors of widely varying sizes. There are the leaders, IBM and Radio Shack. If your competition has no computer and you buy one of the leaders' products, you can achieve an advantage, temporarily. If you are successful, isn't it likely that your friendly competitor will get the message and copy your example? Then you are both back where you were before. Maybe. Suppose instead of copying you, your competitor gets a system that runs rings around yours. How can this be done?

Besides the leaders in the computer industry there are hundreds of small companies. How do they stay alive? No doubt many readers of this book are small-business persons who have to compete against larger rivals. How do you do it? By offering something that your big competitor doesn't. Better product, better delivery, better service, any of a number of things that cause your customer to prefer doing business with you.

It is no different in the computer industry. If you want something special, you look to the smaller firms to supply it. Most often you will be looking for programs or a system that more closely meets your needs than what is being offered by the industry leaders. But it could also be many other things, something as simple as faster delivery.

We spoke above in terms of achieving a competitive advantage. That is only one of the possible rewards. You may look to a smaller firm only because you want a more convenient system for yourself and your employees, to provide better security, more flexibility or growth possibilities, or just because you're ornery, like doing things differently, and that's that. And then there will be cases when the offerings of the leaders will not fit your particular needs under any circumstances.

Doing business with small firms is riskier than doing business with large firms. There should be no mistake about this. However, in the small computer business there are all gradations of size, from the leaders all the way down to one or two moonlighters operating from a garage. As the risks increase, you should expect increasing rewards as compensation. What is a reasonable risk/reward trade-off? Consider the following cases.

Case 1

Mr. X is a good businessman, but he has absolutely no interest in computers. He would, if left to himself, just as soon not have to bother with them. However, he recognizes that the use of computers is good business and he doesn't intend to let the competition get the jump on him. If he learned accounting, he figures he can learn what he needs to know about these damn computers.

Besides, anything that can take some of the paperwork load off his back can't be all bad. But make no mistake about it, that computer better pay its own way or no go.

Case 2

Ms. Y is on a fast track. She wants to make her distributorship grow, and *fast*. Ms. Y sees computers as a way to get a handle on the inventory, control stock and free up needed cash for expansion. She would also like to try out computers as an ordering tool, for accounting and to help route deliveries. So what if she's short of cash. She figures she can swing a deal with some programmers who are looking for an entrée to her kind of business. She'll get free programs in return for teaching them the business. Maybe she'll get a piece of the action, when the programmers market her programs. Ms. Y doesn't know any more about computers than Mr. X, but as far as she's concerned, they're the only way to go.

Case 3

Mr. Z wanted to be an engineer, but had to take over the family business when his father got sick. Business never interested him much until he got a small business computer. Now he's trying out the computer in all kinds of ways. At first he taught himself programming and programmed the first system himself. Now he's too busy planning new systems and running the increasing business. He subcontracts the programming. When he buys equipment he looks for equipment that will do the job he has in mind, and do it right. He just bought a system from a new firm that recently started up in an old abandoned warehouse downtown. It's the best darn business system he's seen yet, and he's seen plenty. Don't talk to Mr. Z about risk. He'll get the soldering iron out and fix it himself if he has to.

These are three extreme cases defining the limits of what should be looked for in risk/reward trade-offs. For Mr. X, obviously, a minimum risk is indicated. Ms. Y will accept a high risk, not because she is a computer expert, but because her business philosophy is to trade off risk for high reward. Mr. Z gets the high rewards without the high risk because he has educated himself in computer technology. He may not be the best businessperson in other respects, but when it comes to computers, he can take care of himself.

Most readers should be able to spot where they fit in between these three people. Are you somewhat technically inclined? Or would you just as well leave the technical part to someone else, but you would like to get a really good computer system, although you're not as freewheeling as Ms. Y. We all have our own best trade-offs between risk and reward. In planning for a computer system you should try to be clear on what yours is. We are back to the question of feasibility and what you can do when the time comes to select a computer system. There is no one answer good for everybody. It depends on where your capabilities lie and what your inclinations are with respect to risk/-reward trade-offs.

HOW TO DO IT

How do you convert your present operations to a computer system? Once you have decided on the application or area that you want to convert, four activities are required:

(1) Data gathering
(2) Development of specifications
(3) Selecting a system
(4) Implementing a system

The first two activities are part of the planning process and, consequently, are discussed in this chapter. Selection and implementation are dealt with in later chapters.

Although most readers will be computerizing present operations, in some cases the computer will be applied in totally new areas. The process is essentially the same in both cases, except that for new systems the data gathering is based on estimates or investigation of similar systems, rather than on known facts of your own operations.

The four steps are presented in a logical order and none of them can be *completed* before all previous steps are completed. However, this does not mean that there won't be overlapping and retracing of steps. Indeed, the selection process should be started as soon as possible. That is, you should not wait until the data gathering is complete to start investigating what's available in computer stores and from dealers. The more you expose yourself to the industry, the more you will learn and gain confidence in your ability to master the subject of computers.

Once you have made a first pass at drawing up specifications and have started the selection process in earnest, you are almost sure to find yourself returning to the data gathering step and the specification steps. Missing data, the need to alter specs and new ideas suggested by the equipment you are examining will require you to retrace your steps. So don't expect to get everything exactly right the first time. Even professionals don't work this way (although some claim to).

Data Gathering

Data gathering provides the facts you need to select the appropriate system. There are hundreds of systems out there, all with eager salesreps promoting their company's products. Which one will you end up with? One that meets your needs and is a pleasure to work with? Or will it be a bomb, a constant irritation, and achieve little of the intended benefits? By gathering data you obtain a means for filtering out the wrong systems and zeroing in on the right ones.

What Data Do You Need?

Data processing, whatever the area of application, usually involves the use of the following elements, all of which we have talked about before:

- Source documents
- Files
- Records
- Reports
- Data fields

Note that fields are the basic elements. Records, files and reports are merely convenient groupings of fields. A field is a unit of data such as a name, a date or a part number. They can be rearranged to suit your convenience. In transferring operations to a computer, rearrangement of fields is a common occurrence. One reason for rearrangement is to facilitate the organization of data to fit the computer. Other reasons are to provide better reports, easier data entry and the ability to call up data on the screen of the display. But whatever the rearrangement, the actual fields of data remain pretty much constant. Therefore, the aim of the data gathering task is to identify the data fields presently used in operations that you plan to computerize. If you need this data in your current operation, chances are you will still need it when the computer is up and running.

There are hundreds of data fields and statistics in your operations, some relevant to computerization, some not. How do you tell the difference? The relevant data answers three questions in three different areas—input, memory and output. The three questions that must be answered are: What? How Much? When? Or, more explicitly: What data is required? How much data is required? When is the data required? Table 9–2 provides a convenient guide for data gathering, with examples.

Table 9–2 lists the major types of input performed in small business and professional systems. The answers to the questions how much and when are typical for the type of input; they are not the only answers. For example, source documents are usually accumulated and then processed in batches at one sitting. Therefore, the relevant question is how long it will take, that is, what is the character rate of entry and what is the number of characters? This type of entry is normally performed at regularly scheduled intervals. However, it could also be performed when the batch of source documents reach a certain size, or when an operator is available, and so on. Thus Table 9–2, as its name states, is only a guide, providing an indication of what might happen in a typical system. You should develop an equivalent table to reflect your own operations before proceeding to the more detailed entries called for in Forms 9–1, 9–2, and 9–3 (pages 207–209).

Forms 9-1, 9-2 and 9-3 provide sample formats for listing the data as you gather it. You may have to add some headings of your own to cover special

Table 9-2   Data Gathering Guide

	What?	*How Much?*	*When?*
INPUT	Source Documents	Number of characters and character rate	Scheduled
	New records	Number per day	Scheduled or when received
	Changes to records	Number per day	Scheduled or when received
	Inquiries	Number per minute	Random
	Transactions	Number per minute	Random
STORAGE	Files	Number	Time of processing
	Records	Number	Order of procesing
	Indexes	Number of entries	Time of processing
	Tables	Number of entries	Time of procesing
	Data fields	Maximum number of characters allowed	Frequency of processing
OUTPUT TO PRINTER	Reports	Number of pages and copies	Scheduled
	Text	Number of pages and copies	Dedicated
	Letters	Number of characters and copies	As required
	Forms	Number of forms and copies	Scheduled
	Graphs	Special requirements	As required

cases. At any rate, these forms should prove useful both for data gathering and later for selecting a system. The column headed Rating is for specifying what is needed, and will be discussed in the following section on specifications. The heading Program or System Check provides for a check list and will be dealt with in Chapter 11.

How to Gather Data

To make sure you gather all the data you need, set up three files—one for input, one for your records, and one for output. In the input file place samples of all source documents and verbal exchanges: bills, orders, inquiries, etc. In the record file place samples of your records of receivables, payables, etc. In your output file place samples of reports and other documents produced for internal or external use. These three files will be the source information for your entries on the three data gathering forms at the end of this chapter.

In order to simplify your task of evaluation, break up your data into logical groups. Use one data gathering form for each such group. Thus, on Form 9-1, under Entry Name would go payments, bills, etc. You will find that the programs you evaluate will be broken down similarly, allowing quick comparisons of like groups.

Input Data

Computers can have many kinds of input devices. However, in small computers for applications of the kind treated in this book, the vast majority of systems will use only a typewriterlike keyboard. Our discussion will, therefore, be limited to this type of input. If you plan to use another type of input and need help, work with a vendor or consultant.

The object of gathering data on input is to determine:

- What data fields are required
- How many terminals will be required
- When data must be entered
- How to schedule operations
- How many operators will be required
- Costs associated with the above points

Use Form 9–1 for input data. There must be one Form 9–1 completed for each entry type.

The Number of Entries depend on the type of entries, as does the When Received data. Thus, new records are usually batched for entry or are entered sporadically, as required. If that is the case, the number of such entries per day and information as to scheduled entry or random entry would be sufficient. On the other hand, transactions, which you will recall are performed rapidly in an on-line environment, would normally require a knowledge of the number arriving per minute in order to adequately plan for rapid response. Refer to Table 9–2 for guidance in making these entries.

The form provides for recording projected volumes. Projections are usually made for periods of from three to five years. Select the period you feel is appropriate in your case, and estimate the percentage growth you anticipate. Then calculate the projected volumes. Even if the system you start with cannot support your growth, you should satisfy yourself that it can be expanded to do so when necessary.

Number and list on Form 9–1 each data field that will be entered. For each field list the average number of characters. Since you are trying to determine the number of terminals and operators required, the average number provides a more realistic result than the maximum. However, if you are uncertain about your figures and want to be conservative, you can use a maximum value.

Storage Data

The object of gathering data on storage is to determine:

- The amount of storage required
- The number of storage devices required
- How best to plan and schedule your computer operations
- What data fields are required in storage that are not required for input or output
- Whether necessary fields for input or output were inadvertently left out
- Costs associated with the first three points

Recall that your records will be stored on disks and that often more than one removable disk and more than one disk unit will be required. Allocation of files to disks and disk units, so as to allow applications to talk to one another and avoid conflicts requires planning, scheduling and care in program selection. Data gathered along the lines called for in Form 9–2 will provide the basis for this planning.

Most of the data fields listed as being in storage will also be listed as either input, output or both. Use this fact to check on completeness of your lists. There are some exceptions, such as indexes and tables, which are entered initially and seldom updated.

Storage data fields, as called for in Form 9–2, must be listed in terms of *maximum* character size, not average. Data fields will be stored in the computer in fixed lengths in order to simplify processing. Therefore, you must select a maximum figure for all variable fields. This is not an absolute maximum, rather it is a practical maximum that will accommodate the vast majority of cases. Thus some people have names or addresses that would be impractical to provide for. These must be abbreviated or cut to fit into the allocated space. Table 9–3 shows some commonly used field sizes that you might use in planning. However, bear in mind that if you purchase a program, different values may be used.

No. 1 and no. 2 data fields in Form 9–2 are key 1 and key 2. A *key* specifies how data is to be accessed. Consider, for example, a personnel file. You may want to access a record by employee number, or by name, or by job classification. Three different keys would be required. All programs provide for at least one key per record. In small computer systems, you are not likely to get more than one key. However, by sorting or other strategies you can get at the data. If you have requirements in this regard, be sure to enter required keys on Form 9–2, so that when you are evaluating programs, you will remember to find out what, if any, procedures are provided that will allow you to access your information in the way you want.

Table 9–3   Possible Sizes of Commonly Used Fields

Data Field	Number of Characters
Personal name	25
Company name	25–50
Address (one to four addresses may be required)	
Street	25
City	25
State	2
Zip	5
Narrative	
(a) Bill description	30–90 per line
(b) Product description	30–60 per line
Purchase order number	10

The Comments heading in Form 9–2 is provided for the following types of miscellaneous information:

• Backup requirements
• Retention periods
• Cross reference to other files processed at the same time

Output Data

There are two important types of output used in small computer systems: displays and printers. Unless you get a customized system, chances are you won't have to get involved with the display. This part of the output will be determined by the program you buy and is not something you specify. However, if you feel you might have special display requirements, set down your requirements on a form similar to those we have been using, and see if what you need is available.

Printers are a different story. There can be considerable differences between models, and these differences can be important to your business or professional activities. Hence, data gathering with respect to printers is provided for on Form 9–3. The object of data gathering on the output to printers is to determine:

• Output data requirements
• Printing speed requirements
• Print quality requirements
• Number of printers required
• Number of copies for each printing job
• How to schedule print jobs
• Number of print columns
• Requirements for preprinted forms, such as checks, invoices, purchase orders, and so on
• Other special requirements, such as type of paper, paper feed, special fonts, and so on

The data required is pretty well spelled out in Form 9–3. If you limit yourself to just the reports generated by programs from one vendor, you can usually rely on that vendor's recommended printer. However, if you plan to add other programs or, especially if you plan to do word processing, then you will probably want to analyze your requirements and select a printer accordingly.

Estimating average number of characters per line or lines per page may be difficult when the format is irregular. Sometimes it is necessary to make what you know is an overly conservative estimate. Note that character positions, not just printed characters, are called for. This is because the printer must move past each position, whether a character is printed or not. Thus, a table with three items of five characters each and two spaces between items would have nineteen character positions.

In Form 9–3, the first six items listed under Document Requirements/Data Fields are document requirements. Questions as to the number of characters do not apply to these items, but they are listed there so they can be rated and checked off in the Program or System Check columns. You can add others to these six, if necessary. Then the data fields required by your reports or forms should be listed and character counts entered as for the other two forms. The maximum number of characters is required to determine number of columns required and the format.

SPECIFICATIONS

How to Rate Your Requirements

You have gathered your data and now you should be able to write the specifications for the system you want. But you can't! Not unless you're planning a custom system. Most readers are going to want to do as little customizing as possible. This means that the vendor of your system is going to set the specs, at least most of them. Hence your task is to find a system whose specs *most closely match* what you need. Forms 9–1, 9–2 and 9–3 were designed to help you do just this.

On each of the three forms is the column headed Rating. In this column you rate the importance of items entered in the second column, most of which are data fields. Three levels of rating should be sufficient. They are:

Rating	Interpretation
1	Data is required—no compromises possible
2	Data is desired—compromises possible
3	Data is not required

This rating system is designed to:

- Quickly filter out unusable systems on which you might otherwise waste a good deal of time and money. If they don't provide for items that you have rated number 1, you can't use the system.
- Quickly filter out those systems that represent overkill for your requirements. The lowest-cost system that satisfies ratings 1 and 2 becomes the strongest candidate (although cost is not your only criterion).

Rating 2 is, of course, a neat way of hiding some tough decisions behind a facade of simplicity. When the time comes for selecting among several possible systems, items whose rating is 2 will play a key role. At the start of the selection process your list will probably be full of 1s, there may be a sprinkling of 2s and no 3s. Then, as the selection process proceeds, and you find no system that meets your tough standards, you may have second thoughts, and the number of 2s and 3s will start to increase.

Planning for a computer system should be like a spring housecleaning. It is a time to cull data no longer required, clean up files, streamline operations and let in new ideas on how to do things. You should use this opportunity to examine critically the information you are now receiving, question its appropriateness and ask yourself what information the computer could give you that you are not getting now. This could alter your distribution of 1, 2 and 3 ratings.

Finally, you should realize that just because an application is computerized it doesn't follow that *every* operation associated with that application must be computerized. If procedures or formats are exceptionally complex or subject to frequent changes, it may be advisable to continue to perform these operations manually. Eliminating one or two intractable operations from the computer can save endless trouble and headaches. Just be sure that you know how the manual operations will interface with the computer operations.

How to Use Specs to Filter Competing Products

The filtering process works like this. When the time comes to select a system, you will review the specs of each candidate's programs and hardware products. The specs can be obtained from vendors' brochures or by contacting the vendors directly. Get all the specs in writing. Check off in the last columns of the forms whether or not the product has the items you need. Some candidates will fail the test. Others will be on the borderline. You will be very lucky if even one meets *all* your requirements. If not, your attention will focus on the borderline cases. It is here that you will have to start making compromises if you want any system at all. There are two directions in which compromise is possible:

(1) Revise your ratings to correspond to what is available in the market.
(2) Abandon your search for an off-the-shelf system, and start planning to have some customizing done.

You may want to do both of the above to achieve the best compromise.

Not all specifications lend themselves to the check-off approach. When we ask questions like how much, we have to supply numbers, put them in formulas and grind out the results. How to do this will be the subject of Chapter 11. There, we will explain some of the items in Forms 9–1, 9–2 and 9–3 that as of now may not be clear to you, and explain how to use these items to calculate your processing requirements.

Form 9–1   Input Data

Entry name: _____

Present number of entries: _____ _____ Per ____

Growth factor: _____

Projected number of entries: _____ Per ____

When received (time of day, week, year, etc.): _____

How received (scheduled, random, is there a peak, etc.): _____

No.	Data Field	Average Number of Characters	Rating	Program or System Check				
				1	2	3	4	5

Form 9–2   Storage Data

File name: _____

When processed (daily, weekly, monthly, on request, etc.): _____

Processing deadline (Friday at 4:00 P.M., EOM, etc.): _____

Applications that will use this file: _____

Characters per record: _____

Present number of records: _____

Growth factor: _____

Projected number of records: _____

Comments: _____

_____

_____

No.	Data Field	Maximum Number of Characters	Rating	Program or System Check 1	2	3	4	5
1	(Key 1)							
2	(Key 2)							

Form 9–3   Output Data for Printer

Name of document: _____

Time available to print document: _____

Average number of character positions per line: _____

Number of lines per page: _____

Present number of pages per document: _____

Present number of documents per job: _____

Growth factor(s): _____

Projected number of pages per document: _____

Projected number of documents per job: _____

When required (daily, weekly, on request, etc.): _____

Deadline (Friday at noon, etc.): _____

Special requirements (forms, print quality, etc.): _____

No.	Document Requirements /Data Field	Maximum Number of Characters	Average Number of Characters	Rating	Program or System Check				
					1	2	3	4	5
1	(No. of copies)								
2	(No. of columns)								
3	(Max. no. rows per pg.)								
4	(Formed characters)								
5	(Tractor feed)								
6	(Graphics)								

Guidelines for Selection

PROGRAMS ARE THE KEY

The proper way to select a small computer is to start with the programs.

Large users do just the opposite. They first find the computer that meets their overall processing requirements and then put their professional staff to work designing systems and writing programs. This allows them to tailor their computer programs to their exact needs, providing efficiency and not requiring them to change the way they do business to suit the computer system.

Small users can't afford this approach. The expense of writing their own programs is usually out of the question. Accordingly, they must use what is available, and adapt to the requirements of programs supplied by vendors. Obviously then, a key concern of the small computer user must be the finding of programs that best match his or her particular way of doing business or performing professional tasks. Changes may be necessary, but they must be kept to a minimum. Only as a last resort should the small user attempt in-house programming, and then only when justified by the expected benefits of the system.

Consider two computers called FAST and SLOW. FAST not only clips along at a higher speed, it is produced by one of the major manufacturers, thousands are in use and there is a large library of programs available. On the surface, it looks like an obvious choice over SLOW. However, when you examine FAST's programs for the application you have in mind, none fit. Your way of doing business, for any number of reasons, is just not accommodated. The vendor of SLOW, on the other hand, has programs targeted right at your type of operations. You find you can use these programs with only minor modifications. You get a better, faster, cheaper system with SLOW than you would with FAST. This is why programs are the key to proper selection of small computers.

Generally, the vendor's approach to program design is as follows. The large companies go after the large markets. To do this they try to design general-purpose programs that can meet the needs of a large number of users. The small companies, not wanting to compete directly with the biggies, design special-purpose programs, programs that are often tailored to specific industries. The general-purpose programs, in order to serve a broad community of users, require more features and memory than programs designed for specific applications with the result that they run slower and require more equipment. Therefore, which you choose should depend on which best fits your particular needs. If the general-purpose program works for you, fine. Take advantage of the support that comes with the products of a large vendor and the higher reliability of programs that are widely used. Otherwise, explore the possibilities of special-purpose programs and their vendors.

The above comments apply to situations in which computers are to be introduced into the mainstream of a business or professional environment. Program considerations are somewhat different when microcomputers are bought and used by individuals in the manner of a personal computer. Numerous professionals, businesspersons and managers have learned to program microcomputer systems in easy-to-learn languages such as BASIC. They are applying their computers in their business and professional work in many unique ways. In these cases, however, the computer is usually not used by an organization; rather it is used by one individual who has programmed it, knows the programs and the use of the computer intimately and may be continually making improvements or expanding the system. The computer is still very much a personal computer even though it is applied in a business and professional environment.

Clearly, the user who does not mind learning to program will approach the whole question of programs from a different angle. Or, at least the emphasis on finding ready-made programs will be less. Still, if ready-made programs are available, it would make sense to take advantage of them. (why try to reinvent the wheel?) Spend the time on other things, development of other kinds of programs that are not available, for example. In any case, except for program selection, the selection process for the buyer of a personal computer will not be all that different.

STEPS IN THE SELECTION PROCESS

Now that we have established programs as the key, we can outline the steps required in the selection of a small computer (actual details of the selection process are given in the next chapter).

(1) Determine your program requirements.   If you have followed the procedures described in Chapter 9, you will have a list of computer applications with assigned priorities, and a set of forms showing your data requirements.

(2) Determine if you need outside help.   If you anticipate problems or just feel that you need the temporary services of a professional, you can tap the services described in Chapter 7—systems houses, consultants, independent contractors and software firms.

(3) Find programs that fit your requirements.   Are your applications fairly typical? If so, you may want to start with the larger firms that sell application programs in order to benefit from the greater support usually associated with them. Otherwise, explore what the smaller firms have to offer. Shop the computer stores, check the ads in the periodicals, go to trade shows, get catalogs of programs.

(4) <u>Find a computer that fits the programs.</u>   Program vendors describe what equipment you must have to run each program. The programs you have selected will be designed to run on at least one type of computer, but they might run on those of several vendors. The latter is an advantage, giving you more flexibility in choice of equipment. You can than look for special features, relative costs, vendor reputation—all those criteria commonly used in the selection of competing products.

(5) <u>Try again.</u>   Although you may have found one or more computers that fit the programs you selected, none may be right for you. They could be too expensive, not have certain features you need, be too small to accommodate your files, not support the right kind of printer, and so on. At this point you may have to go back and renew your search for an alternative program, one that will support the kind of computer system you can use.

(6) <u>Know when to customize.</u>   If no program is found that you can use, or if you're looking for a business advantage, consider custom programs.

The aim of the small computer industry is to make the selection and operation of computers no more difficult than for any standard piece of office equipment. More training and preparation will be required, but essentially the small business computer is viewed as being comparable to a typewriter, copier, or accounting machine. How closely this simplified approach will work in your case will depend on how typical your application is and what your special requirements might be.

HOW TO SELECT VENDORS AND SERVICES

Table 10–1 indicates sources of vendors and services. It is intended strictly as a guide. The industry is too varied to make hard and fast rules that will stand up in all cases. Therefore, it is quite possible that exceptions will be found to the entries in the table. Despite these qualifications, readers should find Table 10–1 a useful guide in the selection process.

Possible systems that may be developed are divided into three categories corresponding to what you are likely to find in the marketplace. Thus, systems and programs are designed to be general purpose, industry specific or application specific. If you do not find a suitable solution in any of these areas, you must resort to a customized solution if you are to have a computer system at all. From the table, it is easy to see the advantage of going with a special-purpose system, if you can find one off the shelf that meets your needs.

The entries in the table are based on the assumption that your chances of requiring some customizing of purchased systems is greater for general-purpose systems than for more specific systems. This is only common sense since the more closely the program is designed for your immediate area of interest, the better fit you can expect. The purchase price (up-front money) of the general-purpose program will tend to be lower than that of equivalent special-purpose

Table 10–1   Sources of Systems and Services

	Purchased General-purpose Systems—Not Industry Specific	*Purchased Special-purpose Systems—Industry or Application Specific*	*Custom Systems for your Application*
1. Minicomputers	Yes	Common	By subcontract
2. Microcomputers	Yes	Rarely, but will increase	By subcontract or by programs written by you for a personal computer
3. From Manufacturers	Some	Possible	No
4. From Systems House	Not likely	Yes	Yes
5. From Service Bureau	Yes	Yes	Possible
6. From Software Firms	Yes	Yes	Some
7. Use Consultants	Maybe	Less likely	Yes
8. Use Programmers	Probably	Less likely	Yes
9. Relative Cost	Lowest up-front but higher over-all	Probably higher up-front but less overall	A good deal higher than both of the other alternatives

products because of the larger market for the former. However, this will be more than offset if changes are required to suit your needs. In the same way, the more customizing you do the more need you have of assistance. This assistance may be available from any of the vendors listed in points 3 through 8. The advantage of using consultants over the other sources, is that you get a more objective view. This is particularly important in the planning and selection stage. Good objective analysis is what you should expect from a consultant, together with a broad knowledge of the industry. Select your consultant with these qualities in mind.

SELECTING THE HARDWARE

So far we have placed all the emphasis on program selection. What about the hardware? Is it true, as some claim, that one computer is just about the same as any other in the same price range? Should you shop for the computer that is the most powerful you can afford? The somewhat paradoxical answer to both questions is no. There can be wide differences between computers of equivalent prices, but you should not try to buy on that basis.

As with most products, computer design is the result of a number of compromises between conflicting requirements. Each designer has his or her own ideas as to the best way to make these compromises. They may also have different markets in mind. The result is that computer designs vary widely and so do their performances. It is not that one design is necessarily better than another; rather, what happens is that one design is better for some things and worse for others. A design might be very good for a large number of applications; it is a good general-purpose computer. However, another might excel at data manipulation, making the general-purpose computer look slow for a certain set of applications.

Unfortunately, you are very seldom in a position where you can take advantage of the differences between computers. Few professionals can tell you which is the best computer for the application you have in mind. It would mean that they have hands-on experience with several systems using the programs you are considering, a very unlikely occurrence. Also, for straight business applications, with a single data entry device, you won't even be *nearing* the limits of the power of the least powerful computer. Most of the time your computer will be waiting for file access, keyboard strokes and print hammers to complete their motion. However, if your application involves lots of computing (project planning, forecasting or modeling, for example) it might pay you to ask around to find out what computers are good number crunchers.

Also, you have to be careful about transferring successful programs from one computer to another. Suppose you know someone who has a successful system on computer SLOW. You decide to buy the same programs and learn that they can work on computer FAST, so you buy FAST instead of SLOW, a seemingly sensible choice. As you have probably guessed, our story ends in disaster, because FAST really is slow with this program, resulting in poor customer service and loss of business. The source of the problem was a mismatch between programs and computer.

Aside from the above example of mismatch, your attention to speed differences between computers in the same class should be about zero. However, there are other considerations which *are* important and which we will now deal with.

Consider point 4 of the Table 10–1 for which the task is to find a computer that fits the programs. This part is relatively simple because if you are purchasing your programs the vendor spells out fairly precisely what equipment is required to run the program. He or she will name all the computers the programs can run on, the smallest model, the minimum amount of main memory and disk storage, type of printer and so on. This will immediately eliminate many computers and thousands of combinations of equipment. Most programs are designed for only one computer, some for two, a few for three. Your choice of hardware has more or less been made for you. That is, if you stay with these particular programs. That is what you now have to decide. You have to evaluate the possible computers to determine if they are right for you. What are your criteria? The answer has to be different for different groups of readers. Those who are interested in professional or personal use will have different criteria from those who are interested in business applications.

Selection for Business Applications

If you are planning to introduce a computer into main-line functions of your business, you must have well-thought-out criteria for selection. These criteria are nothing more than the specifications that you drew up when you were planning your computer system. If you performed the planning steps described previously, you will have specifications that state your requirements for:

- Input
- Storage
- Printing
- Backup
- Maximum down time
- Growth
- Expansion
- Special I/O (input/output) devices
- Communications

The selection process consists in comparing the specifications for each possible machine with your specifications. Check off each requirement on your list. Some you will have rated according to how necessary you feel they are in your application. You now have to make a judgment as to which machine best fits your specs. Maybe they all will. Maybe none. The latter case will be a signal to either revise your ratings or renew your search for appropriate programs. Or should you abandon the project altogether? Not until you have given consideration to customizing. A small change in a program that you were forced to reject might cast the whole situation in a completely new light. Or if you are determined and can afford it, this is the time to consider the services of a systems house. In other words, there are lots of routes to your goal. You start with the shortest, least expensive route: off-the-shelf software and hardware. If that doesn't take you where you want to go, try progressively more expensive routes until you can get what you want or costs have gotten out of reach.

To summarize, hardware selection is fairly straightforward if the proper preparations have been made. First you must decide what you want and where you want to go. Then comes the data gathering and writing of specs. Now you can pick your programs. Computer selection? By now that's the easy part. You already know what's available in the industry. Just match up your specs and choose your computer.

Selection for Professional and Personal Applications

For professionals or those considering a personal computer, your specs on data are probably minimal, but you are likely to have very specific program requirements in a narrow application area. Thus, if you are a CPA you will want programs written for small CPA firms. If you do a lot of statistics you will look for a source of mathematical routines.

Program vendors specialize, so your primary task in the selection process is to find a program vendor who specializes in your area of interest. You can then look forward to an increasing number of program products that utilize the small computer to its fullest advantage in your specialty. Avoid the vendor who has a smorgasbord of products where breadth of product line is stressed over specialization.

A vendor who is specializing in your area of interest is likely to continually expand and enhance the product line in ways that will be of direct benefit to you.

The programs you need may be supplied by the vendor of the equipment, but more likely they will come from an independent software house. The former is preferable, but the latter is entirely acceptable. The overriding consideration is the value of the programs themselves.

Professionals should not get too concerned about equipment. It is easy to get diverted from your main task as you compare the features of various computers and try to decide which to buy. And you can be sure that each model will have something special that the brochure or sales rep will try to entice you with. But this is all irrelevant unless the programs you need are available.

On the other hand, if you focus on the selection of the right programs and program vendor, your options on equipment selection are immediately narrowed to those models that the programs will work on. At that point you should try to take advantage of the program vendor's experience and preference. Thus, if the ad says, "The program will run on machine X, but versions are now being developed for machines Y and Z," you can bet that this vendor's heart is with computer X and he or she is only interested in Y and Z because there are some additional sales out there. Your interest in a particular vendor will stem from the fact that that particular firm is producing programs in your area of interest. Your chances of being able to use this vendor's future products at the earliest possible time will be increased by going with computer X. Also, programs running on computer X will get the most exercise, producing more reliable programs faster. Thus, the criterion for selection should be the focus of your software vendor's programming effort. If you investigate you will find that most vendors do indeed have a machine that gets first billing. Then, other things being equal, you can rely on your own preferences for things like packaging, looks, keyboard, display and any other features not really critical to your application.

Thus, the recommended selection procedure for professionals and buyers of personal computers is similar to that for business applications, but with different emphasis. You must, of course, decide how you plan to use the computer, if there is to be any basis for preferring one system over another. But your idea of where you want to go after your first application may be vague or nonexistent. Depending on the application, it may be necessary to gather data and write specs. On the other hand, you may find just by reading the specs of the programs that are of interest to you, that, without question, they will do the job. Again, the program you select will pretty much determine the hardware you buy.

If you plan to do your own programming, your attention should turn to the programming languages that the vendor is offering. If you plan to be using files and disk storage, you should look for the COBOL language. If not, PASCAL is your best bet. Second best is BASIC, for ease of use, or FORTRAN, for greater efficiency. For those without previous programming experience and who only want to put in a minimum of time and effort in learning to program, BASIC is your first choice, followed by PASCAL. Stay away from FORTRAN and COBOL. Also stay away from other languages not in the mainstream unless there is some good reason to do otherwise. Not that other languages don't provide some good features. It's just that they don't have the following that the others do, and hence limit you to some degree. In this respect, PASCAL's star is rising rapidly while other program languages are just holding their own, or losing ground.

Other things being equal, you should stay with front runners in equipment and program languages. That is where the action is, and consequently that is where you will find the most opportunities for different uses of your equipment. More programs are written for the popular makes and more special devices for input and output are designed to work with them.

What makes a computer popular? To be popular, a computer has to perform adequately and reliably, but need not be exceptional. More important than performance and reliability are promotion, service and availability. For most people, advantages of having a popular make offset any advantage you might get from a more reliable or more powerful machine. But if your needs are in any way special, then, by all means, shop around for the best system for your purposes.

PLANNING AND SELECTION PROCEDURES COMPARED

The planning procedures outlined in previous chapters and the selection procedures discussed in this chapter are based on the fact that for small computers, program selection is the key. This influences how you will proceed in each step of a small computer project. In this section we will review these steps and compare them with the more traditional approach used by computer professionals.

Table 10–2 lists the planning and selection steps of a computer project. The

Table 10–2 Comparison of Planning and Selection Procedures

Traditional Planning and Selection Procedure	*Planning and Selection of Small Computers*
1. Define the problem.	1. Develop a master planning list.
2. Conduct a feasibility study.	2. Select first applications. Try to use the computer for more than one thing.
3. Flow chart present system.	3. Flow charting required only for complex systems.
4. Gather data.	4. Gather data.
5. Design new system and select equipment.	5. Search for suitable programs and evaluate application.
6. Write programs.	6. Select equipment.

left column applies to the traditional planning and selection processes that are used by large organizations that own or rent large computers. It also applies to the use of minicomputers when the organization has available a staff of system analysts and programmers.

The right column of the table corresponds to the planning and selection process for small computers as presented in this book. It is intended for the small-businessperson or professional who doesn't have a staff of systems analysts and programmers to fall back on and must, therefore, rely primarily on his or her own abilities.

Problem Definition

The first step in the traditional process is to define the problem. Recognition of a problem is easy. Its precise definition is harder. You may recognize that an awful lot of time is being spent shuffling papers. However, a problem definition should try to quantify the situation thus:

Problem: to reduce clerical time by two hours per day.

The problem definition would also specify the scope of the problem. Where does the problem begin and end? Will the computer project be broad in scope or narrow? Precise answers must be given before the next steps can be intelligently attacked.

The Feasibility Study

The second step of the traditional procedure is the feasibility study, a key step in the computer project. This is where the solution to the problem is outlined (there may be more than one), costs and benefits estimated, personnel estimated and a schedule for the project presented. The feasibility study is performed by a small group of computer professionals with broad and extensive computer application experience. Also included would be representatives from the user group in the organization where the application is under consideration—accounting, purchasing, etc.

When the feasibility study is complete, a proposal is drawn up, defining the problem and presenting the proposed solution with its anticipated costs and benefits. This is reviewed by a higher body both for its justification and to see how the proposed application fits into the organization's overall plans and objectives. Is it compatible with what other people are doing? Is it consistent with the direction the organization is moving? Is it the best use of resources at this time? Surprisingly, not all organizations ask these kind of questions. Some are content to look only for a favorable financial analysis. Invariably, they pay heavily for this narrow approach.

In this brief review of the problem definition and feasibility study, it must have been made clear to the reader how ill suited these steps are for the small-businessperson and first-time user of computers. Accordingly, steps 1 and 2 in the right-hand column have been substituted to provide for the needs of small computer users.

Step 1 calls for the development of a master planning list as described in Chapter 9. There, you were asked to list those operations you thought might be placed on a computer, and to place priorities on these operations. You weren't asked to define the problem precisely and work up a solution, tasks the first-time user is not equipped to do. Instead, both these tasks will be performed for you by the vendor of your programs. It is the program vendor who will define the problem, its scope and its solution. Your task is to determine if this solution fits your needs.

For example, you may have no idea how much clerical work you can expect to save per day by the installation of a computer. However, once you have a program description in front of you, you should be able to see rather quickly which specific steps can be eliminated and (don't forget this) which must be added. Then it should be a relatively simple task to estimate net time saved.

In addition to serving as a guide in your search for programs, your master planning list takes the place of the higher body that in the traditional procedure checks the proposal for compatibility, consistency and appropriateness. No higher body is going to perform these functions for you. They are your responsibility. The use of a master planning list is your way of avoiding a narrow outlook in the selection process. You want to select programs and equipment that will work tomorrow as well as today. You want to be able to use the computer to do as many productive tasks as possible, not just one. The master planning list helps you see past one, isolated problem, to your operations as a whole.

Flow Charting

The third step in the table specifies the flow charting of the present system. Many readers will have worked with flow charts of one form or another. For those who haven't, a flow chart, like a picture, is worth a thousand words. Using simple symbols connected by lines, the flow of documents and information in a business can be presented in a particularly lucid form. Interested readers can find full descriptions of flow charting in books on systems analysis, business procedures or data processing.

In traditional procedures, flow charting is a practical necessity for proceeding logically from today's operations to the new plans. For the selection of small computers, flow charting is less of a requirement, since the transition to the new design is performed by the program vendor. However, flow charting can always be helpful in forcing you to think through just how your operations are being performed, and as a check in the data gathering step to ensure that nothing of significance has been overlooked. When you are selecting programs a flow chart is useful to ensure that all activities are accounted for both functionally and in cost-benefit calculations. You can check off each task shown on your flow chart when you are satisfied that it will either be eliminated or handled adequately in the new system by the program you are evaluating.

Data Gathering

Point 4, is common to both procedures, an essential step in all business applications. However, the object of the data gathering is different. In the traditional procedure, data gathering is aimed at providing the information needed for the design of a new system. For the buyer of a small computer, data gathering is aimed at evaluating programs that are on the market to ensure that all needed data is accounted for. Thus, the gathered data will be organized differently in the two cases to reflect these differing aims. The data gathering forms, Forms 9–1, 9–2 and 9–3 are designed to aid buyers of small computers in evaluating programs on the market and in selecting those that are right for their needs.

Design, Selection, and Programs

Points 5 and 6 are the critical steps which distinguish the traditional procedure from that for small computers. In the traditional scheme, the new system is designed and equipment is selected to do the job, unless all processing can be handled by already available hardware. Finally, as a last step, the programs are written.

In contrast, small computer buyers, armed with their master planning lists and data gathering forms, search for suitable programs written by program vendors. This is where small computer buyers perform their feasibility study. They find what programs are available, what equipment they require, what the resulting costs will be and then make a business judgment on whether to proceed, back up, or try another route. As we made clear in our survey of the small computer industry, there are many routes to computerization and the more of these you investigate the more options you give yourself in the selection of suitable programs.

How to Select
a Small Computer System

In the previous chapter we discussed general guidelines for selecting small computers. In this chapter we will discuss specific things to look for. In accordance with our guidelines, we will place heavy emphasis on programs as the key element in the selection process. If you talk to hardware sales reps, you will find that they stress things like equipment, support and service. Undeniably, these things are important. But never lose sight of the fact that programs come first.

Every business has things about it that are unique. Recognizing this, the procedures given in this chapter may have to be bent and shaped to your needs.

THE GREAT DEBATE

For some time, a debate has raged within the industry on how best to provide programs for small businesses.

In one camp are those who insist that the only way to go is with off-the-shelf, "canned" programs. While they recognize that businesses differ and, in this respect general-purpose programs are not feasible, their claim is that it's easier and cheaper for a small firm to adapt to the program's requirements rather than vice versa. With this approach, programs can be written for maximum efficiency without regard to making them easy to modify. Their production costs can be spread over a large volume, lowering prices. Through repeated use on a large scale, practically all bugs will be forced into the open, so that the programs will be virtually error-free. With all these pluses going for it, advocates of this approach feel its success is assured.

The other side in the debate insists that firms will not change the way they do business for the sake of the computer, either because they can't or because the resulting chaos would just not be worth it. Their solution is to provide programs written in higher-level languages that can be modified to fit user requirements. Their programs may not be as efficient as canned programs, but at least the user is not straitjacketed into a system that doesn't fit. When overall company operations are taken into account, these tailored programs will result in the best overall efficiency.

Both sides are betting heavily on their views. Which one is right? Given the diversity of requirements by users of small computers, probably both are. There should be plenty of users willing to make some changes, however reluctantly, if by doing so they can buy a system right off the shelf, put it in and get on the air. On the other hand, many users are not going to be satisfied with just having a computer. They will want that computer to work *their* way, give them improved operations and contribute to business success.

Thus, the arguments will continue with both sides winning—that is, the vendors. That leaves you with the task of choosing what your path should be. In this chapter we will present those features you should look for in programs. If you can find these features in an off-the-shelf product, this is the preferred choice. Otherwise, you will have to decide whether to have a program tailored to fit your needs.

The amount of tailoring required might be no more than a few minor adjustments. On the other hand, it could be rather extensive, requiring significant additional cash. You will be able to judge customizing requirements by following the steps outlined in later sections of this chapter. But first it will be helpful to review the elements that make up a good program.

WHAT MAKES A GOOD PROGRAM

Programs are complex and not subject to precise measurement on a scale of good to bad. However, there are certain qualities that experienced users look for in a program. Although there is no way that a nonprofessional can tell if a program is good or bad (short of actually using the program for a period of time) still it is important that he or she recognize those features that determine the quality of a program.

There are a number of sources which can provide valuable information on program quality, either as a result of direct experience or through knowledge of those who have had such experience. Colleagues, associates, trade and professional associations, CPAs and user groups are all good sources of information on what's good and what's not so good about the type of program that you might be interested in. Computer magazines sometimes run surveys to find out how actual users rate programs.

In this section we will review some of those qualities found in a good program, so that you can discuss them with others and ask the right questions. A few readers may contract to have programs written for them, in which case the importance of good programs takes on even greater significance.

Menu Driven

A program is menu driven when the user interacts with the programs through menus, such as those shown in Chapter 3 for the Payroll example. Menus guide the user and minimize keying. If a program is not menu driven, the user must remember command words and type them in every time some action by the program is called for.

Resources Required

The less memory and the less computer time required to run a program the better the program. However, computer time and memory work in opposite directions. By increasing the computer's memory, computer time can often be considerably decreased. Thus, you may find that you have to choose between a higher initial outlay for memory and slower execution of your program over its useful life.

Memory requirements for a program can be pinned down fairly accurately and will be made available by the vendor. On the other hand, running time is more difficult to predict, depending as it does on your particular volume of transactions and how you process them. Here is where bench-mark tests are useful in gauging the relative quality of programs.

Easy to Change

One might think that the only function of a program is to get the job done in a reasonable time and with a reasonable amount of memory. In other words, two programs that produce the same output from the same input in the same time and using equal amounts of memory might be considered equivalent, even if they go about the job in different ways. But this is not the case.

Suppose you were to put out for bids a programming job and received proposals from two programmers working as independent contractors.

Programmer A comes in with the low bid. His proposal shows that he understands the job. In the interview, he appears knowledgeable, talks fast and, best of all, gives the impression that he will work fast.

Programmer B comes in with a slightly higher bid than A. Her proposal is thorough, with much attention to details you don't understand the need for. In the interviews she appears competent, but gives the impression that she might be a slow worker and you want to be up and running for the Christmas season.

Naturally you pick Programmer A. He lives up to expectations. Six weeks before Thanksgiving he comes in with his product, runs it and demonstrates that it performs as requested. Pleased as punch, you pay him, whereupon he promptly takes off for parts unknown.

Within one week you are ready to tear your hair out. Your precious program has more bugs than a flea circus. In desperation you shamefacedly call Programmer B and offer her a handsome fee if she will get you up and running for Christmas.

After what seems to you like an impossibly long time, Programmer B returns with her verdict. Your program is not salvageable. Programmer A has delivered a product that looks like Figure 11–1(a) (page 224). It's unreadable and it will be easier to write a new program than to untangle this can of spaghetti.

Programmer B then does her thing. The result looks like Figure 11–1(b). You have missed the Christmas season, but, older and wiser, you are a happy computer user ever after.

Although the programs in this example were the product of contract work,

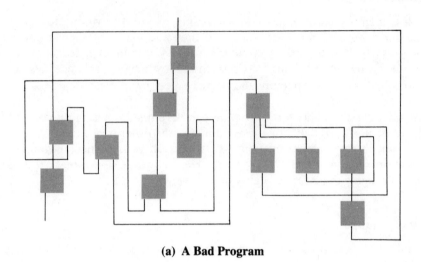

(a) A Bad Program

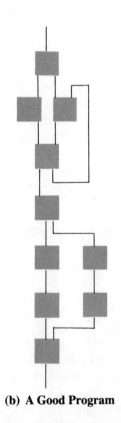

(b) A Good Program

the same problems can arise when programs are bought from vendors. The program structure may be tangled and intertwined, as in (a), so that customizing and maintenance is a major task. Or it may be simply structured as in (b), allowing modifications with a minimum of effort. Therefore, if you find somebody who has experience with a program you are considering, one of your key questions should be: How easy is it to change?

From the above, it is clear that the speed, and therefore the cost, of modifying a program depends on two things: the proficiency of the programmer and the structure of the program. If either of these is poor, there will be problems.

If you buy a ready-made program from a dealer, a store, or the source of the program, it can be delivered in one of two forms: a high-level language or machine language. Remember that a program written in a high-level language is relatively easy to read and change. Programs written in machine language, on the other hand, are difficult to change and are not meant to be changed.

If you are buying systems software, such as a data management system or data base system you should never make changes in this type of program. However, with application programs, changes are often necessary. If you want to have changes made, you must be sure to get a source program.

Error Processing

A good program filters out errors. Not all, because this is impossible, but most errors are detectable and can be dealt with without bringing the system down and tying up operations.

As a minimum, you should look for the following input error checks:

- No alphabetic characters in numeric fields.
- Dates within bounds. For example, a "payment received" date greater than the current date should be flagged.
- Money values within bounds. Thus, prices for paper clips would have one limit and trailer trucks would have another. Both maximum and minimum values may be called for.
- Quantity values within bounds. Again, different bounds for different items.
- Consistency checks.
- Direct checks against known values. Many cases could be cited. Account numbers, part numbers, area codes and invoice numbers are some examples.

When the program detects any of the above errors, the result should be an error message that is prominently displayed and explicit in what the operator is to do next.

If you have the opportunity to try out a demonstration system, input is one program quality on which a nonprofessional can actually hope to do some limited testing. Try entering errors—high values, alphabetics in numeric fields, blank fields, invalid dates, etc. If entered at random points in the program, you should get a reasonable feel for how much input editing has been built into the program. Use your own judgment on whether this appears adequate for your purposes.

Transaction Reports

Transaction reports list all entries made to a system. They include entries of new master records, changes to these records, entry of payments, orders—in short, all entries except those not accepted by the computer because of error.
   Transaction reports serve two important functions:

- Provide an audit trail whereby the contents of all records can be traced back to the original entry. This is highly desirable, to discourage fraud or to find its perpetrator.
- Provide backup to the system. If a file becomes damaged, an occurrence guaranteed by Murphy's Law, a previous version of that file, together with the transaction report can be used to recreate the damaged file. Better yet for this purpose is a transaction file that can automatically recreate the damaged file from a backup copy. However, if the transaction file is also damaged, the transaction report provides the backup. It is the ultimate, last line of defense if a major crash hits your system.

Exception Processing

Some programs work fine for routine processing but fail to deal adequately with exceptions to the rules. Exceptions to the rules abound in the real world. There are power failures, computer malfunctions, key people are absent, customers move without notifying you and payments are received without a return document. All such situations must be handled in one way or another. Obviously, it is not easy to plan for exceptions, nor is it possible to anticipate all possibilities. And each case must be evaluated on its merits to determine whether exception processing must be included in a program and, if so, what it must do. However, there are certain things you can look for in a program that will tell you how well exceptional conditions can be handled.

(1) Much exception processing involves a change in dates and schedules. Therefore, a program should not be dependent on fixed dates or fixed time intervals.
(2) Often some key data is missing in a source document, but it is nevertheless important to get what data is available into the records. If you can anticipate that this will be a problem, adequate *suspense files* would be something to look for in a program.
(3) When failures of any kind occur, the program must be able to recover without damage to existing records. To do this, the program must be able to create and use backup copies of files. A *log file* of all entries can also be useful in preventing the loss of a day's work if a crash occurs before a day's backup file can be created.

Documentation

One of the most frequent complaints heard from users is poor program documentation.

When you buy a program, besides the program itself, you will receive printed documents describing the program and how to use it. The quality of this documentation varies widely from vendor to vendor. Ideally, it should spell everything out and leave nothing to the imagination. Obviously, the best program in the world is useless if you don't know how to use it.

Areas that should be covered in the documentation are:

- How to initiate and terminate the program.
- How to perform all the routine operations connected with the program.
- Descriptions of each error condition and possible operator responses.
- How to proceed in case of abnormal terminations and lock-ups.
- Description of safeguards built into the program to prevent complete loss of data.

With respect to documentation, users may have to settle for something less than the ideal or they may find themselves without programs at all. While the situation seems to be improving, it is still far from satisfactory. This is where the quality of vendor support becomes important. Good vendor support can fill in for gaps in program documentation. A reliable vendor who provides assistance to users should supplement your search for well-documented programs.

Vendor Support

Although not a direct determinant of program quality, vendor support is an important consideration in the selection of any key program in business applications.

Both users and vendors recognize that computer programs cannot be delivered bug-free. Instead of trying to pretend that their software is perfect and will never need corrections, updates or important improvements, reputable vendors provide for these contingencies by providing an ongoing service for which they charge what they consider an appropriate fee.

Support services to look for and determine prices for are:

- Changes.   As programs are corrected and revised, new copies should be provided in a form that can be easily entered into the computer. Floppy disks are good for this purpose.
- Documentation.   When a change is made that affects the user, he or she should be notified with new documents or inserts to old documents. The changed parts should be highlighted in some way to alert the user that something new has been added.
- Hot line.   Fast customer service by telephone to a vendor's representative. Problems can be outlined and solutions suggested immediately or dealt with off-line and a return call.
- Consulting.   For intractable problems that can't be resolved over the hot line, on-site visits by a vendor's representative may be required. This will, of

course, be costly and can become a finger-pointing exercise if the hardware and software have been purchased from different vendors.

- <u>Announcements.</u>   When an error is found or a change is planned, it is important to know these things as soon as possible. The vendor should have a policy of providing users with these facts through special mailings.
- <u>User groups.</u>   User groups are not official vendor organizations, but they are useful in learning what others have found out about the programs you will use. The vendor should have a cooperative and supportive policy toward such groups.
- <u>Training.</u>   Seminars and workshops prior to installation are very important, as is follow-up on an "as needed" basis.
- <u>Cutover assistance.</u>   Assistance in getting the system up and running should be provided.

Integration with Related Programs

Programs are said to be *integrated* when the results from one program are automatically fed to a related program. If an accounts receivable program is not integrated with a general ledger program, the accounts receivable output must be manually keyed into the general ledger program before it can be run. If integrated, the computer performs this function.

The importance of having related programs integrated is obvious. Less obvious is which programs are sufficiently related to require integration. Ultimately all business programs are somehow related and in the ultimate system all business programs would be integrated. Even large users don't achieve this level of sophistication. However, small computer users should look for integrated programs in closely related applications, such as accounting, order entry and inventory, order entry and sales analysis, personnel and payroll. A good program will keep the need for data entry to a minimum.

Good Programs for Word Processing

Word processing programs have their own special requirements. They are usually geared to certain types of documents, although unfortunately you won't find this out from the vendor. For example, a word processing program may be great for producing letters and memos but inadequate for reports. Or a program that has all the bells and whistles required for reports and articles may not be able to handle a long novel or textbook. Therefore, the first step in finding a good word processor is to know where your priorities are and then search out the right program.

HOW TO FIND A PROGRAM THAT FITS YOUR NEEDS

Suppose you decide that you want to computerize your accounting operations. There are dozens of programs on the market for processing general ledger, accounts receivable and accounts payable. They may be sold together with a computer by computer vendors or separately by computer stores and by mail order. In any case, it might appear that you are confronted with an embarrassment of riches and your only real problem is to select one from many possible candidates. However, when you start looking into the details of one or two programs, of what you need and what the programs actually supply, you might be somewhat shocked to find that these programs won't do the job for you at all. If you look further, you may or may not find what you need. But in any case, you cannot simply assume that just any off-the-shelf accounting package will do the job for you. Here are some examples of where mismatches can occur.

- Amount fields are not large enough.
- Total amount fields are not large enough.
- Totals are not broken down the way you need them.
- Account numbering system is not adequate.
- There is a lack of flexibility in allocating receivable and payable to different accounts.
- Cash is not handled the way you want.
- Reports are not adequate for your operations.
- Departmental reporting is inadequate.
- The program lacks the facility for applying interest charges.

These are just some of the possible problems in one example. Similar lists could be presented for order entry, inventory, payroll or any other business application.

Where to Find Programs

Programs are available from many sources—hardware vendors, computer stores, mail order. Mail order is the largest source of programs and should be included in any program search. Check the ads in computer magazines.

There are two routes to the location of programs: through catalogs or directories, and through the vendors directly.

Table 11–1 lists some sources of catalogs and directories. These kinds of publications have a way of coming on the scene and disappearing without a trace. Check current availability and use only recently dated publications. Check computer magazines for ads of possible new sources not included in the table. Also, check ads in the periodicals of your own profession or industry.

Table 11–1   Catalogs and Directories

Datapoint Corporation
9725 Datapoint Drive
San Antonio, TX   78284
512 699-7151

Application Software Catalog. Field-developed programs for Datapoint computers.

Table 11–1   Catalogs and Directories *(Continued)*

National Bureau of Standards
Commerce Department
Washington, D.C.   20234
NBS Special Publication 500–22, A Guide to Computer Program Directories
Government Printing Office
Washington, D.C.   20402

Check for latest price and date of latest edition since publication is not regularly scheduled.

Computer Programs Directory
Macmillan Publishing Co., Inc.
866 Third Avenue
New York, NY   10022

$25.00

Datapro Directory of Software
Datapro Research Corp.
1805 Underwood Blvd.
Delran, NJ   08075

Provides some 3,000 program listings plus monthly supplements.

International Directory of Software
CUYB Publications, Inc.
633 Third Avenue
New York, NY   10017

Over 3,000 listings with equipment on which programs will run.

ICP Directories
International Computer Programs, Inc.
9000 Keystone Crossing
Indianapolis, IN   46240
ICP Directories
   MINI—Small Business Systems: Cross Industry.
      Twice yearly, in April and October, $65 per year.
   MINI—Small Business Systems: Industry Specific.
      Twice yearly, in May and November, $65 per year. $104 for both.

Minicomputer Data Services
20 Coventry Lane
Riverside, CT   06878
203 637-1755

Minicomputer Software Quarterly
Applied International Management Services, Inc.
70 Boston Post Road
Wayland, MA   01778
617 358-4903

Libraries, especially business and technical, often carry program directories.

Vendors of business systems sometimes have catalogs of programs, limited, of course, to their own products, but written by software firms and others.

Table 11–2 lists some sources of programs, together with the types of programs offered. Also, the type of computer for which they are written is given, if known.

Table 11–2   Sources of Programs

Here is just a small sample of program vendors. Included are software firms, dealers, manufacturers and other vendors. The list includes some very large and some very small firms. No endorsement of the firms or their programs is implied by inclusion in the list. Some vendors sell to end-users and some don't, but can direct you to those who do in your area. The types of programs listed are not necessarily a complete list of the vendors' offerings.

Amcor Computer Corp.
1900 Plantside Dr.
Louisville, KY   40299
502 491-9820

Accounting, financial, sales, order processing, payroll, data base and others

American Management Systems, Inc.
1515 Wilson Blvd.
Arlington, VA   22209

Accounting, project accounting and billing, education, financial.

Apple Computer
10260 Bandley Dr.
Cupertino, CA   95014
800 538-9696

Accounting, word processing, retail store mgmt., financial, mailing list, statistics.

Argonaut Information Systems, Inc.
383 Grand Ave., Suite 6
Oakland, CA   94610
415 444-5954

Accounting, sales order/invoicing, sales forecasting and many other business applications. Standard COBOL. Run on many small computers.

Automated Bookkeeping Corp.
55 W. 42nd St.
New York, NY   10036
212 354-7666

Accounting, payroll, insurance and real estate.

Baker Associates, Inc.
300 Marquardt Dr.
Wheeling, IL   60090

Manufacturing systems/purchase order, warehouse distribution, route distribution and accounting.

Bankroft Computer Systems, Inc.
P.O. Box 1533
715 Trenton
West Monroe, LA   71291

Financial, payroll accounting, inventory, mailing list, line graph printing; for IBM System 3, System 34 and others in RPG.

Basic Four Corp.
14101 Myford Rd.
Tustin, CA   92680
714 731-5100

Accounting, order processing, sales analysis, inventory control, purchase order, payroll, fixed assets, word processing; for their own Basic Four computers.

Computer Strategies, Inc.
300 N. Main St.
Spring Valley, NY   10977
914 356-7770

Tax programs for tax consultants; for PET computer.

Computer Systems, Inc.
539 Durie Ave.
Closter, NJ   07624
201 767-7299

Accounting, payroll, inventory, clinical accounting, word processing, and systems for doctors, attorneys, accountants and others; for their own CSI computers.

Data General
Route 9
Westboro, MA   01581
617 366-8911

On-line languages for writing your own programs: FORTRAN, COBOL, RPGII, BASIC ALGOL, PL/I.

Digital Equipment Corp.
Merrimack, NH   03054
603 884-5111

Accounting, invoicing, inventory, word processing; for their own computers.

Digital Systems Corp.
Walkersville, MD   121793
301 845-4141

Accounting, payroll and inventory control.

Table 11–2   Sources of Programs *(Continued)*

Finar Systems Limited 132 Nassau St., Suite 212 New York, NY 10038 212 222-2784	Financial analysis and reporting; for DEC's PDP-11. Written in BASIC-Plus.
GRI Computer Corp. 320 Needham St. Newton, MA 02164 617 969-0800	Job estimating, competitive bidding and job cost control; for their own GRI computers.
Hewlett-Packard 1507 Page Mill Rd. Palo Alto, CA 94304 415 857-1501	Manufacturing-oriented programs for their HP250 computer, and Image, a data base management system.
IBM System Prod. Div. Boca Raton, FL 33432	Accounting, electronic work sheets, word processing, communications, Dow Jones financial, education.
Interactive Management Systems 375 Concord Ave. Belmont, MA 02178 617 489-3550	Financial planning and reporting, accounting; for PDP-11.
Information Unlimited Software 146 N. Broad St. Griffith, IN 46319 219 924-3522	Word processor for Apple computer.
Lifeboat Associates 1651 Third Avenue New York, NY 10028 212 860-0300	"The Software Supermarket" Microcomputer programs, business, word processing, operating systems, compilers and data base systems.
Mini-Computer Business Application, Inc. 4929 Whilshire Blvd., Suite 940 Los Angeles, CA 90010 213 247-1050	Accounting, order entry/inventory, billing, taxes, mailing list, payroll; for Digital Equipment, Data General and Wang computers. No retail sales.
MICRO.AP 9807 Davona Dr. San Ramon, CA 94583 415 828-6697	Accounting, sales activity, inventory, client-patient record, name and address, appointments, special events, library; for small microprocessor systems.
Microsystems Engineering Corp. 106 Barrington Rd. Streamwood, IL 60103 312 289-8828	Word processor on PDP-11.
Modern Microcomputers 63 Sudbury Lane Westbury, NY 11590 516 333-9178	Package for CPAs.
Peachtree Software Sold through computer stores.	Accounting, payroll, word processing, inventory, timekeeping, mailing list; for Intel-type micros.
Percom Data Company, Inc. 211 N. Kirby Garland, TX 75047 214 272-3421	General ledger, data base management system; for Motorola 6800 micros.

Table 11-2 Sources of Programs *(Continued)*

Plycom Services, Inc. P.O. Box 160 Plymouth, IN 46563 219 935-5121	Accounting, payroll; for Digital Equipment computers.
Radio Shack One Tandy Center Fort Worth, TX 76102 817 390-3011	Accounting, payroll, inventory, statistics, mailing list, math and word processing.
VisiCorp, Inc. 592 Weddell Drive Sunnyvale, CA 94086	Programs for micros, problem solving program (Visicalc) for professionals and data management systems for business.
Structured Systems Group 5204 Claremont Oakland, CA 94618 415 547-1567	Accounting, mailing, letter writer, data/query system; for Intel-type micros.

Screening Programs

All programs should be screened for suitability irrespective of their source.

The best way to screen a program is to find somebody who has used it, preferably over a full processing cycle. For accounting programs, a full cycle would be one fiscal year. For other programs a cycle could be a month, a year, or a day. In any case, the person who has used the program can provide invaluable screening information. CPAs, user groups and the vendors themselves can lead you to people with hands-on experience. Probably no single step you can take in screening programs can be as effective as contacting those who have used them. Make every effort to do so. However, as useful as this step is, it will not tell you if the program is a good fit for *your* requirements. For this, further screening is needed.

A good method for checking out programs is to actually enter data and run the program before buying it. Sometimes arrangements can be made to do this, either at your site or the vendor's. Although the technique is good for screening, it is not always possible and has definite timing limitations. Full processing cycles have to be simulated and time limitations restrict how much testing you can do.

The following are screening steps which should be taken to supplement those described above, and which can replace them when necessary.

If you send for information by mail or pick up some material at a computer store, what you will get will vary widely from one software firm to another. Some will send you a glossy brochure that gives very few hard facts, others will load you with almost everything you need to know and then some, and there are all types of responses between these two extremes. This variation merely reflects the vendor's idea about the best way to interest you and sell the product. The material usually includes an invitation to contact them for more information. Once you have shown interest you should expect willing cooperation in providing all the information you need. *Then* you can start evaluating the product and the company, not on the first response.

In the first go-around you can concentrate on the following information to weed out unsuitable program products, some firms will supply this information in response to a first inquiry.

Program Features

Program features are, of course, application dependent. For example, a payroll application might list the following features:

• Weekly, biweekly, semimonthly and monthly processing
• Accommodates both hourly and salaried employees
• Federal, state and FICA tax processing
• Annuities and voluntary deductions based on employee preferences
• Printing of checks, 941-A and W-2 forms
• Adjustments for overtime

In reviewing these features you would quickly notice the absence of anything that was important to your operations. Just because it isn't listed doesn't necessarily mean that the program doesn't have it, but your suspicions will be aroused and its absence will be noted for further investigation.

You will also notice those features that you don't need. In the above example, several of the points listed above might be considered overkill by a small business. You pay for each program feature in three ways: (1) in the cost of the program itself, (2) in the amount of memory required to run the program, and (3) in computer power. It takes a more expensive computer to run a program that is loaded with features than it does to run a program that is lean and mean. Reviewing the features of the program listed by the vendor is a quick way to eliminate unnecessary sophistication. Leave these programs for those who need them and pick the simplest program you can find that will do your job, but remembering to take into consideration your future needs, as well as those of the present.

Sample Reports

Sample reports and all other printed output are an absolute necessity for any kind of intelligent program evaluation. If you like the program features, but don't have samples of printed output, request these from the vendor. Any dragging of feet on this is a signal for skepticism about the firm and its programs.

Reports are key because they tell you what the program is doing to your records, what information you will get on your operations and how the information will be presented. The first two points are obvious things any sensible user would want to know. However, the third point is often overlooked.

Nothing is easier than producing computer printouts that look like somebody randomly threw letters at the paper and left them there for some poor manager to untangle. Compare a few sample reports from different programs and you will see what a difference good spacing, formatting and well-thought-out headings make.

The appearance of printed output becomes even more important if you have clients, customers or bankers who will see and use the results. The fact that "the computer did it" will not impress these people. They probably have computer printouts of their own to contend with and have taken pains to make them readable.

Equipment

All vendors of programs state clearly at the outset the equipment required to run their programs, and often they will state various limitations. If there is a shortcoming in this area it is that information on the types of printers that can be used by the program is usually lacking. Data is given on the makes of computers, the models, memory, and storage requirements, but nothing about the printer. Practically all programs for small computers rely on keyboard entry, a video display and a printer—of some sort.

After presenting this information, it may be stated that the program supports multi-user systems, meaning that more than one operator can use it at a time. If this is not the case, it may be stated that a more powerful and expensive version is offered that does provide for these capabilities.

If the literature doesn't say anything about support of communication equipment, chances are it is a missing ingredient. When they have it, vendors like to proclaim communication capability loud and clear.

What you do with this information on equipment is, of course, to start adding up costs. Somewhere, if only on the back of an envelope or in the back of your mind, you have a budget. Now is the time to see if you can *afford* to use this program you have found, which is going to cut costs, increase profits, make your job easier and beat out the competition.

If you can't get cost estimates directly from the program vendor, take the list of required hardware to a computer store or dealer. Get their estimate. Remember, you're still in the screening process, so you're only looking for ball park estimates.

Hopefully, your preliminary screening has resulted in at least one, preferably several, candidate programs that seem to have what you need. If so, you have reached the point where you now have to start looking into all those niggling details that make the difference between a successful and an unsuccessful computer system.

How to Use the Data Gathering Forms to Select a Program

Before starting detailed analysis of a program, get from the vendor samples of all reports and data that must be entered, both recurring and one-time entries. This will generally require a second or third request for information.

If you have done your homework, you have filled in a set of forms based on the sample data gathering forms presented in Chapter 9. These forms tell you what data you need, together with your intitial evaluation of their importance. Now you should check off each *data field* on the chart for which you find equivalent data in a candidate program. Start with the printed output, Form 9–3. If you are getting all the output from the computer you need, that is the main thing. But it is still necessary to check the other forms, so that you know *what*, *how* and *when* data is required by the program.

Now the above process should be repeated in reverse. That is, check off all input information the system needs that you are now entering into your current record keeping system. Any item not checked off is cause for concern. The program may be doing processing that requires data you do not presently have. If this data is not forthcoming, the program may not know what to do and the system could stop working.

When you did the preliminary screening, you might have seen features that you hadn't been looking for, but that you would certainly like to have. The trouble is that these features might require data input you are not presently able to provide. Therefore, any input required by the program that doesn't have a check mark next to it requires that you determine whether you can supply the missing data with reasonable effort and cost; and if not, whether the missing data is necessary for the program to run.

The answer to the second question can only come from the vendor or a professional after detailed program analysis. In any case, you will be treading on thin ice. Accurately predicting the result of missing program data is not a simple task. Even with the best of intentions, the answer could be wrong. The best course of action in such cases is to find another candidate program. Of course, the situation would be completely different if the vendor publicly states in the published specifications that the program can run without the data in question. Programmers can easily design the programs to perform in this manner if this is part of the original specifications.

If the candidate program is still in the race, the time has come for you to start thinking about compromises. Look at your forms. Are there check marks next to each item listed? If so, consider yourself lucky. Chances are you have found a program that you can use "as is." More likely, there will be some missing checks. What does the Rating column say about these fields? Not required? Desirable? Necessary?

At this point you may decide that desirable items are not really necessary and that necessary items are only desirable and, if pushed, you could find ways to do without. The alternatives are:

• Customize the program to better fit your requirements. Who will do this? Refer to Chapter 6, a profile of the industry, for guidance in obtaining professional programming.
• Drop the candidate program, and find another.

Bear in mind when considering program modifications, that all modifications are not equally difficult. Here are some guidelines that may help in deciding to accept or reject a program.

- Reports and screens.   Headings and formats are fairly easy to change, especially if the vendor has taken pains to provide for this. The content of reports and screens can be changed if the data is available in some part of the program. Otherwise, major surgery may be required.
- Validity checks.   These are easy to change or add to.
- Capacity.   Difficulties are likely due to equipment and software compatibility.
- Program logic.   Changing the *way* a program performs its functions, or *what* functions it performs is asking for trouble.

ESTIMATING INPUT REQUIREMENTS

In the selection of a computer system two important considerations are (1) the time required for data entry and (2) the number of work stations or terminals that must be included. The former affects labor costs and the latter affects equipment and program costs. Both weigh in the economic justification of the system.

Operator Time

Operator time can be easily calculated from the two items: (1) average entry time per screen and (2) the relative frequency of each screen. These should be obtained from the program vendor for each type of data entry, even if there is no corresponding entry type in your present system. If you can't get entry time data from the vendor, you may have to estimate these times yourself, based on the number of characters, operator keying rates and expected screen usage. The advantage of getting these figures from the vendor, in addition to convenience, is that the vendor can base the figures on measured times under conditions where the operator actually interacts with the screens. On the other hand, the vendor's figures may be on the optimistic side, so it is a good idea to check them for reasonableness against your own calculations.

Consider, for example, a screen requiring the entry of the following fields:

Customer number	4 characters
Customer name	10 characters, average
Address	15 characters, average
City	8 characters, average
State	2 characters
Zip	5 characters
Telephone	12 characters
Average number of characters per screen	56

Keying rates for data entry vary widely, depending on the skill of the operator, the legibility of the source documents, the efficiency of screen layouts, and whether the operator is subject to interruptions and the general working environment. Planners use a range of 1 to 2 characters per second for estimating purposes. Then, the 56 characters derived above would require at least 56/2 = 28 seconds. Any lower times quoted by the vendor would be suspect. This doesn't mean you should necessarily reject the program, but at least you should ask for reasonable explanations of the difference.

If you are relying on your own estimates, you might want to work with more conservative values, in which case you would assume an entry rate of 1.5 or even 1 character per second or less, depending on the keying skill of those who will enter data.

Consider, for example, a business that prepares 100 bills per week and receives 100 payments per week, on an average. The program vendor states that the entry of bills requires three screens as follows:

	Seconds	Rel. Freq.	Product
Screen 1	30	1	30
Screen 2	30	1	30
Screen 3	6	0.1	0.6

Screen 3 is negligible, giving 60 seconds as the entry time per bill.

For payments only, the vendor states that only one screen is required and that entry time per payment is 15 seconds. Therefore, total operator time per week to enter bills and payments is,

$$100 \text{ bills} \times 60 \text{ sec. per bill} + 100 \text{ payments} \times 15 \text{ sec.}$$
$$\text{per payment} = 7500 \text{ sec. per week or about 2 hours}$$

If there are other applications, their entry times would be calculated in a similar manner and added to the above to get total operator entry time.

Terminals and Operators Required

How many operators will have to use the computer at the same time? As pointed out in Chapter 2, multi-user systems can be a necessity imposed by the quantity of data that must be entered, or they may be the best way to provide full service or to best utilize the computer. In the latter case the number of terminals will be dictated by convenience considerations and, therefore, is not the subject of this section. Here, we will consider the cases where the quantity of data entry dictates the *need* for a multi-user system.

All computer systems require data entry. However, the time at which this data must be entered is not uniform throughout the working day. Data arrives in batches and often it must be processed within a certain time period. End of week, end of month and end of year are times when peaks in activity are likely to occur. Daily transaction processing also has its peaks—early morning and noontime are common.

It is the *peak load* which will determine the maximum number of operators your system must have. This peak may exist for only a small percentage of the total time that the system is up and running, but you may judge that, nevertheless, this peak load *must* be handled. It is often possible, however, to reduce the peak load by proper scheduling, thereby avoiding the need for a multi-user system. Whenever this is a possibility it should be enthusiastically grasped, since a single-user system is always much simpler and less costly.

The procedures in this section provide for obtaining rough estimates. Before actually committing yourself to a multi-user system, it is recommended that you obtain the help of a professional.

A multi-user system is a system having more than one operator entering data. For each operator there must be one work station or terminal (the term we will use here). The terminal, at a minimum, consists of a keyboard and a display. Terminals may all be in the same room with the computer, or widely separated; it makes no difference for the purpose of this discussion.

In order to get a feel for the numbers involved, consider an operator who works from nine to five. Such an operator has a theoretical working day of 420 minutes (one hour for lunch).

If each input document can be keyed in in one minute, 420 documents can be entered per day, assuming 100 percent, nose-to-the-grindstone working time by the operator. However, since no operator works continuously for seven hours at peak speed, this figure has to be derated. Assuming 80 percent operator efficiency, 336 documents can be entered per day. This is a fair number for a small business, indicating that many small businesses should be able to live with one operator and one terminal. You might want to do your own calculations, using different worker efficiency, hours per day and daily input rate. But, whatever the result, provide a 10–20 percent contingency factor.

There will be cases where volumes are too large or timing considerations beyond the user's control force the use of more than one terminal.

One note of caution: When the entry time of a screen is less than 20 seconds, response time becomes significant and should be included in total screen entry time. Response time is the time it takes the system to process one screen entry and to present the operator with a new screen. Response time should not be greater than 5 seconds and should, preferrably, be closer to 2 seconds. It is very sensitive to the number of operators using the system and the amount of memory available to each operator. Only the vendor, or somebody with hands-on experience, can tell you what kind of response time to expect under various conditions.

As an example of a multi-user system, consider an order inquiry and entry application. Telephone calls from customers tend to be most numerous on Monday mornings, or after holidays, when they can reach a volume of about one per minute. An inquiry results in the following screen usage:

	Seconds	Rel. Freq.	Product
Screen 1	30	1.0	30
Screen 2	30	0.8	24
Screen 3	30	0.4	12
		Total	66 sec. per entry

Here we are illustrating a situation that is somewhat different from the previous example. Customers call in to inquire about delivery times and prices for products. If the delivery time is satisfactory, they will usually place an order. The vendor has stated that only one screen is required per inquiry and that only ten seconds is required for entry and response time. However, it is known that in this particular business 80 percent of the time there will be an inquiry on at least two products, and 40 percent of the time customers will inquire about three products. The number of inquiries on four products is negligible.

This data has been entered above in the relative frequency column.

Further, a call results in some conversation between the customer and the order takers. This customer relationship is considered important and rather than discourage it, order takers are encouraged to discuss customer anticipated requirements and get a feel for what others are doing. Therefore, the 10 seconds quoted by the vendor is extended to 30 seconds in our example. This may be too small or too large in any particular case, but nobody can determine this but the person who knows the business for which the computer system is to be selected. This example illustrates the point made at the beginning of the chapter: No hard and fast rules can be made on how to carry out the selection process. Each organization must use numbers and methods that are appropriate to its way of doing things.

Now assume that on Form 9–1, the number of this type of entry (inquiry) is given as one per minute in the period between 10 and 12 A.M. on Mondays and after holidays. From this we can easily estimate the number of terminals required. One inquiry per minute is 0.017 inquiries per second. Multiplying this times the 66 seconds per inquiry (determined above) gives 1.1 terminals as the required number.

If other entries are required in the *same* time period, these also must be accounted for.

We must allow for other entries at the same time period. In our example, we know there will be orders entered in the same time period and we will assume no other data entry is required in the same time period. Then, for orders, we might have:

	Seconds	Rel. Freq.	Product
Screen 1	10	1	10
Screen 2	60	1	60
Screen 3	5	0.2	1
		Total	71 seconds per order

Assume order rate is 0.8 per minute, or 0.013 per second. Multiplying this times 71 seconds per order, gives 0.92 terminals for order entry.

The total terminal requirements for inquiry and order-taking is:

Inquiry	1.1
Order	0.9
Total	2.0 terminals

Based on this result, you might be tempted to go with just two terminals. This would be a mistake. A contingency of at least 10 percent should be allowed. In addition, a loading factor of about 1.4 should be used to allow for the random arrival of phone calls. This decreases the probability of a customer being put on hold and calling another vendor. In the present example 2 Terminals × 1.1 for contingency is 2.2 Terminals. A 1.4 loading factor gives 2.2 × 1.4 or 3.08 Terminals. Therefore, in this case, three terminals should be used with one operator per terminal.

The loading factor is a technical term and the use of the value 1.4 can be justified only for rough estimates. Readers who do not have professional help are advised to make sure their system can handle additional terminals if experience indicates that the above type of calculations underestimated terminal requirements.

In this section we described how to calculate the number of terminals and operators you will *need*. This is not the same, and should not be confused with, the number of terminals a given system can *handle*. The latter is difficult to determine, even for experienced professionals. It is best done based on experience with a working system, and the vendor is in the best position to do this. Work with a reputable vendor. Try to implement your system in small pieces, so that you can more easily adjust to underestimated requirements.

THE OPERATING SYSTEM

In Chapter 5 we described the various types of operating systems in use. Here we will discuss what to look for in selecting a system.

The type of operating system you must have will depend on the number of terminals that are simultaneously using the system. If you have only one terminal, you should not encounter major problems unless the operating system you get is brand new. Even the simplest operating system is a complex program and requires a good deal of use to get the bugs out. Avoid new operating systems or new versions, just as you should avoid new application programs. Try to determine the reputation of the system and vendor. If this checks out, you can proceed with reasonable confidence.

Since vendors of applications programs target to a particular operating system, you will be using the operating system specified by the vendor for the product. Vendors don't knowingly use a poor operating system, but mistakes have been made.

One operating system that has been very successful and is widely used in microcomputers is Digital Research's CP/M™. A good deal of software has been designed to work with this operating system on low-end computers.

The situation with respect to multi-user operating systems is similar, but all potential problems are magnified. These operating systems are a good deal more complex. Often they come on the market unable to perform satisfactorily. It can take over a year to whip a complex operating system into shape. Accordingly, you should not select a multi-user operating system that has not been around for at least two years, has a good number of users and has a good reputation.

Your exposure to trouble depends on how close you must work to the operating system's limit. For example, if you require only three or four terminals and the operating system can accommodate twelve terminals, you should be on safe ground. However, if the limit of the operating system is five terminals, you're on the ragged edge and should proceed cautiously.

In order for the operating system to handle multiple terminals, you will probably have to add memory. How much depends on the system. 32K bytes per terminal plus 32K bytes for the operating system would be reasonable for a medium system. Memory prices have been dropping fast. As of now, 32K costs about $500.

ESTIMATING MEMORY REQUIREMENTS

Users should have little need for actually estimating memory requirements themselves. Vendors of systems and programs determine memory requirements and, for single-user systems, these are more a function of the vendor's products than your application. However, as pointed out above, the picture changes when several terminals share one computer and its programs. There is a complex relationship between number of users, the application, the input rate and the amount of memory required. Trying to estimate this without direct experience with the same or similar conditions is extremely hazardous. Vendors who have this experience or who have run benchmarks on their equipment can help in this matter. The user should always allow for error in such estimates and assume that at least one more increment of memory may be required.

Even though users need not plan the memory layout themselves, it is useful to know what will determine memory requirements. The amount of memory must be enough to provide for:

- The portion of the operating system that must be in memory to run the application programs. The rest of the operating system can be stored on disk and called into memory as needed.
- The application program. Depending on the operating system, only the part of the program which is currently executing need be memory-resident. The rest is held on disk until needed. However, the speed of processing can be very sensitive to the amount of program stored in memory. Too little could mean impossibly slow processing.
- Miscellaneous storage for tables, directories, indexes and records and transactions. This is usually a relatively small amount of memory.
- Interpreters. BASIC or other higher-level languages designed to work with interpreters must be translated each time they are run, requiring the interpreters to be in memory at run time.

All of the above can be translated into numbers by the following rules of thumb:

Type of System	Bytes of Memory
Professional or personal use	16K to 64K
Low-end, single-user business systems	32K to 128K
Medium, high-end or multi-user systems	128K to 256K and up

Estimate $15 per 1K of memory.

ESTIMATING STORAGE REQUIREMENTS

You can usually get a good handle on storage requirements from the program specs supplied by the program vendor. These should tell you the number of disk drives the program will require. Also, information on record lengths and maximum number of records will be supplied for both the master and transaction file. With this information in hand you must determine if the program is adequate for your needs.

The key item for estimating storage requirements comes from Form 9–2, Projected Number of Records. Using this value, you can quickly calculate program adequacy.

Consider the following program spec:

Records: 1,500

If your projected number of records from Form 9–2 is close to or greater than this, you should reject the program. Never buy programs that don't provide some margin for error in estimates of variation in activity. A rule of thumb for this is at least 10 percent.

You may want, in some cases, to estimate storage requirements. The calculation is straightforward: Record length in characters (or bytes) times your projected number of records. Add all files used at the same time.

ESTIMATING RUN REQUIREMENTS

How often will you have to run a program? Can the program be run an arbitrary number of times without creating problems?

Consider the first question first. The situation here is similar to that for estimating storage requirements. The program spec might include:

Transactions per run: 300

Now, from Form 9–1, we find projected number of entries. Assume this comes to 500 per month. Clearly, we must plan to run the program at least twice a month.

This brings us to the second question. Suppose this is an accounting program. It can't be assumed that such a program can be run at any time or at any frequency without creating problems. For example, if an accounts receivable program ages amounts due and computes year-to-date amounts, running the program more than once per accounting period could result in invalid data. In any such case, check with the vendor. Also, consider if you wouldn't be better off going to a program with greater capacity to handle more transactions.

ESTIMATING PRINTING REQUIREMENTS

In order to select the proper printer, it is necessary to know how fast it must print and how rugged the printer must be. Many printers sold for small computers are low-cost printers designed for light duty, that is, one or two hours of operation a day. They are fine for light-duty use, but will not hold up if overworked. Thus, you need to know what your printing load will be, and must select a printer to match this load.

The difficulty in estimating printer speed and loading varies greatly from one situation to another. It can be quite simple or rather complex. In this section we will outline procedures that should enable you to calculate speed and loading for most of the conditions likely to be encountered with small computers.

Printing Speed Requirements

The speed with which you can do a printing job depends on (1) the rate at which characters can be printed, and (2) the rate at which the paper can be advanced. The relative importance of these two items depends on formats and layouts of the printed documents.

More and more of the printers used with small computers are bi-directional. That is, they have the ability to print in both directions, saving carriage return time and thereby effectively doubling the character print rate. Further, they can take the shortest route, left or right, to the start of the next line.

The information you need to select a printer is:

- The character-per-second print speed. This ranges from about 15 CPS to 200 CPS.
- The paper advance speed. Common rates are 5 to 15 inches per second.
- The number of lines printed per inch.
- Whether the printer is unidirectional or bi-directional.
- If unidirectional, the carriage return speed.
- Your own printing requirements.

The first five items come from the vendors. The last item you derive yourself from the information entered on the data gathering forms, and calculations made, as described below.

Consider, first, the printing of blocked text, which has a fairly simple format, so the average number of character positions per line can be estimated easily and fairly accurately. If there are 60 character positions per line and print speed is 100 CPS, a bi-directional printer will print a line in 0.6 seconds. A unidirectional printer will add to this carriage return time. This is often the same as the rate for printing an entire line, and can be used for estimating purposes. Therefore, a unidirectional printer would require a total of 1.2 seconds to print the same line and be in position to print the next one.

Assume the paper advances at 5 inches per second, and there are 6 lines per inch, or 30 lines per second. This adds only 0.033 seconds per line, and can be neglected in this example. The line length would have to drop below about 30 character positions per line before paper movement time becomes significant for a bi-directional printer. At 15 character positions per line, paper movement time becomes one fifth of print time.

For a unidirectional printer, line length would have to drop below 15 character positions before paper movement is significant.

These figures are based on a line feed rate of 5 inches per second. Higher rates would reduce even further the line length at which paper movement is significant.

All this should give you a feel for how print speed is determined and how to estimate it. The important thing is to get average time per line. This is difficult only when line lengths vary considerably and at random, in which case a small reduction from the maximum might serve as a conservative estimate.

The above considerations apply to character printers. In the case of line printers, which print a full line at a time, the time per line is constant, and the printer is rated in lines per minute rather than characters per second. This greatly simplifies the task of estimating print time.

Knowing the average time to print a line, it is a simple matter to calculate the time to print a page by multiplying by the number of lines per page. Since blank lines and margins must be included in the average line time, it is often simpler to average only lines with print. Then, the time per page is given by,

$$(A \times l) + (P \times L)$$

where

A = average time to print a line
l = number of lines with print
P = time to move paper one line
L = total number of lines per page

In some cases it may not be enough to know the printing requirements for just one job. There may be time constraints that require more than one job to be run in a certain time frame. Consider the situation where printing requirements are as follows:

Monday	Job A
Tuesday	Open
Wednesday	Open
Thursday	Jobs B and C
Friday morning	Open
Friday afternoon	Jobs D and E

Assume you have a candidate printer, and, using the methods outlined above, you have determined the following:

Job	Time per Page	Projected Pages per Document	Projected No. Documents per Job	Product: Time per Job
A	1.0 min.	100	1	1.7 hrs.
B	0.1	60	70	7.0
C	0.3	1	100	0.5
D	0.5	2	200	1.0
E	0.2	10	100	3.2

Then, the load for each time period is:

Time period	Job	Time per time period
Monday	A	1.7 hrs. per 8 hrs.
Thursday	B and C	7.5 hrs. per 8 hrs.
Friday P.M.	D and E	4.2 hrs. per 4 hrs.

The peak load is Friday afternoon. Clearly, this printer is not adequate, since jobs D and E can't be completed in the allotted time frame. Either a rescheduling of jobs or a faster printer is in order.

These examples demonstrate that estimating print speed requires some juggling with numbers. Yet this will have to be done if you plan to do lots of printing other than just standard business reports. In the latter case, you can rely on your vendor's recommendations. Otherwise, determining printer speed will be your job.

Printing Load Requirements

The best way to express the load on a printer is in terms of *duty cycle*. Sometimes the terms light duty and heavy duty are used, but these are less precise and open to misinterpretation.

The duty cycle expresses the percentage of time the printer operates per day. A printer rated at 100 percent duty cycle is designed to operate continuously for eight hours a day. A 25 percent duty cycle will indicate two hours per day operation. By calculating your daily printing requirements, you can determine the duty cycle of the printer you should get.

Unfortunately, not many vendors rate their printers in terms of duty cycle. Some rate them in terms of mean time between failure, MTBF, or simply "light duty" or "heavy duty." However, if you know your printing load, you will be in a position to determine if a particular printer is suitable or not. Assume the print load varies from week to week, as follows:

Week	Number of Characters
1	2,050,000
2	1,000,000
3	75,000
4	2,000,000

Total 5,125,000 characters

Average 1,375,000 char. per week

Average 235,000 char. per day

Now assume a 100-CPS printer has been selected. Convert this to characters per day, assuming an 8-hour day.

Char. per Sec.	Char. per Hour	Char. per Day
100	360,000	2,880,000

Obviously, the printer in this case will be lightly loaded and a light-duty printer is called for. We can get the actual duty cycle by dividing the actual use of 235,000 characters per day by the printer's continuous rate of 2,880,000 characters per day. The result is 0.08, or a duty cycle of 8 percent.

Suppose, however, the results had been a duty cycle of 80 percent. Then, a heavy-duty printer would be needed. Finally, if your duty cycle is between 30 and 70 percent, try to get the duty cycle of the printer. If this is unavailable, play it safe with a medium- or heavy-duty printer.

Another figure of interest is the vendor's mean number of characters between failures, referred to as MCBF. MCBF can be related to your calculated duty cycle to determine the expected number of failures per year.

Of particular concern in dot matrix printers is the MCBF of the print head. Assume the MCBF for such a unit is 250 million characters, the duty cycle 50 percent and print speed 200 characters per second. Then, converting characters per second to characters per day,

$$200 \text{ CPS} \times 3600 \text{ SPH (seconds per hour)} \times 8 \text{ HPD (hours per day)} \times 0.5$$
$$\text{duty cycle} = 2.88 \text{ million characters per day}$$

The time to failure will be

$$250 \text{ MCBF}/2.88 \text{ MCPD} = 87 \text{ days or about 4 months}$$

at 50 percent duty cycle, or 3 times per year.

Suppose, however, the actual duty cycle, as in the previous example, is only 8 percent. Then time to failure is

$$50/8 \times 4 = 25 \text{ months}$$

By underutilizing the printer, long life is achieved. *Over*utilization, of course, produces the opposite result. Unfortunately, not many vendors provide MCBF values. When they are available, take advantage of them to estimate down time.

SELECTING A PRINTER

Most vendors will offer a choice of several types of printers with their computers. Your selection should be determined by these considerations:

- Speed and load.   These requirements have already been discussed in the previous section.
- The program specifications.   These will indicate number of columns, forms and other characteristics the programs are designed for. Here, again, the program is the key. Be sure your printer corresponds to what the program expects to find out there.
- Print quality.   If print quality is important for your application, check if lines are straight, or if they have a wavy appearance. Also, is there uniformity in the darkness of different characters. On daisy wheel printers, compare a period to a "B" to get an indication of how much variation to expect. The relative print quality available on dot matrix and daisy wheel printers has already been discussed and will be a major determinant in printer selection.
- Number of copies.   Lower-cost printers don't generate the printing power of the more expensive units. Get samples of printing of multi-part forms and check the readability of the last part.
- Ease of use.   If the printer is going to be used extensively, someone will be doing a lot of paper loading, print wheel changing, ribbon changing and, in general, tending to the printer. A good printer should make this easy for someone who is not a born mechanic.
- Fail safe operation.   What happens if the printer runs out of paper, or the paper jams, or other things go wrong? The printer should stop before damage can be done. An attention-getting signal is desirable.
- Paper width.   Many low-cost printers today work with paper 8 inches or less in width. You may want less cramped output.
- Noise.   Impact printers can be noisy. Listen to the printer in full-speed operation. Evaluate its noise impact in terms of where it will be located. Ask the vendor about enclosures for deadening the noise.

While the above descriptions of the selection process may appear rather complex to the first-time user, most of the difficulty can be traced to unfamiliarity with a new subject. As you investigate what is on the market and plan for your own computer, you will find things falling into place as you master the basics of small computers. For most readers, the programs you select will determine the equipment, thereby simplifying your selection task.

Negotiating a Computer Contract

When you buy a computer system or arrange to have work done for you, a contract should be signed that spells out the responsibilities of both parties. In dealing with computer vendors the rules are substantially the same as for any other industry. There are people and practices you have to guard against, and the watchword has to be *caveat emptor*. Naturally, you work with your lawyer.

In previous chapters we have had several occasions to mention that you should negotiate compensating advantages when a vendor's product, for whatever reason, entails greater than average risk. But in any case, you should try to negotiate the best deal possible.

The following points in the contract should be discussed with your lawyer:

• Patent and copyright infringement protection
• Warranties
• Rights of cancellation and termination
• Right to assign ownership
• Right to sell

Other points may be suggested by your lawyer.
  Points you should be prepared to negotiate are:

• Deliverables—what they are and what they will do, i.e., their specifications
• Performance
• Prices (software and hardware)
• Testing
• Criteria for acceptance and payments
• Who will get investment tax credit
• Training
• Provisions for maintenance (software and hardware)
• Percentage ownership or other benefits of any products developed or tested at your expense

Include all specifications and put everything in writing.

PART 3
The Application of Small Computers

Five Pitfalls

Even with the most careful evaluation of programs and equipment, computer systems can fail. In this chapter we will discuss a number of issues that are often not considered in the process of applying a computer. These are easy to state, but it is hard to describe precise steps by which they can be avoided. They involve intangibles which can't be measured and for which there is no sharp dividing line between the right and the wrong way to proceed. The biggest pitfall is to disregard these points altogether. However, with reasonable judgment and planning there is no reason why you can't deal with these areas and have a computer system that works well and is productive.

PITFALL 1: THE SYSTEM IS NOT EASY TO USE

You can have a powerful computer and beautifully written programs, but if the system is not easy to use it will be a failure.

What does "easy to use" mean? We have discussed ease of use in previous chapters in relation to equipment and programs. Here we are talking about ease of use of the *system as a whole in it's day-to-day operations*. How will the computer appear to those operating it and to those who depend on it for information? Will it make life easier or will it get in the way? Will people *want* to use it, or will they have to be *forced* to use it? Will they look for ways to get more of their work done by the computer or will they end up looking for ways to bypass it?

When people find that the computer is hard to use, they start looking for alternate routes. If it is easier to yell across the room to get information, this will be done. If it is hard to get information out of the system, personal records will be kept on scraps of paper in desk drawers. Important data will fail to get entered into the computer. The files will deteriorate in accuracy. The original problem will be compounded. Nothing turns users off a system more than data that can't be relied on. And once users become antagonistic to a computer system, its days are numbered.

A successful computer system requires dedicated users and operators willing to do what's necessary to keep things moving smoothly. All the rules and written procedures you can devise won't produce a successful system if those using it are antagonistic. A computer that is hard to use will become even harder to use. A computer that is easy to use requires continuous effort and cooperation on the part of users to keep it that way.

The above comments apply whether the number of people involved in the use of the computer are many, just a few or only one person—you. Suppose you were to get a computer with the idea of streamlining your personal record keeping. The system will store various memoranda, keep track of your appointments and bring up important dates and reminders of things to do. You buy a system that performs all the functions you want and with great enthusiasm you enter the world of the "electronic office." The first week you conscientiously enter your memoranda and appointments and are pleasantly gratified when, by entering a command, you get a display on your computer screen of all the things you are to do that day.

Your electronic office is performing as expected, but nevertheless scraps of paper start accumulating in the top drawer with scribbled notes. After a week or so of this, the old calendar comes out of a bottom drawer back on top of the desk. Soon after, the electronic office is moved off the desk and given other assignments, sold or junked.

What went wrong? The problem was not that the computer was necessarily *hard* to use but that it was *not as easy* to use as the older methods. Writing notes while talking to a customer on the phone with another customer on hold is easier then keying in records. Scanning your calendar for an opening and jotting down an appointment beats hitting keys and scrolling through an electronic calendar. Can't the entries you have made while talking on the phone be entered into the computer later? Never! At least, not after the first week's enthusiasm is dissipated. Nobody but a fanatic would take the time to do it.

Files, to be useful, must be complete. Who would use an appointment file if they knew that even a single appointment had been left out? A successful computer system must be easy to use under stress situations as well as for routine operations. If, under stress, the computer is bypassed, files will no longer be complete and the door to the computer's exit will have been opened.

In small organizations, ease of use is more difficult to achieve than in large ones. And this difficulty can shift an evaluation of a computer system from feasible to unfeasible. In large organizations, the actual entry of data and the operation of the computer can be delegated to specific employees who know this is their job and will accept it as such. A small organization may not be able to justify this kind of employee. This forces the mechanics of using the computer onto people with other responsibilities. How will they react? Will they view the computer as an aid or an impediment? The above example of the computer used as a memoranda file and appointment monitor illustrates this. The basic idea was good but not good enough to justify data entry. If the computer could understand spoken English instead of insisting on keyboard entry, ease of use would have been achieved. But, instead, the computer was more of a hindrance than a help. Similar problems arise when payroll, inventory or any other application is attempted in very small organizations. You have to be careful about who will do the "dirty work" and what their reaction will be.

How can you plan your system so that you can be sure it will be easy to use? You can't. Planning is only one part of what is required. Often it is not possible to know in advance what will, and what will not, be easy to use. What looks easy on paper may not be easy in actual day-to-day operations. In order to provide for this uncertainty it is necessary to perform testing and fine tuning of the system. We will treat system testing and fine tuning in Chapters 13 and 14 respectively. But here are some guidelines on the planning part.

Equipment Selection

Try to stay in the mainstream of small computer usage. As we mentioned in the beginning of this book, small computers are designed for ease of use. They are the product of years of development and testing to determine what works best when a computer is moved out of the computer room and into the office. If you stick with equipment specifically designed and tested for working in an office environment, you will have laid a foundation for ease of use.

If you do find that for some reason you have to deviate from mainstream equipment, then you should take special care to determine how ease of use will be affected.

Data Entry

In order to get a computer to process data, you have to enter data into it. Plan carefully who will perform the data entry, when it will be performed and under what conditions. Try to make data entry a natural part of operating procedure. On-line entry helps in this respect. For example, an inventory and order entry system allows quick response to a customer's inquiry and then easy entry of data if the inquiry is followed by an order. On the other hand, accumulating orders on order slips for later keying into the computer adds extra work. The rule here is to move the entry of data as close to the source of the data as possible, cutting out intermediate steps and reducing chances for error.

If data entry cannot be made a natural part of workflow and has to be batched for input, then in a small organization the questions of who will enter the data, and when, take on added importance. The question of how data will be entered has to be carefully analyzed and should be an important consideration in the decision to go ahead with the project.

File Handling

If you are contemplating a simple system with one file that can fit on a single disk, file handling should be no problem. If, however, your system uses several files which have common data fields, the passing of data between files may make your system difficult to use.

In the previous example, if the system contained an inventory file on one disk and an order file on another disk with only one available drive, the system would be hard to use and on-line inventory would not be possible. This situation could be corrected by (1) adding another drive, (2) using a larger drive that could accommodate both files on a single disk or (3) combining the two files into one. Note, however, that each of these cases would require the right software for the solution selected. So, here again, we see that software is the key. When looking for software for your application, evaluate candidates in terms of how easy or hard it will be to handle files.

Output Data

Nothing will cause people to bypass a system faster than the inability to get the data they need when they want it. As we have stated before, one of the most important justifications for using a computer is that it can provide better, more timely information on what is happening. However, you should avoid assuming that this will occur automatically. The most frequently overlooked point here is in not providing the information to all who need it. Consider an inventory system again. On-line access is great, but if it is confined to one display unit that isn't easily accessible to all who need it, the system may end up being harder to use than the original.

An important capability of computers that you should try to exploit is *exception reporting*. We described in Chapter 5 how computers make decisions on things like inventory reorder points. This same capability can be used to decide when or when not to report data. Thus, an exception report could show all inventory below a certain level, those items that have sold below a certain rate and those above a certain rate. Reporting by exception focuses attention on those pieces of information most likely to require action, instead of leaving them buried in a mass of printed output. Exception reporting makes a system easy to use. Voluminous computer printouts that don't pinpoint the items requiring action are hard to use.

Decisions on what exception reporting and what detailed reports are required are usually made by analysts and programmers based on what they feel will be best for most of the users of their programs. Sometimes programs are written without a correct knowledge of users' needs. Therefore, do not assume that a program has the type of reporting you need. Consider here your requirements for exception reporting, detailed reporting, legal requirements for reporting, and archival records for backup and historical reference.

PITFALL 2: DOING IT ALL YOURSELF

Unless yours is a one-person operation, you have either partners, employees, associates and, if you are a manager, bosses to whom you are responsible. In planning for a computer in a small organization there is a tendency for one person to take charge, do all the planning and then announce the results to the others. The result is usually one very enthusiastic "computer expert" with the rest of the staff harboring feelings varying from indifference to hostility. This is the wrong environment in which to introduce a computer and an important pitfall to avoid.

Experience has shown that to lay the groundwork for a successful computer system, all those who use it or will otherwise be affected by it should be involved not only in the later stages of conversion, but also in the planning. And the earlier the better. By bringing your associates aboard early you accomplish the following:

- Provide them with a sense of participation. The project becomes partly theirs, they become committed and support, rather than oppose, it.
- They can see what their future role will be, so that fears of the computer are dissipated.
- The chances of the system performing well are increased. No one person can think of everything. Those most familiar with a particular area of operation will anticipate problems that can save hours of work later.
- Early involvement allows people to learn about computers and their system in the most natural way. No training class can provide the kind of background that comes from actual involvement in planning. These people are going to have to use and operate the system, not just when things are working right, but also when things go wrong; when you are there, and when you're not. To do this they need to understand the system, not just memorize rules of operation.

How do you involve others without turning the project into a free-for-all? Organizations with a small number of people who work intimately on a daily basis should have no problem and an informal approach should be possible. Larger organizations may want a more formal approach. Here is one method that is used.

A committee is set up, consisting of a few people who will be most involved in the completed system. No rules can be set down here as to how the committee should be run or decisions arrived at. This is strictly a management decision and must reflect management philosophy.

Once a working committee is established, all those who will use or be affected by the system should be co-opted to the committee when their sphere of interest is under consideration. In addition, there should be open meetings or other methods by which participants can learn the whole system as it is being planned and offer suggestions for its improvement. When possible, data gathering should be done by those currently involved with the data in question. Similarly, they should be involved in planning tests, setting up test data and evaluating test results.

With this kind of approach, by the time the new system is cutover you will have a knowledgeable team, committed to the success of the new system.

PITFALL 3: POOR DOCUMENTATION

Recently, the owner of a successful small business installed a computer system, and, because he was in the habit of carefully planning his business activities, the system was quite a success. Then, one day, his office manager, who was responsible for operation of the computer, came down with a virus infection.

This still left a clerk who was trained in all the operations connected with the system. However, when she too contracted the virus a few days later, there was nobody who knew the system well enough to run it. Although the owner tried to fill the gap through repeated phone conversations, it was found that more harm than good was being done when the system was operated by inexperienced personnel. This businessman, despite careful planning in most areas, had failed to plan for a loss in experienced people. There was no adequate documentation on the operating procedures that could be used by those temporarily required to assume the duties of operating the computer.

Good documentation is required in three areas:

- Documentation of equipment
- Documentation of programs
- Documentation of your own data processing flow and operating procedures

Documentation of equipment and programs is furnished by the vendors of those products. The quality of the documentation varies widely. To be acceptable, at a minimum it should provide all data necessary to get the product up and running, and to keep it running. Phone calls to the vendor are time-consuming, costly and not always possible. Beyond these minimum requirements, the quality of vendor's documentation will depend on how helpful it is in handling special cases, the malfunctioning of equipment and exception processing of programs. We are not referring here to documentation required by a service technician or a programmer. There are certain things that a user should know to help overcome special problems and avoid damage to the products.

Finally, a vendor's documentation should be accurate and up to date. This is not always the case. As you will find with respect to documentation of your own system, under the pressure of day-to-day business, documentation gets the lowest priority. When there doesn't seem to be time to do all the things that have to be done, documentation is the activity that is allowed to lapse.

It is possible to determine to some extent the quality of a vendor's documentation by inspection. This can give an indication of how well the use of the product and the handling of special situations is provided for, although the first-time user will not know, except in a very general way, what to look for. However, this limited method is of no use in determining whether the documentation is accurate and up to date. For this, you will have to fall back on the overall reputation of the vendor.

The documentation of your own processing flow and operating procedure is, of course, no one's responsibility but your own. If yours is a one-person operation, there is little need for documentation, as long as you can rely on your memory. Even here, there are risks, but people rarely take the trouble to provide documentation for their own use.

However, as soon as there is more than one person in an operation, documentation becomes important. Even with just two people, without documentation the possibility of mix-ups is enough to warrant making the effort needed to document.

Documentation performs several functions:

- It provides for standard procedures so that everyone is doing the same thing under the same circumstances, instead of having to guess what is right.
- It describes what to do in special cases. Normal procedures are quickly learned and become ingrained. But when nonroutine or exceptional conditions occur we need to look up what to do.
- It provides for backup so that personnel whose main responsibility is other than working with the computer can step in and take over in an emergency.
- It provides training material, greatly increasing the speed and accuracy with which new people can be brought on board.

There are two ways of producing documentation. One way is to put it off until last, and then, when everything is running smoothly, make a special effort to document the results. This has the advantage of not taking time and effort away from the main task, that of getting the computer up and running. Also, upon completion of the installation all the details have been finalized and everything is neatly in place. This avoids, at least in theory, the need to revise the documentation.

The trouble with postponing documentation until the end of the project is that it will probably never get done. There will always be something more pressing to do. And the idea that revisions can be avoided is a chimera. In the real world things are always changing. The day when you can say the system is complete, finished, unchangeable, will probably never come.

Rather than postpone documentation to the end, a better approach is to make it a tool of the planning process. Start the documentation while you analyze your present system and plan how you will convert to a computer system. Put it all in writing and continue to do so as you select your facilities and set up your operating procedures. Use diagrams, charts and tables liberally. It doesn't have to look like a sales brochure, but it must be legible and thorough. Besides, there are going to be a lot of changes. But when the computer is finally installed and running, you are going to have really good documentation, because if you do it right, the documentation you produce cannot but help mirror the flow and operation of your system as it actually is. In addition, your planning process should be improved, because the act of putting things in writing forces you to be more precise and to think things through.

PITFALL 4: THE ONE-GIANT-STEP APPROACH

The one-giant-step approach tries to solve too many problems in the first go-around. An unmanageable number of business data processing operations are converted to computer processing all at once. The system becomes too complex and begins to choke on its own problems. To avoid this pitfall, conversion to computer operations must be planned in small, manageable increments.

In theory, a great case can be made for adopting the one-giant-step approach. After all, business operations are usually closely related. Orders trigger inventory withdrawal which triggers orders for additional inventory which, in turn, triggers accounts payable processing, and so on to the financial reports. There is an obvious advantage in planning and implementing all procedures at one time.

Despite the apparent advantages of the giant-step approach, experience has shown that these advantages are more than offset by the added difficulties of trying to do too much at one time. Especially for first-time users, the watchword should be: "Learn to walk before you run." Implement your computer system in easily manageable steps. Start with a simple system. When that is installed and is working smoothly, proceed to the next most complex system. As you gain experience and learn about your computer and programs and how to deal with them, you will be in a stronger position to tackle more complex systems, with the ultimate goal being the integration of your smaller systems into one larger, smoothly working system. This is the "small-step" approach to computer implementation.

The small-step approach poses one serious danger. If each step is implemented without regard to the others, there is the possibility of incompatibility between subsystems. Suppose you were to buy an accounts receivable program from one vendor, an accounts payable from another vendor and a general ledger from a third. This could be like trying to fit together a motor, a body and wheels from three different auto manufacturers.

Even within the products of a single vendor problems can arise. Programs are continuously being improved, resulting in new releases, which may not be fully compatible with previous versions. Vendors are fully aware of the need for compatibility within their own product line; it greatly increases the attractiveness of their products. Nevertheless, problems can arise in the following two areas:

(1) Unintentional incompatibilities can creep in whenever there are program changes, due to the complexities involved and the impossibility of checking every possible combination of events.
(2) When new versions of a program are created, they are often designed to be "upward compatible" with existing programs. Upward compatible means that your present system can work with the new program, but it cannot use *all* the improvements. This means that if you try to combine two subsystems, either of which is an advanced version of a previous release, care must be taken to ascertain which features will and will not be compatible.

The ideal approach to computer implementation is first to *plan* the total system, ensuring that all the parts are compatible, and then to *implement* the plan in small, incremental steps. This may be asking for more foresight and devotion to planning than the average small computer user is likely to have, especially in a changing world where plans are being continually outdated by events. Nevertheless, total planning prior to implementation is a worthwhile goal and should be the model and aim of how to proceed, even if not adhered to completely.

PITFALL 5: LACK OF INVOLVEMENT

This pitfall is the reverse of pitfall 2, doing it all yourself. Instead of trying to do everything yourself, all of the work of planning, selection and implementation is delegated to others. Then you more or less wash your hands of the project and turn your attention to other things. This situation is apt to occur when you have little interest in computers, but somebody working for you does. You will feel the project is in good hands, the person delegated knows his or her way around computers and you would only get in the way.

Avoid this pitfall! Experience shows that the chances of success for a computer system are greatly increased when the person in charge is actively involved. The more a computer system is integrated into main-line business functions, the more this is the case. The reasons are not hard to discern.

The installation of a new computer system is bound to generate fears, conflicts, power struggles and antagonisms. Some will see the computer as a benefit; others as a threat. Accordingly, some will work to achieve a successful system while others will be uncooperative. Nine people may work enthusiastically for a good computer system, but if one person opposes it, the system could be in trouble. The person in charge must be involved, know what roles people are playing and take appropriate measures to ensure the computer's success.

Further, throughout the project, policy questions will arise which only the person in charge can reasonably answer. Installation of a computer can affect how firms conduct their business, their relation and image with customers and vendors. In order to provide intelligent direction, knowledge of the issues is required, which can come only through involvement in the project.

Finally, if, as is common, more money and time are needed to complete the project than were budgeted, you will not be able to judge whether allocation of further resources are justified unless you have been actively involved.

Obviously, not all businesspersons and managers will be involved in computer projects and become knowledgeable about computers to the same extent, nor should they. However, in all cases *some* involvement and *some* knowledge of computer operations is necessary. As computers are introduced into the main-line operations of small business, it will be just as necessary for the businessperson and manager to be involved in the data processing function as they are now involved in legal, sales and accounting activities.

You don't have to be an accountant or lawyer to run your business, but you do have to know those aspects that are vital to its operation. You cannot afford to turn all problems over to others and walk away. The situation with respect to computers is similar. Whether or not your inclinations are to become involved in the technical aspects, you can't afford to ignore the business side.

Converting to a Computer System

If you are introducing a computer into an existing business or into any other type of operation which must continue to function during the transition period, you will want to minimize disruptions, shift smoothly from current operating procedures and ensure that after the shift your new computer system works the way you planned it to work. If, on the other hand, your computer system is a brand new application, your task is much simpler. Nevertheless, you will probably find that new files must be created, and you will certainly want to test and evaluate the system before relying on it for day-to-day work. For any but the simplest system, conversion requires planning in advance and the conversion itself should be performed in a methodical way.

Planning for conversion requires that you answer the following questions:

- Should you accept the system?
- How are you going to test the system?
- What procedures will be set down for working with the system?
- What documents are necessary for explaining rules and procedures?
- What training will be needed?
- Who will be participating in the conversion?
- What method of cutover will you use?

ACCEPTANCE TESTING

You are about to convert to a computer system, a step that could have a profound impact on your business or profession. How are you going to determine whether the computer system you are contemplating is acceptable? Can it do the job? Should you convert now or are modifications or enhancements called for?

To answer these questions, it is necessary to perform acceptance tests. You must have a clear idea what levels of performance will and will not be acceptable to you. In other words, you should have a set of specifications that the new system must meet. If the new system performs according to specifications it is acceptable, otherwise it is rejected, at least until the deficiencies can be remedied.

The specifications for acceptance will be different in each case. If you feel at all unsure as to what the criteria for acceptance should be, look for professional assistance. Here are some points that should provide useful guidance:

Qualitative features
• Report content
• Display screen content
• Print quality
• Keyboard functions
• Printer functions
• Validity checks
• Backup facilities
• Shutdown, restart, and recover facilities
• Immunity to electrical "noise" in the expected office environment

Quantitative features
• Program run time
• Response time under worst-case conditions, such as maximum number of work stations at peak load
• Print speed—the ability to handle maximum expected print load

Acceptance testing assumes special importance when payment is contingent on the results of the tests. This could be the case in the following circumstances:

• You have contracted for customized programs or equipment. The programs might be brand new or only minor modifications to existing programs. In any case, payment should be contingent on acceptance testing. The tests used must be agreed to by both parties prior to the work being done and should be part of the contract.
• A vendor of a turnkey system has represented the system as capable of doing a specific job for you. Here you should reach an understanding that the system must pass specified tests before payment and acceptance.
• A computer store or computer vendor agrees to let you try out a system for a limited time. In such cases, a deposit to cover safe return of the system will usually be all that is necessary. You can establish any acceptance test you wish. If you don't like the system, you can return it and get your deposit back.

If you purchase a computer or program not specifically tailored to your use, you should still test it, but you will have no claim against the vendor if it doesn't meet your needs.

In the following sections we will discuss specifically how and what to test.

HOW TO TEST YOUR SYSTEM

Tests should be made for (1) the correct functioning of programs and equipment, (2) ease of use and (3) backup operations.

Testing Equipment

If you are buying a system in the minicomputer class, you should expect a customer engineer to come to your site, install the system and check it out. The cost may be included in the equipment cost or it may be priced separately, but one way or the other, it is a service you should use to be sure things are functioning properly after packing, transporting and unpacking.

Lacking the services of a customer engineer, you will have to combine equipment testing with overall system test. Any major equipment problems will show up at that time, although it is not always a simple task to disentangle equipment failure from other system problems.

System Test

This phase of the test determines whether the system will perform correctly. Since you usually can't test all possible situations, you try to pick critical areas to make your judgment on acceptability.

If, for example, you test ten situations and there are no problems, you will begin to have confidence in the system. If you test ten more situations and there are still no problems, your confidence will more than double—you will begin to think you have a perfect system. The more successful tests you complete without problems, the greater your faith in the system.

And where successive tests keep turning up problems, you will soon lose faith in the system and be tempted to scrap it.

These are extreme cases not likely to occur in real life but useful to make the point that you will judge the acceptability of a system, not by trying to check out *all* possibilities, but by how many sample cases work right and how many don't. There is no set rule here. However, as you run your tests you will soon get a feel for whether the system feels solid or shaky. As you continue testing, this first impression will either be reinforced or undermined. If reinforced, you will soon (maybe *too* soon) be tempted to reach a decision. Otherwise, you will remain undecided and continue with further tests.

Your assessment of test results will be tempered by where you got your system. If it is a turnkey system using seasoned programs, you will not tolerate many problems. On the other hand, if there is a lot of custom programming, you will probably be more tolerant of the results, knowing that new programming requires plenty of use to get the bugs out.

In order to test a computer system, you have to feed it data. Where does this data come from?

Efficient testing requires two kinds of data: *artificial data* and *live data*. Artificial data is data you make up to test specific features or cases. Live data is actual data taken from your files. The more of this live data you use in your tests, the more comprehensive they will be.

The advantage of artificial data is that you can quickly test conditions that under live testing would occur too infrequently to show up. Testing system response to error conditions is a particularly good example of how to use artificial data. By creating test data with errors you can see if the errors are detected and what messages are displayed.

In planning your tests and in creating artificial data, you should keep two phrases in mind: "at the end of . . ." and "at the start of . . . ." That is, you should test how the system performs at the end of day, at the end of the week, at the end of the month, at the end of accounting period, and at the end of the year. Similarly for the start of the day, week, and so on. These periods mark times of special occurrence in data processing systems. Reports are printed, checks are mailed, accounts are aged and books are closed. Also, dates change, the system is initialized for a new period and processing begins anew. If there are problems in the system these are the places they are most likely to be.

Other places where these two phrases can be used are:

- At the start of disk when a new disk is inserted
- At the end of disk when the disk is fully occupied and an attempt is made to add more data
- At the start and at the end of tape if you are using tape for backup
- At the end of a file that is accessed sequentially
- At the end of a page
- At the start of a new page
- At the end of groups in reports where total breaks occur
- At the end of reports

When you are convinced that the system works properly with artificial data, it should be tested with live data. Live data will test a wide range of conditions that the system will be called upon to process in day-to-day activity. To try to reproduce these conditions with artificial data would be time-consuming and is unnecessary. At some point you are going to have to convert your files. In the process, you can make a copy that can be used for test purposes. The further you are from cutover the smaller your samples will be. But as you approach cutover, you should have a copy of complete master files for testing. In addition, transaction files, created from live data that represents a very active day, should be used for running against files.

The hardest conditions to simulate in testing are on-line transactions. Since on-line entries are manual, and therefore slow and time-consuming, it is difficult to get a large enough sample for test purposes. At a minimum, you can test the ability of the system to perform the basic functions of record creation, record update, inquiry and end-of-session processing. In addition, incorrect data can be entered to test the computer's error processing functions. When you are satisfied that the computer has passed these tests satisfactorily, you will have to use your own judgment on how extensive an additional test program you want to engage in. The more on-line test data you put in, the greater your chance of smoking out problems, but you have to stop somewhere, and here, again, the performance of the system in past tests is the best guide as to how much further testing is necessary.

When testing systems with several interrelated applications, always start at the top and work down. If an order entry application feeds accounts receivable, which in turn feeds the general ledger, don't start your tests with the general ledger. If you do, changes made later in order entry can force you to retest general ledger. Order your tests *in the direction of data flow* to minimize retesting.

Testing for Ease of Use

In testing for ease of use it is not the correctness of the processing which is being tested but how the system works with people under real-life conditions. The ways in which ease of use can be determined vary considerably. In some cases ease of use can be determined from brochures; in others, by trying the system out in the vendor's showroom. However, to really determine ease of use, you should try to simulate actual conditions under which the system will operate. Since this is not always easy to do, this testing may have to be postponed until the time of conversion. Then, any problems in using the system can be determined during a parallel run, if this is included in your conversion process, or postponed until after cutover. Both alternatives leave open the possibility of some unpleasant surprises. They can be justified, however, on the basis of practicability, and if it is understood by all involved that later adjustments to the system may be required.

Testing for ease of use should try to reveal the following conditions:

Menus and prompting screens
- Unclear prompting messages.
- Error messages that don't pinpoint the source of the problem and tell the operator what to do next.
- Difficulty in getting the cursor to successive entry positions. In most cases this should be accomplished with one key depression.
- Closely related data split between different screens.
- Untitled screens.
- Cluttered screens or screen layouts that make them hard to read and make it hard to locate the cursor.

Reports and inquiry response
- Poor layout. Numbers squeezed together. Individual items hard to locate.
- Important items like total breaks and limit points not highlighted.
- More information than required. User gets "drowned" in numbers.
- Insufficient information. Items not listed in the order needed. Needed items not present.
- Fast access to urgent information is not possible.

File handling
- Data has to be transferred between files manually.
- Excessive changing of disks required.
- Disk switching is required at inopportune moments.
- Insufficient disk storage.

- Record layouts don't provide sufficient flexibility.
- Difficulty or impossibility of accessing needed information by groups such as size, color or price.
- Excessive sorting required.

Data entry
- Data entry places an excessive burden on those doing it.
- Flow of data not planned so that data entry will occur at the most propitious time.
- Data entry assigned to the wrong people.
- Poor planning of file handling results in more data entry than expected.
- Program lets too many data entry errors into the system.
- Person assigned to data entry not available at the right time.
- There is no good substitute when the one person assigned for data entry is absent.

Performance
- Excessive response time to inquiries.
- Data entry slowed due to long wait times between screens.
- Processing seems to take forever.
- Printer keeps the computer tied up most of the time.
- Reports don't get printed when needed.
- Computer not accessible to all who need it.

Procedures and documentation
- It is not clear who is responsible for what.
- Document flow has not been established.
- Methods for capturing all necessary data for input has not been spelled out.
- Input documents get lost and reports fail to get circulated to those who need them.
- New employees have no way of learning the system except by word of mouth.
- Users can only handle the routine operations. The slightest unusual situation results in a crisis.

Note that ease of use involves much more than just the hardware and software of the system. Poorly planned operations or incorrect assignments can make an otherwise good system hard to use. Thus the importance of finding the cause of the problem before deciding what to do about it. Good computers have been junked for the wrong reasons.

Also note the desirability of learning about these kinds of problems *before* cutover. Good planning and thorough investigation can prevent some of them. Those that are left should be smoked out as early as possible.

Testing for Backup Procedures

As stated previously, you should know what to do when things go wrong. You should know what to do about the computer, how you are going to continue to operate while the computer is down and how you are going to get it up and running again. Posting a set of rules is not enough. These rules have to be tested and people have to become familiar with them so they know what to do in an emergency.

Just as buildings have fire drills and ships have boat drills, so computer systems should have "crash drills." This is rarely done. In large systems professional computer operators are in charge so that there is no need for the users of the system to know how to restart the system. Technicians are available to get the system back on the air quickly. In small systems there are no professional operators and service could take much longer. Still, little thought or testing is usually given to backup procedures. Understandably, the vendors don't stress this point and most users would rather not think about it or are under the illusion that it is not a problem.

Testing for backup should include the following:

- Test that all those who use the computer know how to copy a file, and how to use a backup file.
- If you have backup equipment, test switchover procedures and operation in the backup mode.
- Simulate a crash. Test backup operations. Then test start-up and recovery procedures.
- Repeat the above for each application and each mode of operation you have.

CUTOVER

There are three ways you can cut over from your present system to a computer system: (1) use a pilot installation, (2) run in parallel and (3) throw the big switch. The first two allow the testing phase to be blended into the cutover process. The third method assumes all testing is complete and that all systems are GO before cutover.

The Pilot

A pilot installation is a small, manageable piece of the total system. It can start separate from the actual working system during initial testing, and then it can be moved into the working system for cutover.

For example, consider a parts distributor with three order takers. The plan is to provide each order taker with a work station with keyboards and displays, so they can each answer phone inquiries and take orders on-line. A pilot is first set up consisting of only one work station. After the pilot is tested with artificial data and any manifested problems corrected, the pilot is moved into the real operating environment. To do this a small portion of the inventory is entered in the computer's master file and all calls for those parts are referred to the computer work station. This is an inconvenience but one which usually is manageable during the cutover period.

Now the system can be tested in a live environment with minimum risk. If serious problems arise, it is a simple matter to fall back to the old way of doing things. When the system is operating as it should, the pilot can be expanded. More inventory can be added or an additional work station added. In this way the pilot can evolve into a full working system.

It is impossible to overemphasize the importance of testing your system in a live environment. No amount of forethought can anticipate the kind of problems that will turn up in a live system. And for getting people used to the newer system, a pilot provides the fastest training with the least risk.

There are ways of installing a pilot other than the one described above. Instead of selecting a group of parts, it might be better to start off with the entire inventory, again limiting the system to one work station. But in this case we have an example of a problem inherent in the conversion process: how to maintain both the old and the new files during the conversion process. At some point the new files have to be created by copying the current files. Unless the system will be immediately cut over after the copy process is complete and before changes to the files are required, a method must be found for keeping both files up to date.

In the above example, the parts inventory changed by those order takers not working with the pilot system would have to be entered into the computer. The best way to do this has to be determined for the case in hand. It might be best to update the file on-line, or it might be better to note the changes, batch them and make the entries all at once, after hours. In any case, how and when to convert files requires careful consideration and planning.

Summarizing the advantages of a pilot for cutover, the following points can be made:

- The pilot allows testing under real-life conditions.
- The new system can be introduced gradually into your operations, minimizing the overall risk and chances for traumatic situations in the event of system crashes.
- File conversion can be simplified if the file can be converted a small portion at a time.

Pilots are not a feasible approach when the system doesn't lend itself to partitioning. Then another method of cutover must be used.

Parallel Operation

When using parallel operation as the method for cutover, files are completely converted and both systems run at the same time—in parallel. Identical data is entered into both systems and the results compared. Any discrepancy is a signal to find the source of the error and correct it.

Parallel operation provides real-life testing and training conditions. It also provides an excellent way of checking results since you can refer to the results of the old system for comparison. As confidence is gained in the new system, the old system can be phased out, allowing a smooth transition from one to the other. But if anything should go wrong, the old system can be relied on for continued operations.

Parallel operation can start with old versions of files, or summaries of files. Thus, tests might start two months back from current operations, compare results of processing each month and then catch-up to current operations. Staff must be available to run both systems throughout the duration of the testing. Special care is required to ensure that both systems get identical treatment. Otherwise comparison of results will be meaningless and more problems will be created than solved. All this is often beyond the resources of small organizations. Also, not all systems lend themselves to parallel testing. If the computer system is substantially different from the system it is replacing, there may be little basis on which to compare results. For these reasons, despite the definite advantages of parallel operation, it may be dispensed with in favor of a third approach to cutover.

Throwing the Big Switch

With this method cutover is abrupt. One day you are operating in the old mode. The next day you are in the computer mode. In effect, you have thrown a switch, shifting operations from one system to another in one big step.

Obviously, before you throw the switch you must have full confidence in the system from previous testing. You must also be confident that all users and operators are adequately broken in to the new system. Finally, your files must have been converted and be current—absolutely up to the minute!

In spite of your confidence, it would be wise to prepare for the worst. The worst is that the system crashes and you have to continue operations without it for a period of time. Plan for this contingency. If you followed the suggestions made in the section on testing backup procedures, this should have been taken care of. However, crashes following cutover can be caused by many factors. Hardware and software failure are not the only reason for a system going down. In a new system, bottlenecks, unforeseen data flow problems, file management problems—in other words problems resulting from system design oversights—can cause a system to go down or to be shut down in order to maintain file integrity.

Despite the risks, this method of cutover is used. It is straightforward and can be used for all types of systems, skirting the problems of the other methods cited above. However, its use is not recommended for cutting over main-line business functions—the risks are too great.

HOW TO PLAN FOR CONVERSION

How much planning is required prior to conversion will depend on the complexity of the application. As a guide, you should draw up a conversion plan in accordance with the following steps:

- Make an assignment chart showing all the tasks that must be performed in the new system and who will be assigned to do them. You should also include an indication of who will substitute for the assigned person in their absence. Computer systems require a disciplined set of procedures—they are very unforgiving about functions not performed. Hence the need to be clear on this and to provide for substitutes when the assigned person for any reason can't fulfill the assignment. It is helpful if the assignment chart is in the form of a system flow chart, so that tasks can easily be related to the flow of data. The assignment chart should be considered provisional. You may want to make changes as you test and use the system.

- Determine the method of cutover that best suits your needs.
- Knowing the method of cutover will help determine how to test the system. Develop a test plan that specifies:

  - Tests to be performed
  - Test data needed
  - Staffing requirements to generate test data and perform tests
  - Testing schedule

- Find out what facilities your equipment or program vendor has to help you in testing and converting files. Take advantage of these as much as possible.
- Provide in advance for assistance in correcting any problems. Depending on the situation, contact consultants, programmers, vendors or software houses.
- Determine what training is required. If you followed the suggestion in a previous chapter to involve all computer users at an early stage of the planning process, training requirements should be reduced, but will still be necessary. Again, your decision on how to cut over will influence your answers to these questions. Training requirements can be easily determined from the assignment chart if the tasks and task assignments are clearly spelled out.
- From this same assignment chart you can see who should do what during the conversion process by keeping assignments during conversion as close as possible to assignments after conversion. Time constraints may require that you do some juggling here but changes should be kept to a minimum. Consider the use of temporary employees during conversion.
- Determine what you want to do about documentation—things like operating manuals, procedural rules, standards and backup procedures. There are some systems, both large and small, which have been operating for years without much documentation. Many small computer users rely solely on the operating instruction manuals supplied by their hardware and software vendors. Our recommendation is that you use your vendors' manuals but examine them critically in terms of your own needs. Then, see that any gaps are filled so that you have the documents you need when you need them.

The conversion process is often a hectic, traumatic experience. Too many important decisions are left till the last minute. You are always in a period of maximum risk when you switch from an old, familiar system to a brand new one. By following the guidelines presented in this chapter you should be able to avoid the worst aspects of conversion and, hopefully, achieve a smooth transition to your new computer system.

After Conversion

You have planned carefully, tested thoroughly, and found the system accepatable. The system is up and running and now you have a working computer system! The project is finished so now you and your associates can forget computers and turn your full attention to other things.

Not quite.

Computer systems are never really finished. The day never seems to come when you can say, "This system is just the way I want it. I can walk away from it and it will take care of itself." There is, of course, the fact that conditions are constantly changing. Your operations are seldom identical from year to year and computer systems must be adapted to changes in operations.

But even leaving these kinds of changes out of consideration, it is unlikely that you will leave your computer system untouched. The fact is that users are seldom content with the system as is. There is usually a desire to make it work better, expand it, add things, take some things out, or install additional systems. Thus, computerization tends to become an ongoing activity never really completed.

After conversion users generally find that they want to fine tune the system, evaluate it and start planning for the next step.

FINE TUNING

When you tested the system you were anxious to get up and running. You probably let certain problems go uncorrected, assuming they could wait until later. Now, after actually using the system for a while, you find new problems surfacing. The system still works well, but it requires fine tuning to make it purr along smoothly.

It is important to be prepared for a period of fine tuning and to prepare others for it. Additional time and costs are involved. If you are a manager and your boss thinks that after cutover the project is complete—finished—you are in trouble. The probable need for fine tuning should be recognized in the early stages of planning so resources can be anticipated and those involved will know what to expect. Otherwise, a successful system could be branded a failure and scrapped.

It is a common misconception that computer systems can be cut over and work perfectly. When this doesn't happen there is disillusionment and resentment. All of this is unnecessary if people understand what can realistically be expected.

The situation isn't helped by the fact that the amount of fine tuning that will be needed can't be predicted well in advance. However, after testing you should have a pretty good idea of what will be required. It is then simply a question of judging whether the necessary resources will be available for post-cutover adjustments. If not, it is better not to accept the system if these adjustments are judged necessary. If not, but you feel you can live with the system as it is, then the system can be accepted with the hope that eventually resources will become available to make improvements.

EVALUATING YOUR SYSTEM

You have invested time and money in a computer system. What are you getting for your investment? Did you anticipate direct savings? A reduction of clerical work? Better record keeping and reporting? What were your expectations and is the computer system meeting them?

Other questions that might be asked are: Has the system created more problems than it has solved? Is the system easy to use? Are those involved with the system praising it or denigrating it?

If applied properly, a computer should produce *substantial benefits*. The reaction should be: How did we ever do without it? What should be our next application?

If the reaction is: Whose bright idea was this? I told you it would never work!—then a thorough reassessment is in order.

WHAT TO DO IF YOUR SYSTEM DOESN'T WORK

If your system doesn't live up to expectation or, worse, if it is an outright failure, the first thing to realize is that a bad system can sometimes be turned into a good system. The trick is to either correct the problem or change direction and use the computer in a more appropriate application. The former is preferable but not always possible.

The first step in attacking a sick system is to find the source of the problem. Experience shows that this is likely to be found in one of the following areas:

• Inadequate planning, so that the system doesn't actually do what is expected of it.
• The system does what is expected, but it is hard to use.
• The system appears basically sound, but many bugs remain, resulting in constant problems and a lot of down time.

These are broad areas but they lead toward specific courses of action. They have been discussed in detail in the sections on planning, ease of use and testing. Go back to these sections and try to pinpoint the source, or sources, of your problems. Then you will be in a position to answer the basic questions posed by a poorly operating system.

Is the Computer Misapplied?

This question goes to the heart of the matter. It is not easy to answer yes after putting a lot on the line to get a computer system going. Yet it must be realized that not all applications are suitable for computerization. An application will be unsuitable if:

• It is harder to use than a manual system.
• Costs for successful operation are all out of proportion to benefits.
• Actual benefits are minimal.

An objective, unbiased assessment is called for. Don't waste time and money to patch up a system that was poorly conceived in the first place.

If you do decide that your computer has been misapplied, you don't necessarily have to scrap it. Maybe you can find a home for it elsewhere in your organization. Try to salvage as much as possible of the knowledge you have gained about your system by applying it elsewhere.

Does the Equipment Match the Job?

For every job there is a minimum computer, storage and printer that can perform the job satisfactorily. Drop below this minimum and performance will suffer. You may be able to accomplish all the tasks required but the system becomes hard to use. Sometimes equipment deficiencies can be helped by program changes but, basically, the most perfect programs can't do the job with inadequate equipment.

One of the most common equipment problems in small business systems is frequent printer breakdown. A number of low-cost printers have come on the market recently. There is a natural tendency on the part of vendors and users alike to cut costs in this area. The result is the use of printers under conditions for which they were never designed with the predictable outcome: frequent calls to the service technician or frequent trips to the service shop. The solution is simple though it will cost money: a heavy-duty printer that can take the beating and that is compatible with your programs and hardware.

Other than printers, no other piece of equipment normally used with small computers is likely to suffer from heavy usage. Rather, your equipment problems may be along the following lines:

• Insufficient disk storage, requiring constant swapping of floppies.
• Insufficient memory, resulting in sluggish performance.
• Screen size too small for your needs.
• Too few special keys on your keyboard.

Basically, the processors used in today's small computers are powerful enough to do the job. If there is an insufficiency it is likely to be in disk storage. Manufacturers are working hard to improve this area and some notable improvements should be showing up soon.

If you can trace your problems to the equipment the solution is fairly obvious. But before automatically going to the next most powerful unit, try to find out where you went wrong in the selection process and what kind of equipment you *really* need. And be sure that what you select is compatible with your programs.

Do the Programs Match the Job?

This is harder to establish than equipment mismatch and the solution is more difficult. First, bad programs can make the equipment look bad. Then, even if you can establish that the programs are at fault, it is not easy to pinpoint the problem area. And what do you do if you can identify what is wrong? Patch up the program? Get a new one?

Both courses are risky and full of problems when done after cutover. If you can back out of your computer system and go back to your previous methods during problem-solving time your task will be much easier. But after cutover the least costly and least risky solution may be to compensate for poor programs by getting more powerful equipment. If the nature of the problem lies not in what the program does, or does not do, but in poor performance, then better-performing equipment at key points can make a world of difference. Adding more memory or faster disks may provide the cure. Even an upward compatible processor might be a less costly solution than opening up the programs to changes.

When performance is bad, upgrading equipment is the path of least resistance. You don't have to know if the bad performance is due to the equipment or the programs—the solution is the same. It would take a good programmer to diagnose the problem. But your vendor may know, upon learning the nature of your problem, where the solution lies. Chances are that others have had the same kind of problem and tried various solutions. Of course, the vendor isn't a disinterested party when it comes to upgrading equipment.

If the software problem is not one of performance, more powerful equipment won't help you. You may be faced with flaws in the design logic; good professional assistance should be obtained to help you fight your way out of this one.

Has the Vendor Misrepresented the System?

If you have purchased a turnkey system which has clearly not performed as claimed in proposal and contracts, then you should strongly pressure the vendor to resolve the problem. In recent court cases a "duty of care" decision has been rendered which could apply to vendors that don't perform as required. If the vendor does not exercise duty of care, it amounts to malpractice. The vendor is liable.

Even if you don't actually go to court, knowing this can be useful in getting vendors to see that their system performs as represented. But you better get it in writing before money changes hands. Some consulting firms specialize in computer litigation. Expert help is often necessary when disputes arise between vendors and buyers. The advantage of dealing only with vendors who will stand by their products should be clear.

PROTECTING YOUR SYSTEM

The value of a successful computer system is much greater than what you have invested in equipment, programs and all the hidden costs required to get the system operational. Here we are talking about the value to *you*, not just the value on the books or economic value. Your computer system has opportunity value for improving your operations and increasing your income. It has value in terms of records stored on disks and tapes. It could be disastrous if these records were lost, destroyed or copied by the wrong person. These are the kinds of things that must be taken into account when considering how to protect your system and at what cost.

Like any other item, protection of a computer and its files depends on their value to you, their exposure to risk and the cost of protection. The difference with respect to computers is the vulnerability of your business or profession. You may not be able to operate without it at all once it's introduced into the mainstream of your operations. And you cannot expect to find an interim solution unless your files are usable.

The subject of protection is rarely given the attention it deserves. Most users who go to the trouble to get adequate protection have had at least one bad experience that convinced them that they had better do something about it. Obviously, it is preferable to forestall such experiences.

Protection can be applied to a number of areas, but not everybody needs the same kind of protection to the same degree. Here is a run-down of what you should consider.

Power Failure

Electric power interruptions can be of such short duration that you don't notice them, but the computer will. These are *transients* which engineers try to guard against, but they can't be eliminated completely. What happens to your computer when a transient hits the power lines depends on its duration and cause. It can cause undetected errors, detected errors, lost information and malfunctioning. A transient caused by lightning can seriously damage equipment.

Some protection against transients is built into the power supply of the computer. For more thorough protection, devices are available into which you can plug, thereby isolating your computer from most transient conditions. Table 14–1 lists some of the companies that provide this type of equipment.

Table 14–1 Companies Providing Power Protection Equipment

Superior Electric	Elgar Corporation
Bristol, CT 06010	8225 Mercury Ct.
203 582-9561	San Diego, CA 92111
Deltec Corporation	Sola Electric
980 Buenos Ave.	1717 Busse Rd.
San Diego, CA 92110	Elk Grove Village, IL 60007
714 275-1331	312 439-2800
Electronic Specialists, Inc.	R. L. Drake Company
171 South Main St.	540 Richard St.
Box 389	Miamisbury, OH 45342
Natick, MA 01760	800 543-5612
Cuesta Systems, Inc.	Dymark Industries
3440 Roberto Court	7133 Rutherford Rd.
San Luis Obispo, CA 93401	Baltimore, MD 21207
	800 638-9098

Larger power failures with which readers are all too familiar—blown fuses and blackouts—are harder to protect against. Users of large computers often go to considerable expense to protect themselves against power outages, installing motor generator units that are switched on if needed. This is like having your own power plant on site, but these users feel that the importance of the computer to their operations justifies the cost. Clearly, for users of small computers, power backup is much harder to justify. But some vendors do offer backup power supplies for minicomputer systems. These backup units may not handle printers, but they can carry the processor through an emergency.

The alternative is to have backup procedures ready—either a fallback to manual operations or an alternative operating site that can accept your programs and files and perform processing for the duration of the outage.

Equipment and Files

Small computer equipment is a prime object for theft. It is easy to sell and makes a nice addition to a computer hobbyist's home computer system.

Computer files can be the object of both destruction and theft. The files are nothing more than thousands of tiny magnets. It requires only one pass of a small pocket magnet over a disk to destroy all its information. A disgruntled employee can do irreparable harm with practically no risk to himself. Even accidental erasure is possible. Tools and other metal objects sometimes become magnetized and a brush past a disk might erase some data.

Floppies are especially exposed to maltreatment and therefore require special safeguards. Backup copies stored in inaccessible places, fireproof boxes or vaults are commonly used. Tape backup to Winchesters may need similar protection.

The ease of copying disk files makes information stealing a simple task. With a few operations all the records of a file can be copied without leaving a trace. Compare this to what is required to copy a file of printed records.

Theft of information has become a big enough problem in big business and government to spawn a whole subindustry of computer theft specialists and auditors. *Encryption devices* are available that use elaborate codes for protecting data. Protection schemes are written into programs to prevent unauthorized use. An armed guard sits at the entrance to the computer area and everyone working there has a badge with his or her picture on it. All this should give you some indication of the lengths large users go to to protect their computer systems.

Readers of this book will probably not consider themselves likely targets of information theft or sabotage. However, if you have valuable customer lists, new products under development or do contract work for large business or government, your requirements for security may not be so very different from large users.

Some insurance firms specialize in computer systems. They will insure not only the equipment, but will insure you for loss of your files. Contact your insurance agent or the following companies: Harleysville Mutual Insurance Co., Harleysville, PA; The St. Paul, whose agents can be found in the Yellow Pages.

Care of Floppy Disks

Floppy disks give all the appearance of being vulnerable, so it shouldn't be necessary to dwell on the need for handling them with special care. Yet floppies have had hot coffee spilled on them, paper clips attached, telephones placed on top of them and who knows what other maltreatment. Office employees are not used to handling things as fragile as floppies. Most objects office employees come in contact with are made to take a reasonable amount of abuse. Thus, the need to impress upon all concerned that floppies are to be handled with tender, loving care. Strict rules should be laid down on the handling of floppies, and these rules enforced. The rules for handling are simple:

- Floppies are never to be left on desks or put in desk drawers.
- Floppies are to be stored in a designated container when not in active use.
- Backup copies are to be stored separately in a secure location.

Various types of receptacles are available for storing and easily retrieving floppies. For critical, archival records a fireproof safe designed for storing floppy disks and tapes is made by Schwab Safe Company, 3000 Main Street, Lafayette, Indiana 47902. Called Fire Guard, the safe is 31″ × 31″ × 41″ and can store 540 floppy disks.

THE NEXT STEP

By the time you have installed your first system and have it working satisfactorily, you will have become fairly knowledgeable in small computers. You will probably have some idea of what your next step should be. Certainly, you will have a better feel for what can be done with a small computer, and how it can best be applied to your operations.

If you have planned wisely and with reasonable foresight, you should be able to move to the next step. One cannot easily foresee at the start where computerization will lead, so that inability to accurately anticipate future requirements should come as no surprise. Still, the dice can be loaded in your favor if you pay attention in the selection process to what your next step is likely to be. There are three possible routes you can take, described below.

Expansion of Your Present System

A system can be expanded either vertically or horizontally. Vertical expansion is accomplished by adding more programs to a single computer and making it work harder. Obviously, there is an upper limit on how far you can go in this direction. Eventually you will exhaust the capabilities of the system. This is most likely to happen first at the keyboard or at the printer, as different jobs vie for the use of facilities.

Horizontal expansion is also accomplished by adding programs, but not to your present computer. New equipment is purchased. There is practically no limit to how far you can expand horizontally. You can extend your system across the room, across the city or across the country—in several directions at once. Thus, while vertical expansion is the least costly approach, it is much more limited in possibilities than horizontal expansion.

It is feasible to expand vertically and horizontally at the same time, by adding programs to your existing computer but also adding work stations and printers, to better distribute the added load on these units.

Starting from a small computer having only the basic components required to do one job, here are the directions in which expansion is possible, listed roughly in order of increasing complexity:

- Memory can be increased.
- More disk units can be added.
- A more powerful processor can be used.
- Program enhancements or more powerful programs can be used.
- Additional work stations can be added.
- The computer can be connected to a communication system—yours or somebody else's.
- Another processor can be added, providing a multi-processor computer system.

Of course, each of the above expansion routes requires that certain conditions be fulfilled: the capability for expansion must be there, compatible units must be used, programs for doing the job must be available.

Expansion capability costs money. Obviously, a manufacturer has to charge more for a box that provides for memory expansion than for one that doesn't. The more such expansion capability provided by the system, the greater the cost. It is easy to say that some capability for expansion should be provided, and that its cost is cheap compared to the alternatives. But the question is, how much expansion? This is where the need for planning and foresight come in. What will you need in the future and how much extra money should you be willing to pay for expansion capability?

If your future needs will be great and you anticipate lots of uses for your computer, you may have to reverse the growth process. That is, instead of starting small and expanding to meet future needs, it may be better to start with a more powerful processor and memory than you need and underutilize it in the beginning. You won't have to start with more disk units, work stations or printers than actually required. But as you need them, they can be added with the assurance that your processor can handle just about anything you can throw at it. Better yet, you can start right away with the software you will be using at a later point, so that adjustments, always required when programs are switched, will not be required.

Of course, underutilization of equipment and programs requires extra money up front, but it can be the cheapest route in the long run. Here again, careful planning is required to evaluate this course of action.

Adding a Related System

Two systems are related to each other if they exchange data. If the exchange is automatic, that is, over wires connecting the two computers, they can be considered parts of one larger system. However, here we are considering the case where data transfer is accomplished manually, so that the two systems are for all practical purposes *independent*, except for a single bridge occasioned by the manual transfer of data.

Data can be transferred manually by generating an output file on a disk in one system, physically moving the disk to the other system, and then using it as an input file. A cruder method is to use the printed output of one computer as keyed input to another. Both approaches are used, because they are simple to implement and software is easier to find than the sophisticated versions required for multi-processor systems.

Rather than running the risks attendant on any change in a system, some users prefer two separate systems rather than upgrading a system that is already operational and doing a good job. The idea is to leave well enough alone, which should always be a strong temptation where computer systems are concerned. Small changes have a way of growing into major projects. For these reasons, if computer prices continue their rapid descent, multiple-computer systems should become quite common.

Another advantage of having two systems is that when one is not working right, the other can back it up. Of course, you won't be able to do all your processing in the same amount of time. However, you should be able to limp along for the duration of the outage, continue your operations and generally be much better off than without backup.

Backup of two systems for each other requires compatibility, preferably identical units. The use of identical units should be a goal in any expansion program. The more identical units you have, the more alternatives you have for backing up one unit with another. In addition, maintenance, training and chances of error are reduced. Unless the applications are so unique that you are left no choice, it doesn't make sense to have two styles of keyboard, a mixture of different disk units and processors that don't talk the same language.

The use of manual transfer of data is not recommended except as a temporary expedient, and then only when it can be shown how the system you choose can eventually be integrated. The manual transfer of data is slow, subject to errors and delays, and runs counter to what should be a principal function of a computer system—the instant display of timely information.

Adding an Unrelated System

Unrelated systems are completely separate, with no transfer of data between them. Naturally, this requires that the applications are also unrelated. Although all operations in an organization are ultimately related, this relationship may be so indirect that unrelated computer systems are possible. Thus, you can have accounts receivable, accounts payable and payroll all working independently. But if you added a general ledger, a personnel system and an order entry, you would have related systems.

Unrelated systems have the advantages of related systems, without the disadvantage of having to manually transfer data. They are easy to plan and implement; they can back one another up, if suitably chosen; and there is no need to change an existing system when adding an unrelated system. It is the path of least resistance and therefore, the one most likely to be taken. However, since no considerations of data transfer are required, it is easy to disregard all questions of compatibility. This can become a problem later, if integration of jobs is attempted; you will find that the road is blocked by incompatible equipment and programs.

SUMMARY

In concluding this discussion of expansion, it will be helpful to summarize the key points of consideration discussed in this chapter and in previous chapters on planning.

- Provide for vertical expansion with expandable processors or by starting with excess capacity.
- When expanding horizontally, select equipment that can be used for backup.
- When adding processors, provide for later integration of jobs by using compatible facilities.
- Data transfer between jobs is a key consideration in planning for expansion.

- Maximum benefits are achieved in computer systems when they are related and integrated and data is transferred automatically.
- Computer systems are easiest to plan and implement when they are unrelated.
- Save time and money, while reducing errors, by minimizing the amount of manual data entry. Key in directly from original documents or exchanges with customers, and enter at only one point in the system.

Appendix

CHECK LIST FOR PLANNING

CHECK

1. Set up a master planning list of the ways you could use a computer. _____
2. Assign priorities to the items on your list, based on those which will be most beneficial overall. _____
3. Have you taken account of the advantages of integrating closely related operations? _____
4. Have you considered how the use of the same computer in more than one way might affect your priorities? _____
5. Can you anticipate changing conditions that might make computerization difficult? _____
6. If you anticipate changes, have you a good idea how to deal with them? _____
7. Have you determined how much down time you can tolerate for the highest priority items on your list?
8. Is your priority rating realistic in terms of expected down time? _____
9. Do you know how you will deal with system failures? _____
10. Have you considered the use of the computer in unusual ways that might give you a decisive advantage or open new areas of business? _____
11. Have you evaluated the risk/reward trade-offs in these new areas in terms of your business objectives? _____
12. Have you evaluated your top priority item in your master planning list in terms of your resources, your commitment and the complexity of the project? _____
13. Have you considered a less ambitious project to start off with? _____
14. Have you tried to plan beyond the first project? _____
15. Have you given sufficient consideration to how you will add new functions to your original application? _____

CHECK LIST FOR DATA GATHERING

CHECK

1. Assemble in one file sample documents of original entry, such as orders, invoices, etc.
2. Assemble in another file sample records. _____
3. Assemble in a third file sample reports and documents which are produced for internal or external use. _____
4. Use the above files to make entries in the data gathering forms. File 1 is for input data, file 2 for stored data and file 3 for output data. _____
5. Have you answered the three questions: what, how much and when, with respect to your use of data? _____
6. Have you accounted for data which is now passed verbally, but will be entered into the computer? _____

7. Rate your data requirements on the data gathering forms.   _____
8. Have you tried to cull out things that are not really useful?   _____
9. Have you given thought to individual operations that, because of complexity or vulnerability to change, would be better off bypassing the computer and remaining manual operations?   _____

CHECK LIST FOR SELECTION

CHECK

1. Have you considered the use of professional help or the help of colleagues and acquaintances?   _____
2. Review the chapters and tables describing sources of vendors and services. List those that apply to your case.   _____
3. Start your search for the right program on as broad a front as possible to get a large sample of candidate programs.   _____
4. Screen out all programs that don't meet your specifications on the data gathering forms.
5. Check out the vendors of your candidate programs for reliability and support. _____
6. Select the program that requires the least modification.   _____
7. Evaluate the equipment that this program runs on in terms of cost and vendor reputation.   _____
8. Have you checked that the programs are sufficiently seasoned in terms of age and number of users?   _____
9. Did you consider the suitability of the equipment for your purposes? Is it in the mainstream of small computer trends?   _____
10. Does the equipment or program vendor have facilities where you can enter your own data to test the programs?   _____
11. Have you tried to locate those with hands-on experience with the program, to get an evaluation?   _____
12. Make a decision to go with this program, or drop it and look for a more appropriate program.   _____
13. Negotiate a contract on any customizing.   _____
14. Make sure all performance requirements are spelled out.   _____

CHECK LIST FOR WORKING WITH PROFESSIONALS

CHECK

1. Have you evaluated the use of a consultant in relation to the complexity of the job and its role in your operations?   _____
2. Have you considered using a consultant just to point you in the right direction?   _____
3. Did you establish that the consultant has a broad enough knowledge of the industry to be really useful?   _____
4. Have you thought out what you want the consultant to do?   _____
5. Are you prepared to give the consultant the data he or she needs to work efficiently?   _____
6. Does your programmer know your line of business and the language and equipment you plan to use?   _____

7. Get a proposal on the work to be done by a programmer or programming firm, preferably three competing proposals.   _____
8. Evaluate the candidates in terms of experience first, cost second, and time to completion third.   _____
9. If using programmers inexperienced in your application, have you tried to get a compensating benefit?   _____

CHECK LIST FOR EVALUATION

                                                                                                                  CHECK

1. Does your application require a detailed financial analysis?   _____
2. Do you have cost figures for current operations?   _____
3. Are you far enough advanced in your planning to estimate costs of a computer system?   _____
4. Have you obtained costs of equipment and programs?   _____
5. Have you estimated or allowed for hidden costs?   _____
6. Have you tried to use the computer in more than one way, so as to get maximum benefits?   _____
7. Can a computer be justified by lowering costs?   _____
8. Is the payback period satisfactory?   _____
9. Is the ROI satisfactory?   _____
10. Have you compared the advantages of leasing and purchase?   _____
11. Does your proposed application have intangible benefits not easily quantifiable?   _____
12. Are these benefits sufficient to make a business decision without a detailed financial analysis?   _____
13. Is your competition using the computer in ways that are affecting your business?   _____
14. Do you view the computer as a necessity for remaining competitive in the future?   _____
15. Are you willing to invest time and money to learn what computers can do and how best to use them?   _____
16. Make a business decision based on the above considerations.   _____

CHECK LIST FOR CONVERSION

                                                                                                                  CHECK

1. Develop a test plan.   _____
2. Does your vendor have facilities that can be used for testing, converting or creating files?   _____
3. Create test data.   _____
4. Assign personnel to perform testing.   _____
5. Develop a plan for conversion.   _____
6. Have you provided for system crashes?   _____
7. Have you tested backup procedures?   _____
8. Are the system's operation and backup procedures documented?   _____
9. Is training adequate for both normal and abnormal procedures?   _____

About the Author

Mr. Rinder has worked with both large and small computers in a wide range of applications. As a consultant and computer specialist, Mr. Rinder has designed or managed computer applications in the areas of accounting, real estate, communications, manufacturing and government. His interest in small computers started with his first assignment: the applications of an early mini-computer to business functions. Mr. Rinder has published several articles on computers, but this is his first book.